WOMEN'S WORK AND WAGES

At a time when women in industrialized countries have a stronger and more permanent presence in the labor market than ever before, why does a gender pay gap still exist and why does this gap differ so greatly between countries? Why have the marked decreases in sex differentials in labor force participation not been accompanied by corresponding decreases in occupational sex segregation in the labor market? These are the issues addressed by the studies in this volume.

Contributors to the first part of the collection examine the current state of the economics of the gender pay gap and the economics of sex segregation. They illustrate how important insights can be obtained, first through introducing the concept of wage structure as an analytical tool and second through applying a more explicit general equilibrium modeling of occupational segregation.

Time allocation has a central role in the economics of gender. A second part is devoted to the empirical study of gender differences in family responsibilities and time allocation and to how such differences affect and interact with women's wages.

In the final part of the book, contributors analyze various aspects of pay structures and wage mobility. The often neglected issues of gender differences in inter-industry wage differentials and fringe benefits are treated in depth. The book ends with a study of the background to the differences in men's and women's pay in the Soviet Union.

Women's Work and Wages is a timely study of some of the most important issues in Gender Economics. Its findings illustrate how educational and occupational sex segregation, as well as family responsibilities, have contributed to the persisting gender wage gap.

Inga Persson is Professor of Economics at Lund University, Sweden. She holds a chair in the Economics of Gender and has published on labor market policy, unemployment, the welfare state and the economic position of women. Her publications include *Generating Equality in the Welfare State: The Swedish Experience* (1990).

Christina Jonung is a University Lecturer in the Department of Economics at Lund University, Sweden. Her research has concerned the economic position of women in Sweden and gender equality policies.

ROUTLEDGE RESEARCH IN GENDER AND SOCIETY

1. ECONOMICS OF THE FAMILY AND FAMILY POLICIES *Edited by Inga Persson and Christina Jonung*
2. WOMEN'S WORK AND WAGES *Edited by Inga Persson and Christina Jonung*

WOMEN'S WORK AND WAGES

Edited by Inga Persson and Christina Jonung

A selection of papers from the 15th Arne Ryde Symposium on "Economics of Gender and the Family," in honor of Anna Bugge and Knut Wicksell

Routledge
Taylor & Francis Group
LONDON AND NEW YORK

First published 1998
by Routledge
2 Park Square, Milton Park, Abingdon, Oxfordshire OX14 4RN

Simultaneously published in the USA and Canada
by Routledge
711 Third Avenue, New York, NY 10017

First issued in paperback 2014

Routledge is an imprint of the Taylor and Francis Group, an informa business

Typeset in Garamond by Florencetype Ltd,
Stoodleigh, Devon

British Library Cataloguing in Publication Data
A catalogue record for this book is available from the British Library

Library of Congress Cataloging in Publication Data
A catalogue record for this book has been requested

ISBN 13: 978-1-138-86617-1 (pbk)
ISBN 13: 978-0-415-14903-7 (hbk)

Publisher's Note

The publisher has gone to great lengths to ensure the quality of this reprint but points out that some imperfections in the original may be apparent

CONTENTS

PART III Gender and pay structures

FIGURES

TABLES

CONTRIBUTORS

Dominique Anxo is Associate Professor of Economics and Director of the Centre for European Labor Market Studies at Gothenburg University, Sweden. His research interests fall into the areas of labor and industrial economics, gender and time use studies, and evaluation of labor market policy.

Rita Asplund is Director of Research at the Research Institute of the Finnish Economy (ETLA) in Helsinki, Finland. Her main research interests lie in economics of education and labor economics.

Francine D. Blau is Frances Perkins Professor of Industrial and Labor Relations at the School of Industrial and Labor Relations of Cornell University and Research Associate of the National Bureau of Economic Research. Her publications include *The Economics of Women, Men, and Work* (with Marianne Ferber).

Lennart Flood is Professor of Econometrics at Gothenburg University, Sweden. His research interests are divided among the areas of econometrics, labor supply and taxes, household allocation of time, data quality and collection of micro data.

Lena Granqvist is a Ph.D. student at Åbo Akademi University, Finland, and the Swedish Institute for Social Research, Stockholm. She studies fringe benefits and their effects on the gender wage gap, industry wage differentials, and income distribution.

Maria Hemström is a Ph.D. student at the University of Uppsala, Sweden. Her interests include labor economics and gender differences in pay.

George E. Johnson is Professor of Economics at the University of Michigan. He has written on comparable worth (with Gary Solon) and has most recently been studying the role of skill-biased technical change in papers with John Bound and Frank Stafford.

Christina Jonung is a university lecturer at the Department of Economics at Lund University, Sweden. Her research involves the economic position of women in Sweden and gender equality policies.

Katarina Katz is research fellow at the Center for European Labor Market Studies, Department of Economics, Gothenburg University, Sweden. Her main research interests are economics of gender and the labor market, feminist and radical economics, and Russian and Eastern European Studies.

Pål Longva is a doctoral candidate at the University of Oslo, and research assistant at the Center for Research in Economics and Business Administration, Oslo. His interests include wage structures, applied microeconometrics and labor economics in general.

Michèle Naur is a Ph.D. student at the Center for Labor and Social Research, CLS, Aarhus University, Denmark. Her research area is gender wage differentials and pension schemes in Denmark.

Inga Persson is Professor of Economics at Lund University, Sweden. She holds a chair in Economics of Gender and her research interests are labor market policy, unemployment and the economic position of women.

Nina Smith is Professor of Economics at Aarhus School of Business and Research Director at the Center for Labor and Social Research, CLS, Aarhus University, Denmark. Her research concentrates on labor supply models, gender wage differentials, income distribution and applied welfare analyses.

Frank P. Stafford is Professor of Economics at the University of Michigan and Director of the Michigan Panel Study. His publications deal with time use, earnings, childcare, human capital and economic growth. These include *Time, Goods and Wellbeing* and *Divergence, Convergence and Gains to Trade.*

Steinar Strøm is Professor of Economics at the University of Oslo, and scientific advisor at the Center for Research in Economics and Business Administration, Oslo. His research interests include microeconometric labor market models, applied welfare analysis and environmental economics.

PREFACE

This volume contains a selection of the papers presented at the 15th Arne Ryde Symposium on "Economics of Gender and the Family", held on August 18–19, 1995 at Rungstedgaard in Denmark. Some of the other papers presented at the symposium are published in an accompanying volume entitled *Economics of the Family and Family Policies*. During two hot summer days, one hundred economists met to discuss about forty papers in this rapidly expanding area of international research. We want to thank all the participants in the symposium for their contributions to the lively discussions that took place in the various sessions. We (and the authors) are particularly grateful to the appointed discussants who helped to improve the papers with their comments and insights.

We also want to express our gratitude to the Arne Ryde Foundation for financing the symposium. The Foundation was established in memory of Arne Ryde, a promising young doctoral student in economics at Lund University, who died in a car accident. Since 1973 it has generously supported international symposia and lectures as well as other professional activities arranged by the Department of Economics in Lund. This support has proved to be of great value for the economics profession in Sweden and in particular, for the doctoral students and economists at the Department in Lund. Professor Björn Thalberg, Chairman of the Board of the Arne Ryde Foundation, initiated this symposium and also, as a member of the organizing committee, saw it through from start to finish. We owe him many thanks for having shared his vast experience with us.

Other crucial members of the team behind the symposium and this volume have been Kristian Bolin, Carole Gillis, Keith Persson and Ann-Charlotte Sahlin. Kristian Bolin helped us in planning the symposium and also acted as our consultant in editing the papers. Carole Gillis worked hard to improve the English. Keith Persson spent part of what was supposed to be his summer vacation at the copying machine producing the conference volumes. Ann-Charlotte Sahlin, in her calm and efficient manner, took care of all practical arrangements and later also of getting the manuscripts into shape for publication.

PREFACE

The Arne Ryde Symposium on "Economics of Gender and the Family" was held in honor of the Swedish economist Knut Wicksell and his wife Anna Bugge. The reasons for dedicating the symposium to them are explained in our short tale of "Anna and Knut" in the accompanying volume to this book. In their own way they were forerunners both in gender relations and in family economics. Their life story provided a source of inspiration and gave us a sense of continuity through the generations in our work with this project.

Inga Persson and Christina Jonung
Lund, February 1997

ACKNOWLEDGMENT

We wish to thank the *Cambridge Journal of Economics* for giving us permission to reprint the article "Gender, Wages and Discrimination in the USSR" by Katarina Katz. As Chapter 10 here, it is slightly different from the original version which is scheduled to appear in the *Cambridge Journal of Economics*, September 1997.

INTRODUCTION

Inga Persson and Christina Jonung

Research on the economic position of women has a long history. In the nineteenth century it was part of the movement towards the emancipation of women, and discussion and analysis focused on the sexual division of labor in society and the very different roles assigned to women and men. While men were supposed to be patriarchal heads of households and breadwinners in the expanding labor markets of industrial societies, women were confined to and responsible for the private sphere – for household work and the care and upbringing of children. In reality the assignment of men to the public sphere and women to the private one was far from complete, and many women had to struggle hard in paid jobs in order to support themselves and their children. But still, this was ideologically the ideal type of family and the one that was challenged by the reformers and heretics of the day. Women's subordinate role and confinement to the home was questioned and the emancipating effects of women's participation in market work and public life was stressed.

More and more women did enter the labor market – gradually the extreme form of sexual division of labor where women were responsible for household work and men for market work lost favor in industrial societies. The first to enter the labor market in significant numbers were single women who participated in market work until they married and/or had children. Then came the reenters, married women who returned to paid work when their children were no longer young. Eventually also an increasing share of mothers with small children joined the labor force. Today most women, be they young or old, single, married or cohabiting, take part in market work, even if many women leave it temporarily when their children are small and even if women's participation is often not full-time.

As women entered the labor market in growing numbers it became evident that their place was not the same as that of men. And when it did coincide, the pay was not the same. Early nineteenth-century research focused on this new, emerging form of gender division of labor. Economists, both male and female, analyzed and discussed the patterns and causes of occupational segregation by sex and the role that discrimination and segregation played in women's low pay. As married women, particularly those with small children, entered the labor force, research interest during the 1960s and 1970s came to focus on the patterns and determinants of female labor supply and the interaction between the (still remaining) gender division of labor within the family and women's supply of labor to the market. Today, when women comprise a large share of the labor force and have a stronger and more permanent labor market attachment during their life cycle, economic research has once again concentrated on the position and outcome for women in the labor market. Thus studies of job segregation by sex in the labor market, its causes and consequences, as well as studies of the pay gap between women and men and its underlying causes, are again high on the research agenda within the Economics of Gender. The contents of this book reflect these priorities.

The book is divided into three parts. Part I contains three chapters which together provide an overview of "where we are" in the economics of the gender pay gap and the economics of sex segregation in the labor market. They are followed, in Part II, by three chapters devoted to the empirical study of gender differences in family responsibilities and time allocation and how such differences affect and interact with wage outcomes for women in market work. The four chapters included in Part III analyze various aspects of pay structures and wage mobility from a gender perspective.

PART I WHERE ARE WE IN THE ECONOMICS OF GENDER?

Why is there a gender pay gap in all industrialized countries and why does the size of the gap differ so much between countries? These are the two questions addressed, theoretically and empirically, by *Francine Blau* in the first chapter of the volume. She illustrates her discussion of the gender pay gap by the examples of Sweden and the USA. Both are countries with high rates of female labor force participation, well-qualified women and a strong commitment to anti-discrimination legislation and affirmative action (the USA) or equal status policies (Sweden). But in 1984 the female–male wage ratio amounted to only 67 percent in the USA as compared to 83 percent in Sweden – a considerable difference. How come?

Blau describes how research on the gender pay gap has traditionally focused on the role of what she calls gender-specific factors, particularly gender differences in qualifications (human capital explanations) and differences in the treatment of otherwise equally qualified male and female workers (labor market discrimination). She reviews the human capital and discrimination approaches and using Swedish and American data on individuals, illustrates how these approaches can be applied and how they provide fruitful empirical insights. But she also shows that they have their limitations, particularly when it comes to comparing gender wage gaps between countries and understanding the evolution of the gender pay gap over time in a specific country. For such purposes, she argues, the introduction of the concept of wage structure as an analytical tool is of great value.

Applying this tool, she solves the puzzle of the large difference between the American and the Swedish gender pay gap. In doing so, she also changes our conception of how women fare in the Swedish as compared to the American labor market. The gender pay gap in the USA is relatively high, not because of relatively high values for the traditional gender-specific factors (gender differences in qualifications and treatment) but rather because of the fairly large penalty that the American wage structure imposes on groups who have below average skills (measured and unmeasured) or are located in less favored sectors. In terms of their placement in the male wage distribution, Swedish women fare no better than American women. But the wage penalty for that placement is much smaller in Sweden with its highly compressed wage structure.

It is often regarded as something of a paradox that the marked decreases in the sex differentials in labor force participation rates and wage rates that have taken place in the industrialized countries over the last few decades have not been accompanied by corresponding decreases in the occupational segregation by sex in the labor market. Sweden provides one clear case in point. But, argues *Christina Jonung*, the paradox may only be a surface one which disappears on closer analytical scrutiny. In Chapter 2 she sets out to show this by surveying the different economic approaches to occupational sex segregation that have been developed in the literature. She divides the approaches into four categories: labor supply theories of occupational choice; labor demand theories of occupational hiring; transaction cost theories of occupational matching; institutional theories. Her focus is on what different theories predict would happen to occupational segregation over time during a process of change such as the one in recent decades. It turns out that several theories of occupational segregation would predict rising, or at least stable, levels of occupational segregation as labor force participation rates of women rise and wage differentials by sex fall. Thus, from a theoretical perspective, there is no paradox in the developments that have been observed, and this is the case whether one supports human capital theories or discrimination theories of occupational sex segregation. Her analysis also demonstrates that in analyzing changes over time one has to consider the interdependencies between supply, demand and the wage and thus between increases in labor force participation, the structure of demand, reduced wage differentials within and between occupations, and occupational segregation. In short, more of a general equilibrium approach is required.

This is also the standpoint taken by *George Johnson and Frank Stafford* in Chapter 3 on occupational exclusion. They set out to construct a modelling framework within which the interactions between occupational exclusion and gender wage outcomes can be investigated. In their model there are four distinct potential reasons to explain why men and women may have different occupational distributions. Two involve forms of discrimination: direct employer discrimination against women in certain jobs and institutional discrimination (legal or otherwise) that restricts women from working in "non-traditional" jobs. The other two reasons involve women's non-pecuniary preferences regarding different occupations and their relative abilities in different jobs compared to men. The questions Johnson and Stafford want to answer are first, what the existence of these types of exclusion imply for gender wage and distributional outcomes and second, how changes in the four types of exclusion will affect wage outcomes and the degree of occupational exclusion once all interactions have taken place. Using a simple, geometric two-sector model (à la trade theory) they first show that occupational exclusion and changes in occupational exclusion will indeed affect the relative economic well-being of women and men. Then they construct an algebraic model which allows them to illustrate more formally the effects of all the four exclusion sources on wage outcomes and the impact of changes in the respective exclusion sources on distributional outcomes and occupational segregation.

One result from their model is that institutional discrimination might increase men's earnings, but less so than the accompanying loss in female earnings: i.e., institutional discrimination involves an economic efficiency loss. Using a bargaining model of the family, the authors show that institutional discrimination of women may still pay off for men. Even if total family income is reduced, the change that institutional discrimination brings about in the relative earnings of women and men might increase male bargaining power within the household to such an extent that the welfare of the husband improves relative to a situation without institutional discrimination. This is but one illustration of the interesting insights that a more explicit general equilibrium modeling of the interactions between the demand for and supply of occupational labor, occupational wage differentials and occupational segregation seem to offer.

PART II GENDER ROLES, TIME ALLOCATION AND WAGES

Time allocation has a central place in the economics of gender. Gender differentials in the time allocated to market and household work, in the time allocated to different sectors and types of jobs in the market, and in the time allocated to different tasks within the household reflect and define gender but also contribute to the perpetuation of gender roles and the economic inequalities between men and women. Patterns of time allocation by gender are not constant, however. There is variation and change, over time and between countries. Evidently, it is also the case that the patterns are responsive to the economic incentives facing individuals and households.

Variation in the gender allocation of time between countries is the subject of Chapter 4 by *Dominique Anxo and Lennart Flood.* They study similarities and differences in time use patterns between France and Sweden, two countries for which similar time use surveys were conducted in the mid-1980s.

In terms of female labor force participation, Sweden is often regarded as a forerunner. About 82 percent of Swedish women are in the labor force, a level nearly as high as that for Swedish men (86 percent). French participation rates are lower (51 percent for women and 75 percent for men) and the gender differences still substantial. Despite the marked difference in female labor force participation between the two countries and despite important institutional and economic differences, a more in-depth analysis based on time use data clearly reveals that both countries are characterized by a rather traditional gender division of labor. The gender specialization is somewhat more pronounced in France than in Sweden, but the gender division is similar, with women and men specialized in typical activities. Males both in France and Sweden are highly specialized in the labor market (they spend on average 35.5 and 33 hours respectively per week on market work). A striking finding is that on average female time spent on market work is exactly the same in France and Sweden. But this equality hides large disparities in labor force participation rates (higher in Sweden) and incidence of part-time work (lower in France). Women in both countries spend more time on household work than they do on market work and they spend on average about three times more hours on household activities than men do. Even if Swedish males spend more time than French males on household work, the difference does not exceed one hour per week.

When the analysis of time use is limited to households with married or cohabiting couples, some interesting findings emerge. In both countries female time spent on household work is strongly reduced for women who work in the labor market, whereas male time spent on household work is hardly affected at all by the market work of their wives. Furthermore, for households where both spouses work full-time, the difference between the time Swedish males and French males spend on household activities amounts to only 12 minutes per week – which makes Sweden no longer look like very much of a forerunner.

In both countries children have a large impact on time use. Women with children reduce their time spent on the labor market (the impact being stronger in France) while men with children spend more time on the labor market than men without children do. Having children leads to a strong increase in women's household work, the increase being larger in France. French males with children actually reduce the time they spend on household activities, whereas Swedish males increase it slightly. Thus, in both countries having children reinforces gender specialization and strengthens the unequal gender allocation of time.

Where labor force participation rates give a picture of radical change, time use data reveal that strongly gendered patterns of time use still persist. Most of us probably do think that much has changed over time: that young women fare better in the labor market than their mothers and their older "sisters". But again, more in-depth analysis of the experiences of different cohorts modifies the picture. Certainly, there is change. But it also seems to be the case that "plus ça change, plus c'est la même chose". At least that is one possible interpretation of the results of the comparative cohort study of Danish women by *Michèle Naur and Nina Smith* in Chapter 5. Their study is based on samples of three birth cohorts of Danish men and women, aged 20–29, 30–39, and 40–49 respectively in 1980 (when the samples were selected). These individuals were observed every year during the 1980s up through 1990.

Comparing cohorts, what stands out is the rather dramatic change that took place in Danish women's time allocation to human capital investments. For the oldest cohort (40–49 years old in 1980) the gender difference in formal education amounted to 0.7 years and in accumulated work experience to 9.4 years in 1980. For the second cohort the gender difference at the same age (in 1990) amounted to 0.4 years for formal education and to 4.8 years for accumulated experience. For the youngest cohort the gender difference in 1990 (when that cohort was aged 30–39) had virtually disappeared for formal education and amounted to only 1.2 years for accumulated experience. These changes were not reflected in diminishing gender wage gaps, however. During the 1960s and 1970s the Danish gender wage gap decreased, but this tendency stopped in the 1980s, and since the mid-1980s the wage gap has increased slightly. This was due partly to changes in the wage formation process during the 1980s, which resulted in a slightly larger wage dispersion in general and a decrease in the public sector – private sector relative wages. Both are changes which, given the character of the horizontal and vertical gender segregation in the labor market, tend to favor men as a group relative to women.

By estimating wage functions for men and women belonging to the three cohorts and decomposing the corresponding gender wage gap, the authors are able to provide an in-depth analysis of what happened to the three cohorts of women in terms of returns on their human capital investments and wage penalties for having a family. A main conclusion of their study is that even though the youngest cohort starts out with a lower gender wage gap in 1980, it ends up in 1990 with approximately the same gap as the older cohorts. But the explanations for the wage gap are different across cohorts. In the oldest cohort, lack of human capital is the major factor. In the youngest and middle cohorts segregation and sectoral and occupational wage differentials seem to be important. Family responsibilities and children do not show up directly as significant factors increasing the gender wage gap. But since the gap seems relatively stable across cohorts once family formation has taken place, family responsibilities may still be important for the gender wage gap in the younger cohorts. But their effect may nowadays instead be indirect and work via (statistical) discrimination on the demand side and/or via individual choices of type of education, sector and occupation on the supply side.

The labor market experiences of today's young women and men are further illuminated in Chapter 6 by *Maria Hemström's* study of the early wage careers of young business graduates in Sweden. Her study is based on a survey conducted in 1992 among former students of the Business Administration program at Uppsala University who began their education in 1983–4 and entered the labor market some years later. The survey data are complemented by register data on taxable income and by data on university grades and degrees obtained. Thus the data set contains excellent controls for investments in human capital and work history prior to the survey. Of particular interest is that we are dealing here with a sample of highly motivated young men and women who have chosen the same type of education and future profession. Still, as the author presents her results, significant differences are revealed in how they fare once they enter the labor market.

A first finding is that the starting salaries for men were 5 percent higher than those for women. This female starting salary disadvantage cannot be explained by gender differences in characteristics, despite the refined measures of investments in human capital and labor force attachment included in the analysis. Seemingly identical attributes yield different returns depending on gender – but we do not know whether this is due to (statistical) discrimination by employers or to women setting lower reservation wages, at given wage offer distributions. By 1992 the male salary premium had increased to 12 percent: only one-fourth of this premium reflected gender differences in characteristics. The study further reveals interesting gender differences in the factors affecting wage levels and wage growth. Men received a huge return to experience, women none. Educational achievements influenced the wage growth (and starting salary) obtained by women, but had no effect on the earnings of men. Time spent in unemployment, on the other hand, had a negative impact on male current wages, but not on female wages. Neither marital status, children or career interruptions (for reasons other than studies or unemployment) had any direct impact on the earnings profile of either gender. One possible interpretation is that "the costs of children" were already paid for by the young women in advance: by their having been assigned to, or having voluntarily entered, different career tracks than male business graduates – a fate only possible to avoid by signalling via educational achievements that you are an "exceptional" and not an "average" young woman. Again, as in the Danish case, the impact of gender for younger generations of women seems to be indirect rather than direct.

PART III GENDER AND PAY STRUCTURES

The analysis of wage structures and of their role in the gender pay gap is taken further in the four chapters included in the last part of the volume. *Pål Longva and Steinar Strøm* (Chapter 7) base their study on a unique and large data set which includes all individuals in Norway who had a full-time job in 1991. It contains information about types of income (including non-wage compensation), personal characteristics, place of residence and industry affiliation (at a two-digit level), which enables them to make an in-depth study of the contribution of inter-industry wage differentials to the gender pay gap in Norway in the early 1990s.

Neoclassical models of the labor market explain wage differences as resulting from differences in productivity related characteristics (individual-specific human capital variables) and/or from deliberate individual choices in which a higher pay is substituted for other attributes of a job (compensating wage differentials). Recently neoclassical models have lost some ground in the explanation of labor market behavior and, hence, of measured wage differences: union power theories, efficiency wage theories, etc., have identified other possible causes of wage differences between firms and industries. In recent empirical studies of wage differentials, the focus has therefore been on explaining wage premiums by industry, after controlling for productivity related individual characteristics. In these studies the gender issue has usually not been addressed, but there are several reasons why industry wage premiums may differ between women and men. In their study Longva and Strøm allow for gender differences by estimating separate wage equations for women and men. They assume that wages depend on productivity related individual characteristics, but that there might be inter-industry wage differentials beyond the return to human capital. This framework enables them to answer questions such as: are women's inter-industry wage differentials as large and varied as men's? Is the ranking of industries by wage premiums the same for women and men? Is there any significant difference between the wage premium for men and women in specific industries?

The observed mean female–male wage ratio in their sample is 76 percent. A decomposition of the gender wage gap, based on the estimated wage equations for women and men, shows that as much as 71 percent can be attributed to discrimination. Gender differences in human capital endowments contribute only about 4 percent. The second largest contribution, 25 percent, comes from the differences in the distribution of male and female workers across industries. Thus, once more, sex segregation is shown to be a main culprit. Gender differences in inter-industry wage differentials account for only a negligible part of the wage gap. This means that on the whole, industry specific wage premiums are equivalent for men and women in Norway, a result which differs from that obtained for the USA.

The study by *Rita Asplund* in Chapter 8 seeks to uncover trends in wage levels, wage dispersion, wage mobility patterns and rates of return to human capital endowments among male and female white-collar workers in Finnish industry for the years 1980–94. Of particular interest is how women fared relative to men during the deep recession in the Finnish economy in the early 1990s. Her study is based on individual-level data collected by employers. The data set covers each year during the period 1980–94, and has the properties of both panel and cross-section data.

At the start of the study, in 1980, female white-collar workers in Finnish industry earned 62 percent of the average male white-collar total hourly wage. By 1994 the ratio had increased to 69 percent. Besides female white-collar workers earning less on the average than their male colleagues, there are marked gender differences in wage distributions and wage mobility. The female wage structure is much more compressed than the male one and there is a remarkably strong concentration of females in the lower half of the white-collar wage distribution, especially in the lowest wage decile where women constituted 95 percent in 1980. For the same year, over 90 percent of those located in the upper half of the wage distribution were men. The relative position of women improved somewhat in the boom years of the late 1980s. But the deep recession in the early 1990s put an end to, and even reversed, this trend. The women situated in the lower tail of the wage distribution have a higher probability than men of remaining there for several years. Furthermore, female white-collar workers tend to have a higher probability than male workers of moving downward in the wage distribution, i.e. of lagging behind in promotions and wage growth. These gender differences in wage mobility patterns intensified during the recession years in the early 1990s.

The gender wage gap for all Finnish white-collar workers, adjusted for gender differences in personal and job-related characteristics, declined from 26 percent in 1980 to 20 percent in 1991 and then increased slightly to 21 percent in 1994. The largest drop in the (adjusted) male–female wage gap was observed among the male-dominated category of upper-level, white-collar workers: from 30 percent in 1980 to 19 percent in 1991. But there was a substantial decline also among technical white-collar workers: from 23 percent in 1980 to 16 percent in 1991 (back to 18 percent in 1994). On the other hand there was no statistically significant decrease in the (adjusted) gender wage gap for the female-dominated category of clerical white-collar workers. Indeed, since the mid-1980s this group has persistently exhibited the largest male–female wage gap. A similar pattern is found for male-dominated versus female-dominated sectors of industry: the adjusted wage gap is smaller for the former and displays a clearly declining trend.

Estimation of separate wage functions for women and men reveals marked differences in male and female rewards to human capital investments. Particularly notable are the differences between the returns to educational degrees for male and female white-collar workers. For female, but not for male, white-collar workers the returns declined steadily at all educational levels over the period studied. By 1993, this development had resulted in a situation where the average return for women to a particular educational degree was of approximately the same magnitude as the average return for men to the closest lower educational degree. Huge gender differences are also found in the rewards to work experience and seniority, differences that widened further during the recession in the early 1990s. Decompositions of the gender wage gap show that the decline in the male–female wage ratio during the period studied is entirely attributable to decreases in the differences in background characteristics between male and female white-collar workers. The component reflecting gender differences in remuneration, often taken as a measure of wage discrimination, remained almost unchanged over the period.

There are many reasons why fringe benefits might differ between men and women. One reason is that fringe benefits tend to be related to the education, occupational status and place in the job hierarchy of the employee, and men and women are very differently placed in these respects. Another possible reason is that employers may use fringe benefits as a "hidden tool of discrimination": showing their favoritism of certain employees, for example males, by using fringe benefits as extra rewards that do not show up in regular wage statistics. Due to lack of data, fringe benefits have often been neglected in studies of the gender pay gap. Based on everyday observations, one suspects that this would lead to underestimates of the actual differences in pay between men and women. But how serious is this underestimate? Do studies that ignore the existence of gender differences in fringe benefits also tend to give a "wrong" picture of the pay-offs to human capital investments for men and women? These are the issues addressed in Chapter 9 by *Lena Granqvist*. Her study is based on data from a Finnish income distribution survey for 1989, which contains detailed information about different fringe benefits. From this information the total value of fringe benefits received by each individual has been calculated. In the sample, the female–male ratio for money wages amounted to 75 percent, whereas the female–male ratio for the total value of fringe benefits amounted to only about 50 percent. This indicates that the gender pay gap may indeed be underestimated when fringe benefits are left out.

Granqvist analyzes two different subsamples of Finnish workers which differ in their degree of labor market attachment. One sample includes full-time, full-year employees and the other employees working at least one month full-time or part-time during the year. For these two samples traditional wage equations are estimated, but with the value of fringe benefits alternatively excluded and included in the wage measure used as dependent variable. Including fringe benefits in the wage measure turns out to increase the gender pay gap significantly in both of the samples, even if the increase is not very large.

As a next step in the analysis separate wage equations are estimated for men and women. The results show that excluding fringe benefits from the wage measure tends to lead to underestimates of the returns to education for males, but not for females. Inter-industry wage differentials are affected by fringe benefits – more so for women than for men. On the other hand, including fringe benefits does not seem to have any significant effect on the returns to experience, either for men or for women. Decompositions of the gender wage gap, with and without fringe benefits, show that an inclusion of fringe benefits causes an increase in the gender differences in the returns to human capital that serves to widen the gender wage gap.

The studies of the gender wage gap included in the volume have been based so far on data from market economies and on wage determination theories developed for the analysis of the labor markets of such economies. In Chapter 10, *Katarina Katz* makes a detailed analysis of the wage structure and the background to the differences in the pay of men and women in the Soviet Union. Her study utilizes data from a survey of a Russian industrial town, Taganrog, in 1989. This was the first set of household data collected in the USSR to be made available for econometric analysis.

While there is general agreement that women in the USSR earned about one-third less than men, detailed knowledge of how this came about has been lacking. Katz's study reveals some particular features of work and wages in the Soviet system: the great importance of "gendered work" for male–female relative wages and the fact that many women coped with their "double burden" by working less than the standard work week, legally, or illegally with the connivance of their employer. Thus job segregation and "part-time" work were part of the gender wage story there, too.

In the Taganrog sample the female–male wage-ratio amounted to 65 percent for monthly wages and 73 percent for hourly wages. The fact that the ratio was smaller (and thus the gender wage gap larger) for monthly than for hourly wages reflects the possibilities of reduced work hours for certain categories of workers: possibilities utilized more by women than by men. Separate wage equations were estimated for men and women, for both hourly and monthly wages. A number of different specifications was tried, since in the case of a planned economy there are no underlying labor market theories to guide the investigation. The results are used to identify gender differences in the pay-off to human capital and job characteristics, and to decompose the gender wage gap into a part reflecting gender differences in characteristics and a part reflecting gender differences in coefficents (pay-offs to characteristics). It turns out that gender differences in experience, education, qualification level and working conditions account for roughly one-third of the male–female gap in hourly wages. Gender differences when it comes to partaking of different forms of reductions in work hours contribute in the opposite direction – decreasing the male–female gap in hourly (but not monthly) wages quite substantially. Taken one by one, few of the pay-off coefficients differ significantly between men and women: the really striking difference is found between the intercepts in the male and female wage equations. This means that Soviet women could improve their wages, both in absolute terms and relative to other women, through choice of education and job and by accepting bad working conditions. But regardless of this, their choices would make a rather small difference when it comes to the wage differential relative to men with the same personal and job characteristics. So, in the last analysis the author arrives at the conclusion that "Soviet women were paid less because they were women."

The results of the studies included in this volume exhibit similarities which tentatively can be summarized in the following way. During the last decades women have acquired personal characteristics more similar to men when it comes to educational level, labor force participation, time allocated to market work and work experience. This did contribute to a decline in the gender wage gap during most of the period, and it also means that gender differences in such characteristics play but a minor role for today's remaining wage gap. Likewise, marital status and children no longer seem to have any marked, direct effect on women's wages. On the other hand, the studies also reveal that large wage differentials still exist between women and men. For example, in the Danish study, the youngest cohort ended up at age 30–39 with approximately the same gender wage gap as older cohorts: it was the factors behind the gap that had changed. Thus the searchlight must now be focused elsewhere. The studies indicate that it should be on the causes behind educational, occupational and vertical (i.e. career) segregation by sex and on the effects of such segregation for the wages and returns to human capital investments of men and women. Furthermore, future research should try to sort out the indirect ways through which family responsibilities and gender today affect the pay gap.

Part I

WHERE ARE WE IN THE ECONOMICS OF GENDER?

1

THE GENDER PAY GAP

Francine D. Blau

While the gender pay gap has been an important focus of modern economists concerned with the economics of gender, it was not necessarily the primary concern of early commentators on gender inequities. For example, in the nineteenth century, with few married women employed outside the home, observers like American feminist, Charlotte Perkins Gillman (1898), and Marxist, Friedrich Engels (1884), focused on the gender division of labor itself and espoused the emancipating effects of women's participation in market work. Among economists as well as the general public, interest in gender issues including the gender pay gap has proceeded hand in hand with the growth in women's labor force participation. As women have come to comprise a larger share of the paid labor force and as market work has loomed larger in the typical woman's life, interest in the determinants of gender differences in labor market outcomes has also grown.

Of these labor market outcomes, the wage is of fundamental importance as a major determinant of economic welfare for employed individuals, as well as of the potential gain to market employment for those not currently employed. Further it serves as a significant input into myriad decisions ranging from labor supply to marriage and fertility, as well as a factor influencing bargaining power and relative status within the family. Thus, I focus here on wages in confidence that I am examining a question of considerable interest to economists and of considerable importance to women's economic well-being. However, I readily acknowledge that wages are by no means the whole story even as a measure of economic well-being.

Research on the gender pay gap has traditionally focused on the role of what might be termed, gender-specific factors, particularly gender differences in qualifications and differences in the treatment of otherwise equally qualified male and female workers (i.e., labor market discrimination). An innovative feature of recent research on gender and race differentials has been to integrate the analysis of the gender pay gap as well as other demographic differentials into the study of wage structure in general.[1] Wage structure describes the array of prices set for various labor market skills (measured and unmeasured) and rents received for employment in particular sectors of the economy.

Wage structure is potentially of considerable importance in determining the relative earnings of groups such as women who tend on average to have lower skills or to be located in lower paying sectors of the economy. In this chapter I will first consider the determinants of gender differentials, highlighting the role of wage structure. I will then illustrate the impact of wage structure by summarizing some of my recent work with Lawrence Kahn on international differences in male–female wage differentials (Blau and Kahn 1992a, 1995, 1996), and on trends over time in gender differentials in the USA (Blau and Kahn 1994, forthcoming). I will then offer some concluding thoughts and suggest some implications for public policy.

DETERMINANTS OF THE GENDER PAY GAP: GENDER SPECIFIC FACTORS

An initial early impetus to the study of wage differentials was provided by the British experience in World War I. Pursuant to the war effort, there was some substitution of women into traditionally male civilian jobs, although not nearly to the degree that there would be during World War II. Questions of the appropriate pay for women under these circumstances arose and stimulated a number of economic analyses of the sources of the gender pay differential – all of which gave a prominent causal role to occupational segregation (e.g., Fawcett 1918; Webb 1919; Edgeworth 1922). Modern efforts to understand the gender pay gap have generally rested on two strong pillars: the human capital explanation and models of labor market discrimination. These are gender specific explanations in that they focus on gender differences in qualifications or treatment as the cause of the pay gap.

Human capital explanations developed by Mincer and Polachek (1974), Polachek (1981) and others explain gender differences in economic outcomes on the basis of productivity differences between the sexes. This explanation is based on the gender division of labor within the family which, as we have seen, was the focus of the nineteenth-century commentators, and traces the impact of this division on the wages and occupations of men and women. Anticipating shorter and more discontinuous work lives as a consequence of their role within the family, women will have less incentive to invest in market-oriented formal education and on-the-job training than men. Their resulting smaller human capital investments will lower their earnings relative to men's. Similar considerations are also expected to produce gender differences in occupations, as women choose those where such investments are less important and where the wage penalties for workforce interruptions are smaller. In the absence of parental leave policies, women will especially avoid jobs requiring large investments in firm-specific skills because the returns to such investments are reaped only as long as one remains with the firm. Since the costs of firm-specific training are shared by employers and employees, employers are reluctant to hire women for these jobs due to their shorter expected tenure on average. The difficulty of distinguishing more career-oriented women from less career-oriented women means that the former may be the victims of such "statistical discrimination" as well (see below).

Thus, the human capital model provides a logically consistent explanation for gender differences in economic outcomes based on the traditional division of labor in the family. Not only will women earn less, but they will tend to be located in different occupations. Gender differences in industrial distribution could also occur if industries vary in their skill requirements. Thus the human capital model provides a rationale for the pay gap based on the voluntary decisions of women and men. Working in a similar direction is Becker's (1985) model in which the longer hours women spend on housework lowers the effort they put into their market jobs compared to men's and hence reduces their wages. But these models may also be viewed as shedding light on how the traditional division of labor in the family disadvantages women in the labor market. Thus, in this sense, they provide some support for the claim of the nineteenth-century observers that the traditional division of labor is of fundamental importance in determining women's status within the larger society. To the extent that gender differences in outcomes are not fully accounted for by productivity differences derived from these and other sources, models of labor market discrimination offer an explanation.

Theoretical work on discrimination was initiated by Becker's (1957) examination of race discrimination. Becker conceptualized discrimination as a taste or personal prejudice against members of a particular group. Models of statistical discrimination were later developed, in part to explain the persistence of discrimination in the long run in the face of competitive labor markets (e.g., Phelps 1972; Aigner and Cain 1977; Lundberg and Startz 1983). Such models assume a world of uncertainty and imperfect information and focus on differences between groups in the expected value of productivity or in the reliability with which productivity may be predicted. Since the real or perceived average gender differences that underlie statistical discrimination against women in the labor market tend to stem from the traditional division of labor in the family, this constitutes another route by which traditional gender roles within the family adversely affect women's labor market outcomes. Another aspect of interest is the relationship between occupational segregation and a discriminatory wage gap formulated in Bergmann's (1974) overcrowding model. Discriminatory exclusion of women from "male" jobs results in an excess supply of labor in "female" occupations, depressing wages there for otherwise equally productive workers.

These two explanations, gender differences in qualifications and differences in treatment of otherwise similar men and women, do not necessarily constitute mutually exclusive sources of gender wage differentials. Both may play a role and empirical studies based on cross-sectional data within countries provide considerable empirical support for each. One problem here is that evidence for discrimination relies on the existence of a residual gender pay gap which cannot be explained by gender differences in measured qualifications. This accords well with the definition of labor market discrimination, i.e., pay differences between groups that are not explained by productivity differences, but may also reflect group differences in unmeasured qualifications or compensating differentials. If men are more highly endowed with respect to these omitted variables then we would overestimate discrimination. Alternatively, if some of the factors controlled for (e.g., occupation, tenure with the employer) themselves reflect the impact of discrimination, then discrimination will be underestimated.

Another challenge to empirically decomposing the gender pay gap into its constituent parts is the existence of feedback effects. The traditional division of labor in the family may influence women's market outcomes through its effects on their acquisition of human capital and on rationales for employer discrimination against them. But it is also the case that by lowering the market rewards to women's human capital investments and labor force attachment, discrimination may reinforce the traditional division of labor in the family (e.g., Blau 1984; Blau and Ferber 1992; Weiss and Gronau 1981; Lundberg and Startz 1983). Even small initial discriminatory differences in wages may cumulate to large ones as men and women make human capital investment and time allocation decisions on the basis of them. Another nineteenth-century observer, John Stuart Mill, touched on this very relationship over one hundred years ago when he advocated women's "admissibility to all the functions and occupations hitherto retained as the monopoly of the stronger sex," claiming that "their disabilities elsewhere are only clung to in order to maintain their subordination in domestic life" (1878: 94).

DETERMINANTS OF THE GENDER PAY GAP: THE ROLE OF WAGE STRUCTURE

Thus, we see that the clear determination of the impact of qualifications versus discrimination in the gender pay gap is difficult for both empirical and conceptual reasons. However, both explanations share a common focus of being gender specific explanations of the pay gap. Analyses of trends over time in the gender differential within countries as well as intercountry comparisons of gender earnings ratios have traditionally tended to emphasize these types of gender-specific factors. The last fifteen to twenty years have been a time of ferment in the labor market with rapid changes in skill differentials and thus wage inequality in much of the industrialized world. Nowhere have these changes been more dramatic than in the USA. It has been a natural extension of the study of these types of realignments to examine their consequences for various demographic groups. Moreover, upon further reflection it is clear that the traditional gender specific factors imply an important role for wage structure.

The human capital model suggests that men and women tend to have different levels of labor market skills (especially work experience) and to be employed in different occupations and perhaps in different industries. Discrimination models too suggest that women may be segregated in different sectors of the labor market. This implies a potentially important role for wage structure in determining the pay gap. All else equal, the larger the returns to skills and the larger the rents received by individuals in favored sectors, the larger will be the gender gap. Similarly, labor market discrimination and/or actual female deficits in unmeasured skills result in employers treating women as if they have lower unmeasured as well as measured skills. Thus, the higher the rewards to unmeasured skills, the larger will be the gender gap, other things being equal.

The notion of a "high" or a "low" return is intrinsically a relative concept. Thus, the framework provided by wage structure requires some frame of reference and is particularly useful in analyzing changes over time in gender differentials or differences across countries in gender gaps. Such intertemporal and cross-country comparisons enable us to measure the effects of wage structure comparatively with reference to the situation that existed at an earlier point in time or that prevails in another country.

Consider the following examples. Suppose that in two countries women have lower levels of labor market experience than men but that the gender difference in experience is the same. If the return to experience is higher in one country, then that nation will have a larger gender pay gap. Similarly, an increase in the return to experience within a country will, all else equal, raise the gender gap. Or, as another example, suppose that the extent of occupational segregation by sex is the same in two countries, but that the wage premium associated with employment in "male" jobs is higher in one country. Then, again, that nation will have a higher pay gap. In like manner, an increase over time in the wage premium for "male" jobs will increase the gender gap, ceteris paribus. This second example suggests that a clear-cut distinction between gender-specific factors and wage structure may be difficult to achieve. A gender-specific policy like comparable worth which mandates pay adjustments across male and female jobs to provide for equal pay for work of equal value within the firm can obviously affect wage structure. Nonetheless, as I hope to show below, the notion of wage structure is quite useful and can shed considerable light on international differences in the gender gap as well as trends over time within countries.

Wage structure itself is determined by a variety of factors, including relative supplies of labor of various skill levels, technology, the composition of demand, and wage setting institutions. In recent years, there has been an increase in wage inequality within most of the industrialized countries (Gottschalk and Joyce 1995). Juhn *et al.* (1993), in their work on the US trends, make a strong case that this trend reflects a rising return to skills, both measured and unmeasured. We do not have full consensus regarding the reasons for this increase in the return to skill, but technological change and the impact of international trade are two of the chief candidates in the USA (e.g., Bound and Johnson 1992; Katz and Murphy 1992; Borjas and Ramey 1995). In addition, institutional factors, including declining union density and a falling value of the minimum wage, appear to have also contributed to rising inequality (Freeman 1994; Card forthcoming).

With respect to international comparisons, Kahn and I have emphasized in our work that systems of centrally determined pay are likely to entail less wage inequality and smaller gender wage differentials for a number of reasons. First, in the USA, a significant portion of the male–female pay gap has been found to be associated with inter-industry or inter-firm wage differentials (Blau 1977; Johnson and Solon 1986; Sorensen 1990; Groshen 1991). The relatively large pay variation across industries and firms in the USA is to some extent an outgrowth of our relatively decentralized pay-setting institutions. Therefore, centralized systems which reduce the extent of wage variation across industries and firms are likely to lower the gender differential, all else equal. Second, since in all countries the female wage distribution lies below that of the male, centralized systems that raise minimum pay levels regardless of gender will also tend to lower male–female wage differentials. In Blau and Kahn (forthcoming a), we find considerable evidence consistent with the view that, compared to the USA, the more centralized wage-setting institutions of other industrialized countries not only reduce overall wage inequality, but that this reduction is primarily due to greater compression at the bottom of the wage distribution in these countries rather than at the top. This tendency to bring up the bottom of the wage distribution in turn reflects not only the impact of conscious government and union policies in some countries, but, more generally, wage-setting institutions in both the union and non-union sector which lead to greater wage compression in each sector compared to the USA. Of particular interest is the greater prevalence in other countries of contract extension and informal mechanisms which extend union determined wages (and thus the more compressed union wage structure) to the non-union sector.

INTERNATIONAL DIFFERENCES IN THE GENDER GAP: A USA–SWEDEN COMPARISON

My work with Lawrence Kahn on international differences in the gender gap addresses a puzzle. While the relative qualifications of American women are high compared to women in other countries and the USA has had a longer and often stronger commitment to anti-discrimination laws than most industrialized nations, the USA has traditionally been among the countries with the largest gender gaps. Our results based on comparisons of the USA to nine other industrialized nations (Blau and Kahn 1995, 1996) suggest that the resolution of this paradox lies in the enormous importance of overall wage structure in explaining the lower ranking of US women. That is, the gender gap in the

USA is relatively high, not because of the traditional gender-specific factors but rather due to the fairly large penalty that the US wage structure imposes on groups that have below average skills (measured and unmeasured) or are located in less favored sectors. We find that the US gap would be similar to that in countries such as Sweden and Australia (the countries with the smallest differentials) if the USA had their level of wage inequality.

I illustrate the role of wage structure in influencing international differences in the gender pay gap in more detail by presenting some of our findings for the USA–Sweden comparison (Blau and Kahn 1996). This comparison is of interest because the USA and Sweden represent cases at the extremes of an international ranking of gender ratios, with Sweden having among the highest gender ratios of the advanced industrialized countries and the USA having among the lowest. This was particularly the case for the year from which we draw our data, 1984, since the gender gap has been narrowing in the USA and widening in Sweden. An additional reason why our results for these two countries are especially interesting is that our data sources, the Michigan Panel Study of Income Dynamics (PSID) for the USA and the Household Market and Nonmarket Activities Survey (HUS) for Sweden, contain information on actual labor market experience and thus permit us to control for this important variable in our wage regressions and corresponding decompositions.

USA–Sweden differences in the gender gap

The extent of the USA–Sweden difference in gender ratios may be seen in Figure 1.1 which shows unadjusted and adjusted gender log wage ratios for each country in 1984.[2] The unadjusted ratios of 66.9 percent for the USA and 82.7 percent for Sweden, indicate that the ratio was nearly 16 percentage points higher in Sweden – a considerable difference. Swedish women also fare better after adjusting for all variables, including education and experience, as well as major industry and occupation: the adjusted wage ratio[3] was 82.2 percent for the USA and 90.9 percent for Sweden. Thus, while adjusting for measured characteristics raises the ratio in each country and reduces the gap between the two countries, a substantial differential in gender ratios of almost 9 percentage points remains.

Interpreting these findings in terms of the conventional gender-specific explanations would lead us to view the smaller unexplained gender gap in Sweden as indicating that, compared to US women, Swedish women encounter less discrimination or have more favorable levels of unmeasured characteristics compared to men or both. The reduction in the USA–Sweden difference in the gender gap when controls are added for measured characteristics would imply that Swedish women, on net, also have more favorable levels of measured characteristics compared to their male counterparts than do US women. These conclusions make intuitive sense in some respects.

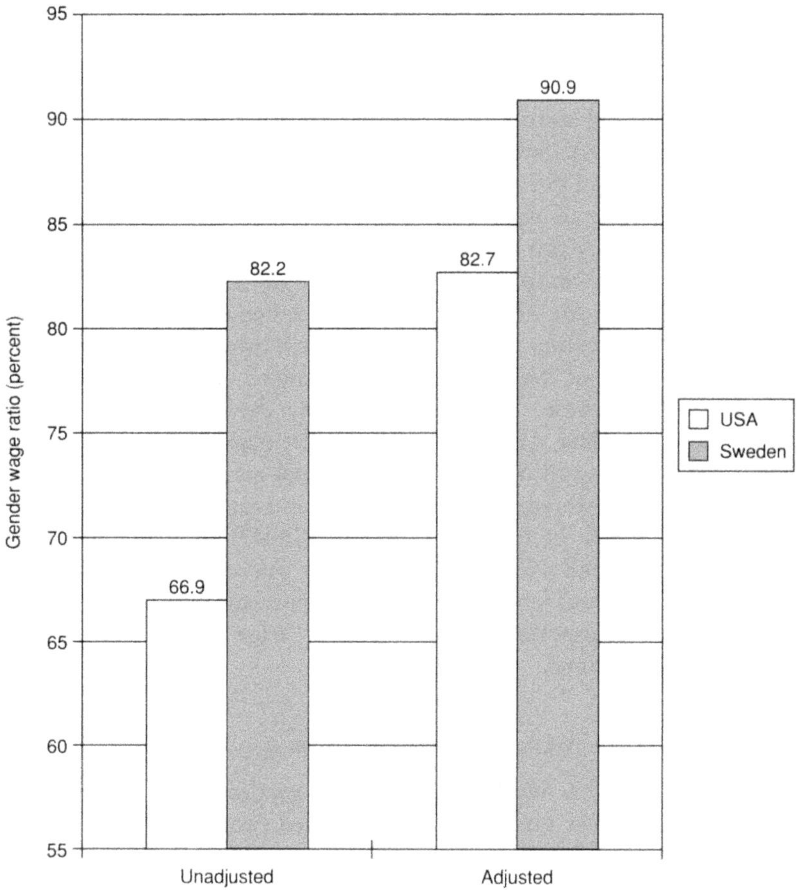

Figure 1.1 The gender wage ratio in the USA and Sweden

With regard to measured characteristics, Sweden's considerably more generous family leave policy may result in Swedish women being more firmly attached to their employers and to the labor market than US women.[4] With respect to discrimination, the results are somewhat surprising in that, as noted above, the USA has a considerably longer commitment to anti-discrimination laws than Sweden. However, it could be that Sweden's long-term commitment to attacking traditional gender roles through a variety of policies is responsible for the smaller unexplained pay gap in Sweden.

The role of wage structure

Despite the apparent reasonableness of the conclusions based on the conventional approach, our examination of the role of wage structure suggests that they are incorrect. Differences in women's qualifications or labor market treatment are not responsible for the larger US gender gap, rather it is differences in overall labor market prices in the two countries. To illuminate the role of wage structure, Kahn and I adapted a framework developed by Juhn *et al.* (1991) to analyze trends over time in race differentials in the USA. Gender-specific factors, including differences in qualifications and the impact of labor market discrimination, are regarded as determining the percentile ranking of women in the male wage distribution, while the overall wage structure (as measured by the magnitude of male wage inequality) determines the wage penalty or reward associated with this position in the wage distribution.

The basic premise here is that males at the same percentile ranking as women may be viewed as comparable in the eyes of employers. Thus, the same set of factors will determine the relative rewards of women and of these comparable males. The portion of the gender differential associated with women's lower ranking in the distribution in country A as compared to country B is ascribed to differences between the two countries in gender-specific factors (i.e., qualifications and treatment), while the portion that is due to the wage penalty associated with that position (i.e., greater wage inequality) in country A than in country B is attributed to wage structure. Some indirect evidence for the assumption that the same factors determine the relative rewards of women and of these male comparables, is that wage inequality is higher in the USA than in the other countries among both men and women (Blau and Kahn 1995, 1996).[5] Similarly, wage inequality in the USA has been increasing among both men and women (Katz and Murphy 1992; Blau and Kahn forthcoming b). This suggests that the same sets of factors – the prices of measured and unmeasured skills and wage-setting institutions – affect the wages of both men and women in a similar way.

It should be noted, however, that the possibility of discrimination complicates this division into gender-specific factors and wage structure because what we have labeled as the impact of wage structure may also include a component which is due to the interaction between wage structure and discrimination. That is, discrimination pushes women down in the distribution of male wages, while wage structure determines how large the penalty is for that lower position in the distribution.

Empirical findings for the effect of wage structure

Figure 1.2 presents the mean percentile rankings of women in each country's overall male wage distribution[6] and residual male wage distribution.[7] Our reasoning suggests that the female percentile rankings may be taken as overall indicators of gender-specific factors, that is the relative qualifications and treatment of women in each country. The placement of women in the overall male wage distribution represents the combined effects of gender differences in qualifications and treatment (or unmeasured characteristics).

The ranking of women in the male residual wage distribution represents the effect of gender differences in treatment (or unmeasured characteristics) only. Differences between the rankings of the two countries in Figures 1 and 2 represent the role of wage structure or the wage penalty associated with being below average in the distribution in each country.

Looking first at the findings for the unadjusted gender wage difference, we see that, despite the large USA–Sweden difference in the unadjusted gender gap, the mean percentile rankings of women in the male wage distribution in Sweden and the USA are virtually identical. On average in each country women rank at about the thirtieth percentile in the male wage distribution. This implies that the large difference in the gender gap between the two countries is entirely due to differences in wage structure, i.e., the larger wage penalty placed on women's lower position in the male wage

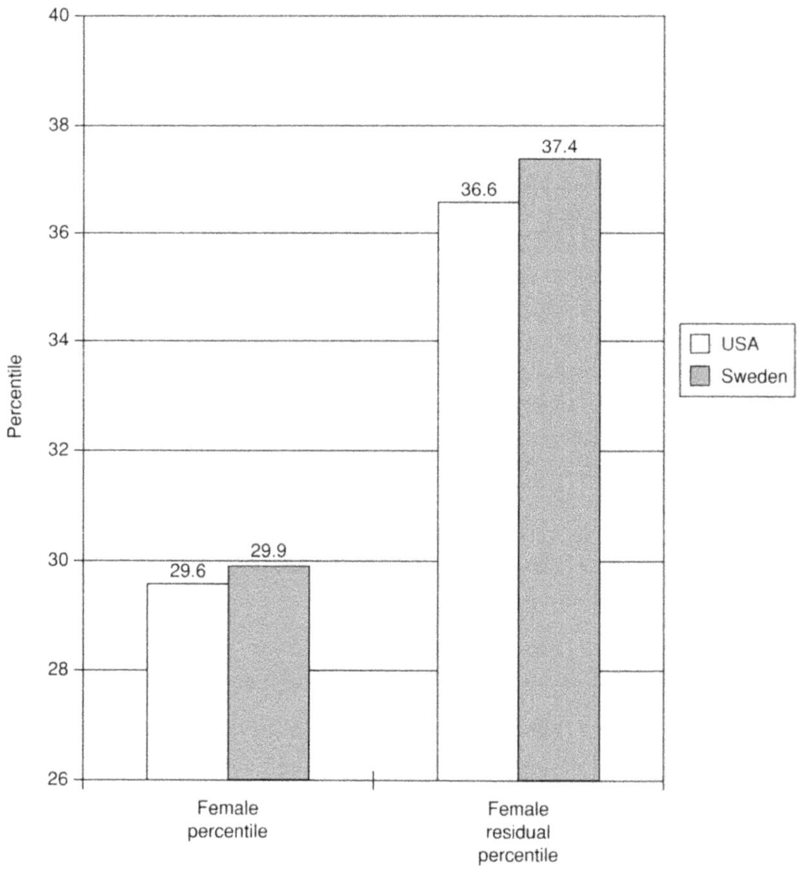

Figure 1.2 The mean female percentile in the male distribution in the USA and Sweden

distribution in the USA. This means that at the same mean percentile ranking, the resulting US gender ratio is much lower than in Sweden.

As discussed above, the overall mean female percentile rankings in Figure 1.2 show the combined effect of both sets of gender-specific factors: qualifications and labor market discrimination. It would be interesting to compare the USA and Sweden with respect to the latter, that is their treatment of otherwise equally qualified men and women. We have seen that the traditional estimate which involves computing adjusted earnings ratios indicates that Swedish women fare considerably better. As noted above, such estimates are subject to bias; and the adjusted ratios presented in Figure 1.1 are no exception. On the one hand, we may lack data on some factors which influence wages, although our inclusion of actual labor market experience at least surmounts this particular problem. On the other hand, we control for broadly defined industry and occupation even though these variables may reflect the impact of labor market discrimination. What is primarily of interest here, however, is the contrast between the traditional measure, the adjusted ratio shown in Figure 1.1, and the female residual percentile ranking shown in Figure 1.2.

For each country, we drop each woman's residual from the male wage regression into the distribution of male wage residuals and find the female mean of the resulting percentiles. This is an indicator of the relative wages of women in each country after controlling for gender differences in personal characteristics, industry and occupation. Unlike the traditional measure, it is not contaminated by differences in wage structure between the two countries. The caveat of course remains that, as with any analysis of this type, differences in the female rankings may also represent cross-country differences in the unmeasured characteristics of women relative to men. Indeed, in the absence of discrimination, one way to think of the rewards (penalties) associated with a higher (lower) position in the residual wage distribution would be as a return to unmeasured skills or characteristics.

Looking at Figure 1.2, we again find that while there are sizable USA–Sweden differences in the adjusted gender ratios, the mean percentile rankings of women in the residual wage distribution are virtually identical; in each country women rank at about the thirty-seventh percentile, on average. This implies that the observed differences in the adjusted gender ratios in Figure 1.1 are entirely due to differences in wage structure between the two countries, i.e., the larger wage penalty placed on women's lower position in the male residual wage distribution in the USA. Putting this somewhat differently, the extent of labor market discrimination against women (or unmeasured productivity differences between men and women) appears to be no greater in the USA than in Sweden.

Our detailed decomposition of the USA–Sweden gender log wage differentials (Blau and Kahn 1996) sheds additional light on the specific factors underlying these general results. Our finding that gender differences in observed characteristics do not contribute to the USA–Sweden difference in the gender gap reflects offsetting effects. On the one hand, there is a somewhat smaller gender difference in actual experience in Sweden (5 years) than in the USA (6 years) and a slightly more favorable relative occupational distribution of Swedish than of US women. On the other hand, this is offset by smaller gender differences in the USA in educational attainment and industrial distribution. At a common set of prices (or rewards for measured characteristics) for both countries, gender differences in observed characteristics contribute about the same amount to the male–female pay gap in each country. As we saw in our discussion of Figure 1.1, however, using the conventional approach, differences in characteristics contribute to a larger gender differential in the USA than in Sweden. This is because the conventional approach uses own-country prices; that is Swedish prices for Sweden and US prices for the USA. In general, the prices of skills are higher in the USA and this means that the female deficits (i.e., the lower qualifications of women compared to men) are more heavily penalized in the USA

Breaking this price factor out separately, we find that the impact of differences in observed prices between the USA and Sweden strongly favors Swedish women. The Swedish–US differences in relative rewards to employment by industry are the most important factors,[8] although less favorable (for women) prices of education and experience in the USA also play a role. Overall, the effect of wage structure, including the impact of prices of both measured and unmeasured characteristics, is more than sufficient to account for the considerably larger gender gap in the USA

Finally, Figure 1.3 presents the female percentile comparisons of the USA and Sweden in greater detail. It shows the female cumulative distribution functions that result from placing women in male wage deciles on the basis of the male log wage cut-offs. [9] So, for example, in the USA, approximately 20 percent of women fall in the first decile of the male distribution of log wages; almost 44 percent in or below the second male decile, etc. The results indicate that our conclusions based on a comparison of the mean female percentiles in the male distribution are fully supported by the more detailed comparison. Specifically, the US female cumulative distribution function is quite similar to that of Sweden. Particularly notable is the larger proportion of women in the lowest male wage decile in Sweden (29 percent) than in the USA (20 percent). This suggests an important role for labor market institutions which tend to "bring up the bottom" in reducing the gender pay gap in Sweden relative to the USA. That is, although the percentage of women who fall in the bottom male decile in Sweden generally exceeds that in the USA, the gender pay gap is smaller in Sweden. This suggests that formal or de facto wage floors in Sweden lessen the wage penalty for those in the bottom male decile.

I would argue that the rankings in Figure 1.2 and the distributions in Figure 1.3 provide an informative basis for comparing the economic status of women in the two countries. The fact that, on average, women in both

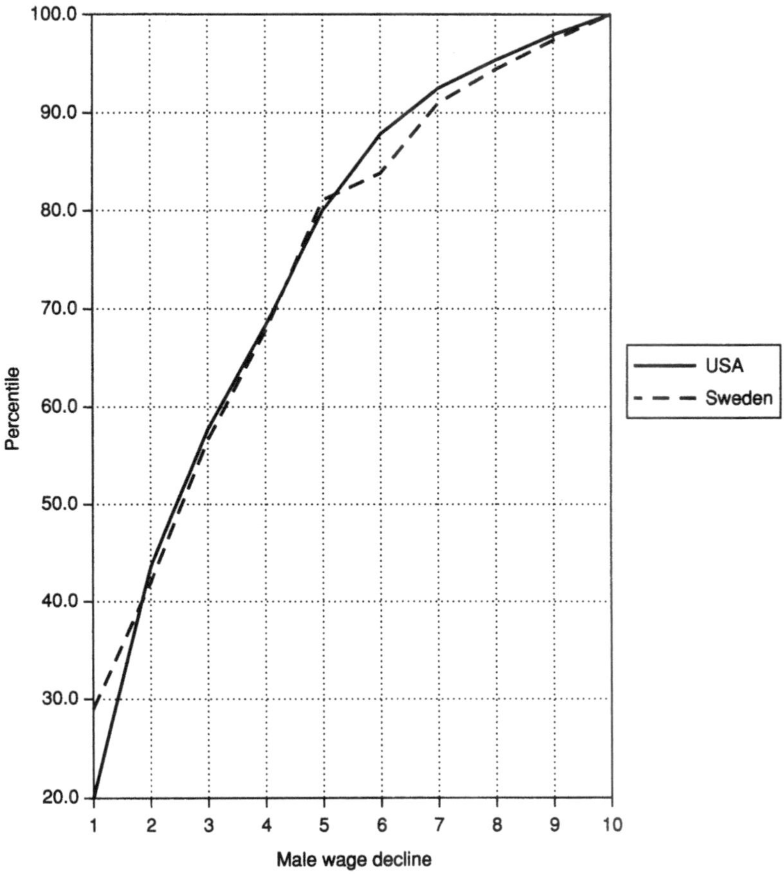

Figure 1.3 Cumulative distribution function, female wages relative to the male wage distribution, USA and Sweden

the USA and Sweden "out-earn" about 30 percent of male workers tells us a great deal about the relative qualifications and treatment of women compared to men in each country. What makes the rankings so informative in this respect is that they are not affected by differences in wage structure between the two countries. Moreover, our finding that US and Swedish women have similar rankings, on average, in the male wage distribution is quite surprising given the large disparities in gender earnings ratios shown in Figure 1.1. However, what this similar ranking in the male wage distribution in each of the two countries buys in terms of relative wage levels is of course also extremely important. The wage is an important indicator of economic well-being in and of itself and also, as noted above, a significant input into decision-making. So I would suggest that both measures, conventional earnings ratios and percentile rankings, are of interest.

FRANCINE D. BLAU

SWIMMING AGAINST THE TIDE: TRENDS IN THE GENDER GAP IN THE USA

While these findings on international differences in the gender gap help to resolve one paradox, they generate another. Wage inequality has been increasing in the USA. Our analysis implies that in the face of rising wage inequality, American women are essentially swimming upstream in a labor market that is growing increasingly unfavorable for workers with below average skills. In the face of rising rewards to labor market skills (measured and unmeasured) as appears to have occurred over the last fifteen to twenty years, women's relative skills and labor market treatment have to improve merely for the pay gap to remain constant; still larger gains are necessary for it to be reduced. Yet the gender pay gap has actually been falling in the USA since the late 1970s. How can we explain this apparent contradiction?

Kahn and I have examined this issue (Blau and Kahn 1994, forthcoming b) and found that women were able to swim against the current during the 1970s and 1980s and narrow the gender gap because gains in gender-specific factors were large enough to counterbalance the negative effect of the trends in wage structure on their relative earnings. Women gained from improvements in their relative qualifications, particularly their relative experience[10] and occupational distribution. A larger negative impact of de-unionization on male than female workers also contributed to a narrowing of the differential. Women benefited from a substantial decline in the "unexplained" portion of the gender gap, particularly when the adverse effects of widening residual inequality are netted out. These reductions in the unexplained gap may reflect improvements in unmeasured characteristics or reductions in discrimination. Both explanations are credible for this period. Since women improved the relative level of their measured characteristics, it is plausible that they also enhanced the relative level of their unmeasured characteristics. Further, as women increased their commitment to the labor market and their other job skills, it is possible that the rationale for statistical discrimination against them diminished. Moreover, while government efforts to enforce the anti-discrimination laws appear to have been reduced during the 1980s (Leonard 1989), it is possible that women's relative wage gains indirectly reflect the impact of government enforcement efforts in earlier years which had the effect of encouraging them to train for and enter traditionally male fields.

Another insight that may be derived from a focus on wage structure relates to the possibility that shifts in skill prices may have impacted men and women differently. In particular men and women appear to be viewed by employers as imperfect substitutes in the labor market. This is suggested by the considerable differences in the occupations and industries in which they work, as well as the substantial pay differences that exist for men and women with the same measured characteristics (e.g., Blau and Ferber 1992).

Thus, while rising skill prices may be expected to widen the gender pay gap, such changes need not affect men and women in precisely the same way. We examined this issue in Blau and Kahn (forthcoming b) and found that, over the 1980s, shifts in demand for output across industry–occupation cells favored women over men for low and medium skilled workers, but men over women among high skilled workers. The growth in the supply of women was also considerably larger at high skill levels.

Such a "gender twist" in the net supply of skill may have affected the relative gains of women within skill groups. We find evidence that this is indeed the case. While the unadjusted pay gap closed slightly faster for high skill women over the 1980s, industry and union representation effects strongly favored women at the bottom and middle of the skill distribution relative to those at the top. High skill women nonetheless advanced at a roughly similar pace as the other groups due to the large improvement in their human capital characteristics and occupational distribution. Further, wage gains for low skilled women would have been greater had the minimum wage not declined in real value over this period. The progress of high skilled women during this period is particularly impressive given the relatively unfavorable demand and supply shifts they faced.

CONCLUSION

As wage inequality has been increasing in recent years in many of the industrialized countries, labor economists have increasingly turned their attention to understanding its determinants and the reasons for changes over time. In this chapter I have endeavored to highlight the role of wage structure in determining the size of the gender pay gap both across countries and within a particular country, in this case the USA, where wage inequality is especially large. In addition to bringing a useful new construct to bear on analyses of male–female pay gaps, such a focus serves to integrate analyses of demographic differentials into the study of wage structure in general. This in itself is an interesting new development in labor economics.

From the perspective of our consideration of the determinants of the gender gap, the analysis of the trends in the pay gap over time in the USA provides an interesting comparison to our consideration of international differences in the gender gap. With respect to the puzzle of the relatively high US gender pay gap compared to other countries, wage structure provides the whole story – the traditional gender-specific factors do not appear to play a role. In contrast, with respect to the narrowing of the gender gap over time in the USA, the traditional gender specific factors, i.e., improvements in women's relative qualifications and declines in labor market discrimination as conventionally measured, are an extremely important part of the story. The insight which wage structure contributes is nonetheless also important; that is, the notion that women were indeed swimming against the tide. In the absence of substantial improvements in the gender-specific factors, the gender gap would have widened not narrowed. A comparison of these findings also serves to illustrate the more general point that the relative importance of gender-specific factors versus wage structure in any particular situation is an empirical question. With hindsight it is perhaps not surprising that wage structure proved to be a more significant part of the story in the international comparison than in the intertemporal one. Differences across countries in wage inequality, particularly between the USA and other industrialized nations, are of considerably greater magnitude than the changes in the level of inequality that have occurred in the USA over time, as significant as those changes have been.

The points made here about the potential importance of wage structure for the gender pay gap can readily be expanded to encompass the relative wages of other demographic groups, such as racial or ethnic minorities or immigrants, which have below average skills and/or face discrimination in the labor market. Thus, the well-being of particular demographic groups depends not only on group-specific factors like relative qualifications and the extent of discrimination against them, but also on the market factors and institutional arrangements which determine the return to skills in general and the relative rewards to employment in particular sectors of the economy. This insight has a number of policy implications. While I will particularly address policies aimed at women, these points can readily be generalized to other demographic groups.

First, in evaluating the effectiveness of "gender-specific" policies, that is policies which are specifically designed to impact economic outcomes for women, it is important to net out the effects of wage structure. On the one hand, policies may be erroneously deemed ineffective, or their impact may be underestimated, because the positive effect of the policies is disguised by adverse shifts in wage structure. So, for example, cross-national comparisons of the gender gap could lead one to conclude that gender-specific policies in the USA have been relatively ineffective in comparison to those in other countries. On the contrary, my work with Kahn implies that US gender-specific policies have been quite successful. US women have lagged behind those in other countries because of the high level of wage inequality in the USA which heavily penalizes workers with below average wages, regardless of gender. On the other hand, gender-specific policies could be incorrectly judged successful, or the extent of their success exaggerated, if they happen to be accompanied by changes in wage structure which benefit women as a group.

A second potential policy implication that follows from our work is that outcomes for women are affected not only by policies specifically targeted at them, but also by wage structure in general. This means that policies designed to alter wage structure, such as the promotion of more centralized wage determination or the establishment of relatively high minimum wages, constitute an alternative approach to improving wage outcomes for women. While this provides a potential benefit of such policies, it is important to bear in mind that they also have costs which need to be balanced against this benefit. These costs may be substantial.

First, there is the concern that minimum wages, particularly the imposition of relatively high wage floors, may create unemployment.[11] Second, centralized wage setting may allow firms too little flexibility to respond to differences in market conditions across industries or at the local level. Moreover, the compression of wage premia for skills may dampen workers' incentives to acquire appropriate training.[12] Finally, overly ambitious attempts to regulate the labor market may result in the growth of an uncovered sector, as appears to be the case, for example, in Italy.

The substantial potential costs to direct government intervention in wage setting make me hesitate to recommend attacking gender (or other demographic) differentials in this manner. An additional issue is that developments in the 1980s and 1990s have led to the decentralization of bargaining in virtually every industrialized country (see Katz 1993; Edin and Topel 1994; Edin and Holmlund 1995). As the protection of centralized wage structures falls away, women who continue to have less human capital on average and to encounter labor market discrimination are left exposed to downward pressure on their relative wages. Thus, in my view, the fundamental answer to the gender pay gap must lie with gender-specific policies designed to increase women's human capital and reduce discrimination against them. In a way, this conclusion is not entirely surprising in that it is these gender-specific differences in qualifications and treatment that constitute the basic cause of women's lower labor market outcomes. Were there no such differences, men and women would be similarly affected by the overall wage structure and by changes in it.

ACKNOWLEDGMENTS

This paper draws heavily on joint work with Lawrence Kahn. I am also indebted to him for helpful comments.

NOTES

1 Work on gender is described below. Wage structure has also been found to play a role in US trends in black–white and immigrant–native wage differentials (Juhn *et al.* 1991; LaLonde and Topel 1992).

2 Wages are equal to average hourly earnings.

3 That is, for each country j, we estimate a male wage equation:

$$Y_{im} = X_{im}\beta_m + e_{im} \qquad (1)$$

where Y_i is the log of wages; X_i is a vector of explanatory variables including education, experience and its square, and major industry and occupation, β is a vector of coefficients and e_i is a residual. The adjusted wage ratio is:

$$R_a = \exp\{-(e_m - e_f)\} \equiv \exp(e_f) \equiv (X_f\beta_f)/(X_f\beta_m) \quad (2)$$

where e_m and e_f are the mean residuals from the male wage regression for men (m) and women (f), X_f is a vector of means of the explanatory variables for women, and β_m and β_f are vectors of estimated coefficients from wage regressions estimated for men and women separately.

4 The expected impact of family leave (disproportionately taken by women even when it is available to men) is unclear a priori. On the one hand, it is possible that such policies raise the relative earnings of women by encouraging the preservation of their ties to particular firms and hence increasing the incentives of employers and women to invest in firm-specific training. On the other hand, the existence of such policies could increase the incidence and/or duration of temporary labor force withdrawals among women, raising the gender gap. Further, the incremental costs associated with mandated leave policies may increase the incentives of employers to discriminate against women.

5 Similarly, across our full sample of countries, male and female wage and residual wage variation are highly correlated (Blau and Kahn 1995, 1996).

6 We assign each woman in country *j* a percentile ranking in country *j*'s male wage distribution. The female mean of these percentiles by country is presented in Figure 1.2 as the "female percentile."

7 We find the percentile ranking of each woman's wage residual from the male wage regression (e_{if}) in the distribution of male wage residuals from the male wage regression (e_{im}). The mean female percentile for each country is presented in Figure 1.2 as the "female residual percentile."

8 This is not surprising given Edin and Zetterberg's (1992) finding that inter-industry wage differentials are much smaller in Sweden than in the USA.

9 Bernhardt *et al.* (forthcoming) use a similar methodology to examine the distribution of women's wages relative to the male distribution over time in the USA.

10 O'Neill and Polachek (1993) and Wellington (1993) also provide evidence of the importance of women's gains in relative experience in narrowing the gender gap.

11 For example, Katz *et al.* (1995) report that in France, where the minimum wage increased from 45.7 to 53.3 percent of median earnings from 1967 to 1987, the problem of youth unemployment has been more severe and the duration of unemployment has tended to be longer than in other OECD countries. Edin and Topel (1994) find that the solidarity wage policy followed in Sweden in the 1960s and 1970s disproportionately raised pay and lowered relative employment in low wage industries. On the other hand there is evidence for the USA which suggests that relatively small increases in the minimum wage do not have adverse employment effects. See Card and Krueger (1995); for responses to their research see *Industrial and Labor Relations Review* (1995).

12 Both complaints have been voiced about Sweden's "solidarity" wage policy by employers, and that country's generous student stipends and subsidized loans for higher education may be viewed in part as a means of offsetting the distortions caused by wage compression (Edin and Holmlund 1995).

REFERENCES

Aigner, Dennis and Cain, Glen (1977) "Statistical theories of discrimination in labor markets," *Industrial and Labor Relations Review* 30, 2: 175–87.

Becker, Gary S. (1957) *The Economics of Discrimination*, Chicago: University of Chicago Press.

—— (1985) "Human capital, effort, and the sexual division of labor," *Journal of Labor Economics* 3, 1(S): S33–S58.

Bergmann, Barbara (1974) "Occupational segregation, wages and profits when employers discriminate by race or sex," *Eastern Economic Journal* 1, 1–2: 103–10.

Bernhardt, Annette, Morris, Martina and Handcock, Mark (forthcoming) "Women's gains or men's losses? A closer look at the shrinking gender gap in earnings," *American Journal of Sociology*.

Blau, Francine D. (1977) *Equal Pay in the Office*, Lexington, MA: DC Heath.

—— (1984) "Discrimination against women: theory and evidence," in William A. Darity (ed.) *Labor Economics: Modern Views*, Boston: Kluwer-Nijhoff Publishing.

Blau, Francine D. and Ferber, Marianne A. (1992) *The Economics of Women, Men, and Work*, 2nd ed., Englewood Cliffs, NJ: Prentice Hall.

Blau, Francine D. and Kahn, Lawrence M. (1992a) "The gender earnings gap: learning from international comparisons," *American Economic Review* 82, 2: 533–8.

—— (1992b) "Race and gender pay differentials," in D. Lewin, O. Mitchell and P. Sherer (eds) *Research Frontiers in Industrial Relations and Human Resources*, Madison, WI: Industrial Relations Research Association.

—— (1994) "Rising wage inequality and the U.S. gender gap," *American Economic Review* 84, 2: 23–8.

—— (1995) "The gender earnings gap: some international evidence," in R. Freeman, and Lawrence Katz (eds) *Differences and Changes in Wage Structures*, Chicago, IL: University of Chicago Press.

—— (1996) "Wage structure and gender earnings differentials: an international comparison," *Economica* 63. 250 (S): S29–S62.

—— (forthcoming a) "International differences in male wage inequality: institutions versus market forces," *Journal of Political Economy*.

—— (forthcoming b) "Swimming upstream: trends in the gender wage differential in the 1980s," *Journal of Labor Economics*.

Borjas, George and Ramey, Valerie (1995) "Foreign competition, market power, and wage inequality: theory and evidence," *Quarterly Journal of Economics* 110, 4: 1075–110.

Bound, John and Johnson, George (1992) "Changes in the structure of wages in the 1980s: an evaluation of alternative explanations," *American Economic Review* 82, 3: 371–92.

Card, David (forthcoming) "The effect of unions on the distribution of wages," *Econometrica*.

Card, David and Krueger, Alan B. (1995) *Myth and Measurement: The New Economics of the Minimum Wage*, Princeton, NJ: Princeton University Press.

Edgeworth, F. Y. (1922) "Equal pay to men and women for equal work," *Economic Journal* 32, 128: 431–57.

Edin, Per-Anders and Holmlund, Bertil (1995) "The Swedish wage structure: the rise and fall of solidarity wage policy," in Richard Freeman and Lawrence Katz (eds) *Differences and Changes in Wage Structures*, Chicago, IL: University of Chicago Press.

Edin, Per-Anders and Zetterberg, Johnny (1992) "Interindustry wage differentials: evidence from Sweden and a comparison with the United States," *American Economic Review* 82, 5: 341–49.

Edin, Per-Anders and Topel, Robert (1994) "Wage policy and restructuring: the Swedish labor market since 1960," unpublished, University of Chicago.

Engels, Friedrich (1972, orig. pub. 1884) *The Origin of the Family, Private Property and the State*, New York: International Publishers.

Fawcett, Millicent G. (1918) "Equal pay for equal work," *Economic Journal* 28, 109: 1–6.

Freeman, Richard (1994) "How much has de-unionization contributed to the rise in male earnings inequality?" in Sheldon Danziger and Peter Gottschalk (eds) *Uneven Tides: Rising Inequality in America*, New York: Russell Sage Foundation.

Gillman, Charlotte Perkins (1966, orig. pub. 1898) *Women and Economics: A Study of the Economic Relation Between Men and Women as a Factor of Social Evolution*, New York: Harper & Row.

Gottschalk, Peter and Joyce, Mary (1995) "The impact of technological change, de-industrialization and internationalization of trade on earnings inequality: an international perspective," in K. McFate, R. Lawson and W.J. Wilson (eds) *Poverty, Inequality, and the Future of Social Policy*, New York: Russell Sage Foundation.

Groshen, Erica L. (1991) "The structure of the female/male wage differential: is it who you are, what you do, or where you work?" *Journal of Human Resources* 26, 3: 457–72.

Industrial and Labor Relations Review (1995) "Review symposium: Myth and Measurement: The New Economics of the Minimum Wage", by David Card and Alan B. Krueger, 48, 4: 827–49.

Johnson, George and Solon, Gary (1986) "Estimates of the direct effects of comparable worth policy," *American Economic Review* 76, 5: 1117–25.

Juhn, Chinhui, Murphy, Kevin M. and Pierce, Brooks (1991) "Accounting for the slowdown in black–white wage convergence," in M. Kosters (ed.) *Workers and their Wages*, Washington, DC: AEI Press.

—— (1993) "Wage inequality and the rise in returns to skill," *Journal of Political Economy* 101, 3: 410–42.

Katz, Harry C. (1993) "The decentralization of collective bargaining: a literature review and comparative analysis," *Industrial and Labor Relations Review* 47, 1: 3–22.

Katz, Lawrence F., Loveman, Gary W. and Blanchflower, David (1995) "A comparison of changes in the structure of wages in four OECD countries," in Richard Freeman and Lawrence Katz (eds) *Differences and Changes in Wage Structures*, Chicago, IL: University of Chicago Press.

Katz, Lawrence F. and Murphy, Kevin M. (1992) "Changes in relative wages, 1963–87: supply and demand factors," *Quarterly Journal of Economics* 107, 1: 35–78.

LaLonde, Robert J. and Topel, Robert H. (1992) "The assimilation of immigrants in the US labor market," in G. Borjas and R. Freeman (eds) *Immigration and the Work Force*, Chicago, IL: University of Chicago Press.

Leonard, Jonathan (1989) "Women and affirmative action," *Journal of Economic Perspectives* 3, 1: 61–75.

Lundberg, Shelly and Startz, Richard (1983) "Private discrimination and social intervention in competitive labor markets," *American Economic Review* 73, 3: 340–7.

Mill, John Stuart (1878, orig. pub. 1869) *On the Subjection of Women*, 4th ed., London: Longmans, Green, Reader & Dyer.

Mincer, Jacob and Polachek, Solomon W. (1974) "Family investments in human capital: earnings of women," *Journal of Political Economy* 82, 2, pt. 2: S76–S108.

O'Neill, June and Polachek, Solomon (1993) "Why the gender gap in wages narrowed in the 1980s," *Journal of Labor Economics* 11, 1: 205–28.

Phelps, Edmund S. (1972) "The statistical theory of racism and sexism," *American Economic Review* 62, 4, September: 659–61.

Polachek, Solomon (1981) "Occupational self-selection: a human capital approach to sex differences in occupational structure," *Review of Economics and Statistics* 63, 1: 60–9.

Sorensen, Elaine (1990) "The crowding hypothesis and comparable worth issue," *Journal of Human Resources* 25, 1: 55–89.

—— (1991) *Exploring the Reasons Behind the Narrowing Gender Gap in Earnings*, Washington, DC: The Urban Institute Press.

Webb, Beatrice (1919) *The Wages of Men and Women: Should They Be Equal*, London: Fabian Bookshop.

Weiss, Yorem and Gronau, Reuben (1981) "Expected interruptions in labour force participation and sex-related differences in earnings growth," *Review of Economic Studies* 48, 4: 607–19.

Wellington, Alison J. (1993) "Changes in the male/female wage gap, 1976–85," *Journal of Human Resources* 28, 2: 383–411.

2

OCCUPATIONAL SEGREGATION BY SEX AND CHANGEOVER TIME

Christina Jonung

INTRODUCTION[1]

Empirical studies on occupational segregation often note with surprise that while the labor force participation of women and men has become much more similar and in some countries wage differentials have become significantly smaller during the last decades, occupational segregation still lingers on. The fact that the increasing labor force participation of women has not led to a corresponding integration of men and women in occupation is considered something of a paradox.[2] My own work for Sweden shows that while the labor force participation rates for women aged 20 to 64 increased from 54 percent in 1963 to 85 percent in 1990, occupational segregation as measured by a dissimilarity index[3] for the three-digit level of the occupational distribution fell from 75 percent in 1960 to only 65 percent in 1990 (Jonung 1993). Thus, increased labor force participation for women does seem to have been accompanied by increased occupational integration, but to a significantly lesser degree.

The empirical findings inspired me to take a closer look at economic theories of occupational segregation by sex in order to find what they imply about the development of occupational segregation over time and whether the persistence of occupational segregation in the face of rising labor force participation can be explained. This chapter surveys such theories with a focus not so much on what the theories have to say about the cause of segregation, as on identifying the mechanisms of change in the amount and pattern of occupational segregation that the various theories describe.[4] What are the factors which retard or encourage change in occupational segregation according to different theories? Under what conditions does segregation increase or decrease? In particular, what relationship do different theories predict between changes in occupational segregation and changes in labor force participation on the one hand and wage differentials on the other hand. My conclusion is that from a theoretical perspective there is no paradox in the empirical developments that have been observed. Several economic theories would predict rising, or at least stable, occupational segregation as labor force participation rates of women rise and wage differentials by gender fall. I further argue that the fallacy in the interpretation of trends arises in part from disregarding work in the home as an occupational option for women.

WHAT IS OCCUPATIONAL SEGREGATION BY SEX?

Before entering the discussion of different theories, there are some definitional problems that I find relevant for the theoretical discussion and for relating any theory to empirical studies.[5] What is meant by occupational segregation? Most articles on the subject do not waste many words on the definition of occupational segregation. They simply state that occupational segregation by sex means that men and women are distributed differently across occupations and then proceed to discuss measures of occupational segregation, theories of occupational segregation or consequences of occupational segregation. But what distinguishes an occupation and what is meant by segregation?

Any analysis of segregation in the labor market has to start from the premise that labor is not homogeneous. Instead the labor offered on the labor market derives from workers with different characteristics regarding preferences, education, work experience, health, age, sex, race, etc. In the same way, jobs offered are dissimilar in the type of labor they require and in the attributes attached to the job. Skills, knowledge and physical strength demanded vary and working conditions differ. This implies that different kinds of labor are not perfectly substitutable for each other. The labor market is divided into segments more or less separated from each other depending upon the degree of substitutability. Segregation relates to how different groups are distributed across such segments.

One method used empirically to delineate markets, and the one in focus here, is through a division by occupations. In order to develop and draw implications from a theory of occupational segregation by sex, one needs to know how the concept of occupation is defined. For the purposes of analysis the occupational classification should represent characteristics affecting the substitutability of workers. The categorization should be such that the ease of substituting one worker's time for another's should be higher within each class of jobs than between each class of jobs. However, the actual borderline is a matter of subjective judgment. The characteristics chosen should be those which are emphasized in theories of occupational segregation. Different theories may, however, have different implicit or explicit concepts of occupations. The criterion most often mentioned in the literature, e.g., in human capital theory, is skill or education. However, in practice the classification of occupations is an empirical construct, not founded on theoretical criteria. Activities of the same general character are grouped together regardless of education or branch and people with simple work tasks and more qualified ones may be put together. The characteristics that link jobs may vary: subject matter dealt with, product produced, material used, etc.

Occupation is thus a vague concept, from a theoretical as well as an empirical perspective. The relationship between the basis for the occupational classification and theories of occupational segregation should be considered when it comes to evaluating the explanatory value of each theory. Any test of a theory is a test of what constitutes an occupation as well as a test of the cause of occupational segregation.

Most analyses of occupational segregation focus on the labor market, i.e., the market where labor services are directly paid for. Work, however, is also performed outside the labor market and we know that this non-market work is especially important for women. From the perspective of economic theory, work in the home is not fundamentally different from work in the market.[6] The form and place of production, and thus for work, is a matter of social organization, where the choice of organizational form depends upon the efficiency of various technologies and business associations. The arrangement changes over time as product demand, prices, wages, technologies, etc., change. This also means that the organization and structure of jobs are not independent of the structure of sex segregation in society.

The recent increase in the rate of labor force participation of women means that they have moved from an extremely segregated area, the home, to a less segregated one, the market for wage labor. The division of work between the sexes on the labor market is not independent of the division of labor between household work and market work (nor indeed of the sexual division of labor within the household). If time is transferred to the labor market, then most likely some of the work tasks women used to do at home will also be transferred. Segregation between home and the market will then be superseded by segregation between occupations in the market. Thus, simply including household work as an occupational option resolves the paradox mentioned at the beginning of this chapter. Disregarding work in the home as an occupational option in the analysis of segregation may lead to misleading conclusions, both in evaluating the extent of segregation and for understanding the factors behind changes in segregation.

ECONOMIC THEORIES OF OCCUPATIONAL SEGREGATION – A CLASSIFICATION

The economic theories put forward to explain occupational segregation are numerous and point to many possible causes. For the sake of brevity and clarity an attempt will be made to group different theories together. Still, some theoretical approaches will inevitably be left out and others treated somewhat cursorily.[7] The reasons for occupational segregation are of course not only economic in nature. Biological, psychological, sociological and cultural forces are also at work. While economic models usually do not explain the original cause of segregation, they can be used to analyze how outside forces enter economic decision-making and give rise to economic outcomes such as wage differentials and occupational segregation.

A comprehensive theory of occupational segregation by sex[8] should ideally be able to explain all of the following: the existence of occupational segregation, the pattern of occupational segregation (job characteristics and the worker characteristics of men and women in male, female and integrated occupations),[9] changes in the level and pattern of occupational segregation over time, and finally differences between countries in the level and pattern of occupational segregation. Of particular interest here is to analyze the relationship between occupational segregation and:

- changes in the life-cycle pattern of time allocation between work in the home and market work for men and women: i.e., changes in labor force participation or other measures of labor supply activity, such as hours of work;
- changes in the development of labor demand: e.g., increased demand for female labor;
- changes in the relative wages of men and women.

This chapter deals with theories of what factors determine the difference in distribution of men and women across occupations. How are people allocated to jobs, or in this case, occupations? In the labor economics literature the theory relevant for the study of occupational distribution is usually not presented under any separate heading such as "theory of the occupational structure": it is rather to be found under the issue of "determinants of the wage structure" or "compensating wage differentials."[10] According to a competitive market view of labor market processes, the occupation, or job structure, is determined jointly with the wage structure. The same factors determine both, one representing price and the other quantity. This also explains why occupational segregation by sex and wage differentials by sex are closely linked to each other.

Workers and jobs are matched through the labor market. On the supply side one finds individuals choosing between various occupations, weighing costs, such as years of education, time and effort against benefits, like pay, power, prestige, according to preferences. On the demand side one finds employers in the same way weighing costs for the employment of various types of workers, such as wages, expenses for non-monetary benefits and costs due to absence from work against benefits like the contribution of workers to output.

The wage structure and employment structure are determined by the interaction of the forces of demand and supply. Both sides of the market always play a role in the outcome, although separate theories emphasize one or the other as the most important or the driving force. For example: employers are willing to pay more for people with certain talents in certain jobs, because they will be more productive. Thus there are incentives for people with those talents to enter the well-paid occupations. The cost of turnover for employers probably varies across different jobs. Employers are thus reluctant to recruit, alternatively will pay less for, people likely to have a large incidence of turnover in jobs where the cost of staff turnover is high. People with an expected life style with high turnover in the labor market are likely to select occupations where they are not punished for this behavior. Discrimination lowers the return for those discriminated against. Therefore they "voluntarily" choose not to enter those occupations where they meet discrimination. One can focus one's analysis on either the supply side or the demand side of the market, but one cannot ignore the feedback effects from the side not chosen.

The adjustment process between labor supply and labor demand to different occupations takes place not only through changes in relative wages, but also through the flows between occupations, either by job changes of people on or outside the labor market or through the occupational choices of new entrants. Employers adjust, besides substituting workers of different types, as well in their use of capital and new technology.

Up till now we have disregarded the fact that the matching of workers and jobs is a process that in itself is resource consuming. The workings of markets, perhaps the labor market in particular, are characterized by what economists call transaction costs: costs for finding information about different products (in this case jobs and workers), establishing contact, negotiating contracts, and following up and controlling such contracts. A number of theories analyzes the implications of such costs for the outcome on the labor market in terms of unemployment, wage levels, wage structure, etc. Employers as well as people looking for work try to economize on transaction costs and this may lead to or reinforce occupational segregation if there are systematic differences between male and female preferences and/or labor market behavior or differences in the characteristics of jobs and occupations.

Some theories question the importance and strength of the competitive forces of supply and demand in determining labor market outcomes. Instead they emphasize, to a varying degree, the role of institutions, laws, traditions, social norms and hierarchies for wage determination and the placement of workers in jobs. Often they claim that individual behavior, ability and knowledge are the result of individuals adjusting to their placement in certain jobs rather than being the reason that individuals select or are recruited to different occupations,

Following the presentation above, this chapter is based on a fourfold division of theories of occupational segregation:

- labor supply theories of occupational choice;
- labor demand theories of occupational hiring;
- transaction cost theories of occupational matching;
- institutional theories.[11]

LABOR SUPPLY THEORIES OF OCCUPATIONAL CHOICE

The first set of theories is those where the major focus in the analysis of occupational segregation is on the decisions of labor suppliers. Of the four supply-side "theories" presented below, only the fourth, "the division of labor theory" has developed an economic rationale for occupational choice and it is also the one that has been the basis of most economic research.

Tastes

The simplest way to explain occupational segregation would be to ascribe it to inherent differences in the preferences of men and women.[12] Men and women are genetically different and these differences shape their preferences. Women are nurses, teachers, cleaners, sales clerks, waitresses, etc., because they prefer these tasks to masculine jobs. Men are engineers, mechanics, miners, etc., because it is in their nature to like these jobs more than caring for or serving others.

Explanations for the division between market work and work in the home would run along similar lines. Women participate less in the market and work part-time more than men because women prefer non-market work tasks to those available in the market, and men prefer market work to household work. Men may even be more interested in monetary rewards than women, who may value more the non-pecuniary, emotional benefits.

The idea of tastes being important for occupational segregation of course builds upon the existence of a heterogeneity in jobs on the demand side as well. However, referring to preferences provides no clues as to what type of occupations will be female or male, nor does the theory predict what the expected characteristics of female–male occupations should be in terms of wages, life-cycle income profiles, unemployment, level of education, on-the-job-training, etc.[13] Men and women are in the occupations they prefer and thus the characteristics of these occupations are those which each sex prefers. One possible prediction is that female occupations in the market are those related to tasks in the home or related to women's role of giving birth to children. Women in caring and teaching roles could thus be expected. But why should women prefer jobs as secretaries to those as administrators, as sales clerks rather than managers, or nurses instead of doctors? And why should women's jobs have a lower pay than men's jobs?

If female jobs pay less than male jobs in a competitive labor market framework, this must be the result of the workings of supply and demand. This is illustrated in Figure 2.1. Suppose we have two occupations, A and B. Both are assumed equal in terms of the non-wage benefits they offer and the qualifications they demand. Employers are supposed to be indifferent regarding the choice between men and women. Initially let us also assume that men and women are indifferent between the two occupations.

The supply curve for women (S_f) is drawn on the assumption that women prefer non-market work to market work. They start to enter the labor market at a higher reservation wage, are in the market to a lesser extent, and are more sensitive to wage changes in their participation decision. Men's supply curve (S_m) is steeper since they consider their place to be in the market almost regardless of wage. D_a and D_b are the demand curves for occupations A and B, respectively. If workers are indifferent between the two occupations and employers are indifferent between men and women, the wage will be equal to w and women and men will be randomly distributed between the two occupations.[14]

Let us now initially assume that all women have similar preferences and that they prefer occupation B, while men are still indifferent between the two occupations. What will be the outcome? At the going wage all women will be working in B together with some men, and A will be an all male occupation. We will thus have complete segregation in the male occupation and women segregated into mixed occupations. The wage will remain the same in the two occupations (assuming that employers do not apply wage discrimination within an occupation). Even if women were willing to work for less in occupation B, men are not.

If women instead prefer occupation A, what will happen? Women will be willing to work in A for a lower wage than they receive in B. Employers will thus want to hire women first. Since the supply of women to A is larger than the demand at the present wage, the wage will fall in A. With women moving out of B the wage will rise there instead. A wage difference will

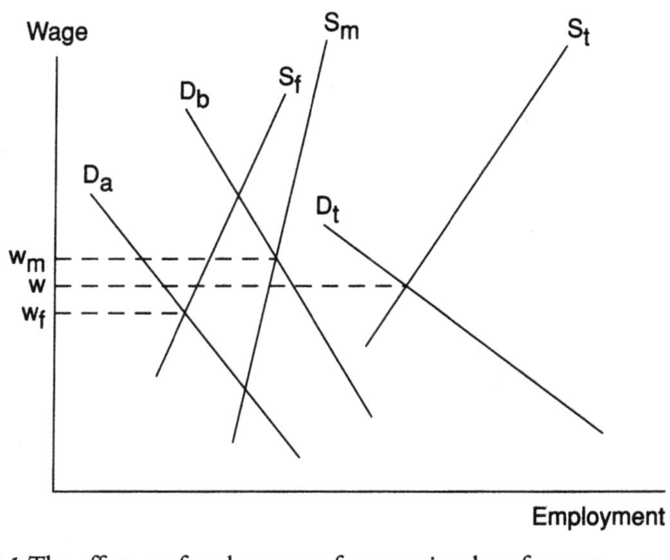

Figure 2.1 The effect on female wages of occupational preferences

emerge between occupation A and B. A will become a female occupation and B a male occupation as long as the wage difference is not large enough to compensate women for their dislike of occupation B. If preferences among women are heterogeneous and some have preferences more similar to men, we will observe some integration of B, and the upward wage pressure there and the downward wage pressure in occupation A will be reduced.

Only in the second case did the assumption of different preferences cause both segregation and a wage difference between occupations. A necessary condition for preferences to explain sex differences in wages and occupational distribution is thus that the occupations that women prefer are also those where demand (and thus productivity) is low relative to their supply to the market or, expressed alternatively, where jobs with attributes that are valued more by women than men are relatively scarce (Corcoran and Courant 1985: 276). Additionally, preferences among women have to be similar enough for the wage differential not to entice a number sufficient to erode the wage differential to move over to occupation B. We have no explanation, however, of why the occupations that women prefer should be those of low demand and low productivity.[15] Such an explanation is attempted in the division of labor theory described below.

Assuming preferences are stable and tastes do not change (since they are assumed innate) does the theory describe an immutable state where segregation and wage relations never change? No, changes in demand, due for example to changes in consumer demand or technology, will cause changes in segregation and wage relations. Additionally, economic policy changes, such as introducing subsidies to out-of-home childcare will influence decisions as well. Suppose we are in the situation where women prefer occupation A and thus receive a lower wage than men. If demand increases in male occupations (B), wages will increase in this sector and wage differentials will rise. When the wage difference becomes large enough to compensate for their dislike of type B jobs, women will start entering. Some integration will occur in male occupations, but wage differentials between male and female jobs will remain. If we have more than two occupations we may find that some, namely those originally male occupations which women dislike the least, switching in gender.

Suppose instead that the increase in demand for labor arises in female occupations. Wages in these occupations will rise and more women will enter the market. As the wage gets closer to that of men, men with more "female" tastes may enter the female sector. Segregation in female jobs will decrease in connection with the narrowing of wage differences, due to men moving into female occupations. Male occupations will remain segregated. If women's labor supply is very elastic, labor force participation will rise rapidly and wages in female jobs may not rise much even with strong shifts in demand. Thus, there will not be a marked change in segregation within the labor market.

If the major explanation of occupational segregation is distinct preferences according to sex, it is easy to understand the persistence of occupational segregation within the labor market despite increases in female labor force participation. In this case female entry to the market would be expected to occur primarily in connection with increased demand in typical female occupations. Increases in the labor force participation of women and the proportion of women in the labor force should be due to structural changes, where the numbers employed in female-dominated occupations grow in relation to male-dominated ones, and not to an increased proportion of women in male occupations. If women do enter some male occupations, we should observe a tendency towards a shift in gender composition of those occupations, as women will change home work for the least disliked male occupations. The result may even be increased segregation. If we include work in the home as an occupation in evaluating segregation the situation should be characterized by stability.

What is the relation between occupational segregation and wage differentials with the assumptions about preferences made above? Integration of women into male occupations should occur only in connection with widening wage differentials between male and female jobs. Integration of men into female jobs should occur in connection with diminishing wage differentials (if men do not all prefer male jobs). What if one tries to implement a policy of administratively reducing wage differentials between occupations such as a solidaristic wage policy or comparable worth policy? The result of such policies will be that incentives for women to work in male areas will be reduced and segregation may increase.

The first criticism that can be leveled against simply ascribing segregation to differences in tastes is that it provides no explanation as to why women should prefer low demand, low productivity, low wage occupations (and men the opposite), as characteristics necessary to create a pattern of occupational segregation where women's occupations are less well paid than men's. Second, actual data on occupational segregation indicate an extreme sex distribution in many occupations with well over 90 percent women or 90 percent men. This means that in order to refer to preferences only as a rationalization for segregation, we have to assume a very wide variation in tastes by gender indeed. Third, "natural" tastes seem to vary widely from country to country. Even though women's and men's occupational distribution within industrial countries shows similarities, there are also significant discrepancies between countries (Rubery and Fagan 1993). The distributions also vary widely over time, and some occupations that were once all male are today virtually all female, while others that were dominated by women have been taken over by men. This casts doubts that tastes can be considered intrinsic, and suggests rather that they are socially constructed.

Ability

A second explanation of occupational segregation, also starting from an assumption that men and women are biologically and/or psychologically different, asserts that men and women have different innate abilities, for example, in physical strength, mathematical and linguistic ability, motivation or nurturing. This means that each sex brings different endowments of human capital to the market. With this approach occupations are separated by the requirement of different skills. Distinct talents give different pay-off in terms of wage and other benefits in different pursuits. Women choose the type of education and occupation in which they have a comparative advantage and which gives the best pay-off for their inherent talents. Men do the same.

Starting from assumptions of differences in ability we would expect wage differentials within occupations. With an absolute advantage these should be such that women have a wage advantage in female occupations and men a wage advantage in male occupations. With a comparative advantage it should be enough for women to do relatively better than men within female occupations. If costs of entering occupations are the same, women should earn more in female than in male occupations. Normally, we find that wage differences favor men in all occupations, but that the female/male wage ratio is higher in female occupations. Average pay in female occupations is less than in male occupations (Sorensen 1994).

Why should men be paid more for their talents? The answer is the same as the one provided above in the discussion of taste: because they are scarce in relation to demand. Women have directed a large share of their talents to non-market work where demand for them has been high. If women's talents and services can be enjoyed for "free" outside the market, why pay dearly for them in the market? If men are more achievement oriented than women, they will also be motivated to seek positions and occupations of more power, prestige and pay than women.

Again changes in the occupational distribution may come about through shifts in the demand for labor that may affect the relative profitability of occupations. If demand for female talents rises in the market, women could easily shift from work at home to work in the market. Again we see nothing contradictory in rising labor force participation rates and a stable or rising level of occupational segregation. If demand rises in male occupations, it may be worthwhile for women, especially those whose abilities do not differ much from men's, to enter male occupations. However, this requires a wage differential within the occupation. If wage differentials are "artificially reduced," employers will not be willing to hire women, whose productivity is assumed to be less than men's. Thus, reduced wage differentials could be related to increased segregation. We may also think of a situation where as the demand for labor rises, women successively take over the male occupations where ability differs the least and men move into other occupations where their productivity is higher. This would give rise to the often alleged effect that average wages fall as women enter an occupation (in this case due to average falling productivity).

A problem with the "ability" as well as with the "taste" explanation is that neither can be assumed to be neutral to the gendering of occupations. With respect to taste, if each sex prefers to work with members of its own sex, women will be reluctant to enter occupations with a greater proportion of men and vice versa. We can also imagine that the social and cultural factors in each occupation, i.e. the way people interact, communicate, and the values they stress in their work, adjust to the preferences of the sex in majority and thus interact with "taste." With respect to ability, if there are only a few women in an occupation, tools, methods of work, even the way to manage and solve problems may be adjusted to men in a way that reduces the ability of women to be productive (and vice versa for men in female occupations). Thus, even if there are innate differences in men's and women's tastes and abilities, they may not be relevant for their interest or productivity in a specific occupation unless the occupation is gendered to begin with. If the gendering of occupations is what keeps men and women out, the entry of men and women into non-traditional occupations can be expected to stimulate integration at a quicker pace than if taste and ability have a more direct effect on the choice of occupations.

A factor which may bring about change in occupational segregation with either divergent tastes or variations in ability between the sexes is technological change. New technology may change the work tasks within occupations in ways that make new abilities important and/or other abilities obsolete or in ways that make them appealing to new groups (e.g., requiring less physical strength, becoming less dirty, demanding higher or different education). Consequently the pattern of sex segregation will change, but not necessarily the level. The influence of technological change on segregation is relevant for all of the theories and will not be further discussed below.

Again, ascribing segregation to differences in innate ability seems too simplistic to motivate the profound occupational segregation by sex. Even if research has been able to identify what appears to be basic differences between the average man and average woman in personality traits, the variation within and the overlap between the groups is great.[16] Differences in the occupational distribution between men and women are far greater than what could be expected from only differences in innate taste and ability, which suggests that economic motives and considerations add to and amplify whatever initial differences there may be.

Sex role socialization

In economic models both tastes and initial endowments are typically assumed to be exogenous. Tastes and ability were discussed above as if they were biologically or psychologically intrinsic to men and women. However, preferences and "natural talents" as we see them in the labor market are also, many will say mainly, socially constructed through children's upbringing and through a continuing lifelong process of adjusting to sex roles. This is what is termed pre-market discrimination, societal discrimination or sex role socialization.[17]

Sex role socialization is the process by which we learn gender-appropriate values and competencies through our interaction with family, friends, school, books and media, working life, and social life in general in the society we live in. Our gender-specific tastes and skills are acquired through this process of observing, listening, imitating, practising and in some cases obeying. Many of these traits are relevant for occupational choice. Gender stereotypes about family obligations and the role of work shape men's and women's expectations. Characteristics valued in male fields such as physical strength, competitiveness, achievement orientation, authority, and mathematical and technical ability may be encouraged in boys, and nurturing, cooperation, subordination and linguistic ability encouraged in girls.

The result is gender differences in the values attached to different activities as well as in the skills acquired through the socialization process. Choosing in accordance with "feminine" or "masculine" values may seem particularly important for young people, who want to strengthen their sexual identity. Since people around you are socialized in similar ways, the occupational selection process is reinforced. A woman entering a male field will have to overcome not only her own feelings of acting inappropriately for her sex, but possibly also the disapproval of her friends, family or coworkers. In addition, socialization adds to the tendency for employers to screen in a statistically discriminatory way (see below).

Short run analysis of the effects of socially acquired tastes and abilities is similar to the analysis of innate tastes and abilities above. In the long run, if tastes and abilities are the result of social influences, they may be revised as the economic consequences of given sex roles change for individuals, employers or for society as a whole.

Socialization has not been explicitly incorporated into economic models. Depending upon which theoretical approach is taken, socialization can be looked upon in two ways from an economic perspective: either the process is an efficient investment in skills in anticipation of future roles in family, work and society, which conforms to human capital theory; or it is a societal discrimination that prescribes specific roles for men and women and upholds them through a gendered social structure, a view which is close to models of discrimination or institutional models.[18] Each of these approaches is treated below.

Division of labor in the home

The most elaborate economic theory of gender differences in occupational choice, and one where gender divisions are based on economic reasoning to a greater extent than in the theories above, is the theory of division of labor in the family, usually combined with human capital theory. The theory can be seen as providing an economic rationale for what superficially appears as differences in taste and ability and for the socialization of boys and girls in different directions. The logical consistency and internal coherence of the theory make it possible to derive more detailed implications than from other theories. It has also been subjected to extensive empirical testing. In its most extended form the theory rests upon three propositions.

1 Division of labor within the home is profitable for the family.
2 Investment in human capital depends on labor force attachment.
3 Occupations differ in terms of the human capital they require and/or offer.

The starting point for the division of labor theory is the time allocation decisions within a family. According to the "new home economics" (Becker 1965, 1991), the family is viewed as a production unit, a small firm, trying to maximize its utility by producing final commodities for the family: good meals, clean clothes, a cozy home, sleep, health and care.[19,20] The theory argues that in activities where family members' time is substitutable, the family can make gains from specialization if the partners' productivity in the household or earnings capacity in the market differs. The person who can receive the highest market wage will spend more time in market work, while the person most productive in household work will take the major responsibility in this area. If the same person is most productive in both areas, the division of labor will be determined according to comparative advantage. The specialization results in differences between men and women in the extent and pattern of their labor supply and consequently in the size and type of investment in human capital they choose to make. Inequalities in the labor market with respect to wages, occupational distribution, unemployment, etc., reflect differences in the labor force experience and the human capital acquired by men and women.

According to the household model, specialization may be beneficial for the family.[21] There is nothing in the model, however, that implies that members of one sex will always be responsible for household work and members of the other for the main share of market work. The division of labor according to gender is only explained given differences in men's and women's productivity in certain activities. The theory has no explanations of why these productivity differences arise.[22] Such explanations have to be found outside the theory. So we return to relying on biology, psychology, history, traditions, sex role socialization, etc., as the sources of the comparative advantages of men and women in the family. Another possible assumption that will introduce productivity differentials, although usually not brought into these models, is labor market discrimination of women.

The added insight provided by the division of labor theory is a mechanism through which these factors may work: by creating differences in women's and men's productivity and as a consequence in their allocation of time. The model also tells us that any difference in taste with respect to market and household work, any difference in ability with respect to market and household work, any difference in the socialization of each sex, or indeed any degree of discrimination, will have its effects amplified by adjustment to the gains of specialization described by the model. Thus the theory is well apt to illustrate how the forces of segregation described by the different theories reinforce each other.

According to the model (and the ad hoc assumptions added to it) women's priority occupation will be work in the home. If women enter the labor market it should be for occupations with requirements compatible with the demands of work at home – that is part-time, flexible work hours, short commuting distance and not much overtime work or traveling involved.

In addition – which is an implication stressed by the theory – the family allocation of time influences the human capital investment that men and women choose to make: their level and type of education, and their on-the-job training. The returns to human capital accrue over a long time period and it is necessary for the individual to use his/her own time in certain activities for the returns to be actualized. This means that the expectations which a person has about the future allocation of time are crucial for evaluating a human capital investment. It is also a reason why non-pecuniary aspects of a job have an important influence on such investment decisions.

According to the household model above, while a man can concentrate on maximizing his lifetime income stream, a woman has a more complicated decision to make. The specialization of labor within the household implies that women expect to spend less, and possibly more discontinuous, time in the labor market than men, and more time working in the home. A woman will consider the probability of participating in the labor force, of having to interrupt a market career, to work part-time or at flexible hours. As a result of these calculations, women's investments in human capital are likely to be less oriented towards the market than those of men. Women are likely to favor education that increases the productivity of time used in the home as well as in the market. The content will be such that it relates to the functions at home and can be used in both sectors. If the major return to education accrues through the market sector, women will choose shorter education than men. It is not profitable to spend years on an education that is not certain to be used as intended.

The theory of human capital relates naturally to occupational choice. From the perspective of this theory occupations are seen as characterized by their human capital requirements: first, by the amount and type of education required to enter the occupation or occupational group; second, by the amount and type of investments in human capital offered during the pursuit of an occupational career; third, by the amount and type of human capital required to advance within the profession. The choice of an occupation is an implicit choice of what skills to develop. Certain occupations involve a lot of learning and possibilities of career development. Others offer little new knowledge. According to human capital theory, investments in on-the-job training often have to be paid for by initially accepting a relatively low wage at the beginning of working life, then receiving rapid wage increases later on as returns on investments come due.

If women intend to supply less of their time to the market than men, they demand less and different human capital than men, which is likely to show in their choice of occupations. Women are hypothesized to be in occupations with relatively high starting salaries, but flat experience earnings curves, which is assumed typical of low investment careers (Zellner 1975). They are considered to give priority to general training, usable in many areas of the labor market, over specific training usable only in a particular firm. If women plan interruptions in their market work due to childcare, they have incentives to choose occupations where the wage penalty (due to depreciation of their market capital) for such behavior is minimized, e.g., where technological progress is slow (Mincer and Polachek 1974, Polachek 1981). Becker (1985) has suggested that even if women work the same number of hours as men, family responsibilities will reduce the effort they can put into market work and they have to choose less demanding jobs which are compatible with a family life. Women will be less productive than men in the high investment careers and thus unable to reap the returns that make the investment worthwhile.

The division of labor theory, focusing on the role of labor force attachment for human capital investments thus offers a possible explanation for the absence of women in professions demanding a high level of education or much on-the-job training, entailing travel, overtime or geographic mobility. However, it should be stressed that it cannot explain the occupational segregation by sex between occupations with similar amounts and type of human capital: within the higher professions, within blue-collar work, between blue-collar work and service work, etc.

The new home economics and its explanation of the difference in men's and women's labor force status as deriving from the division of family labor and specialization has been accused of defending the status quo and women's "natural roles." I find instead, that the theory puts the spotlight on a large number of factors, which if they change will induce changes in occupational segregation. What are some of the factors that will alter occupational choice according to the division of labor theory? The crucial factor behind occupational choice in this model is the time allocation within the family and the resulting degree of labor force activity. Labor force activity has several dimensions: participation in the labor force, labor force attachment (the extent and frequency of labor force interruptions), the number of hours put into market work, the effort put into market hours. All can be expected to influence human capital investments and thus occupational choice. In this model anything that will affect present or expected time allocation between home and the market for wife and husband will have ramifications for the occupational distribution – e.g., the development of women's real wage, the female–male wage ratio, tax and transfer policy, the development of the demand for labor, technological change, fertility, the price of market and public childcare, the probability of divorce, family law, the price of substitutes for home production (other than childcare), the demand for home production.[23]

One may easily draw the misleading conclusion that an economic development or an economic policy that results in rising labor force participation rates for women should lead to a greater and more market-oriented investment in human capital among women and thus to reduced occupational segregation. This fallacy follows from ignoring work in the home as an occupational option. At low levels of labor force participation, women with a high incentive to work, higher education, and no or fewer children are likely to be over-represented in the labor force. These women will also have greater possibilities for buying low price service from other women. As labor force participation rates rise, women who previously would have chosen full-time homemaking as their occupation, decide to allocate some of their time to the labor market. However, according to the division of labor theory, we can still expect a division of labor with women taking prime responsibility for the family. The women providing the increase in the labor force are likely to make exactly the very traditional choice of occupations described by the model occupations compatible with family responsibilities. This should hold even if the rise in labor force participation occurs through a reduction in labor force interruptions. Young women expecting a longer and more continuous working life should invest more in formal education and on-the-job training. But as long as women bear the major burden of work in the home, they now need to find jobs compatible with childcare and will keep their investments within the female areas. There will be a reduction in the division of labor as women allocate some time to the market (and men maybe some more to the home). There will also most likely be a reduction in segregation, including work in the home as an occupation (unless all of the increase in the labor force is added to occupations as exclusively female as work in the home). However, occupational segregation as measured conventionally, excluding work in the home, is likely to persist or even increase as a result of rising labor force participation rates.[24]

Only if the labor force activity of the women in the market rises, does the division of labor theory predict a falling occupational segregation within the labor market. If women who are already in the labor force are able to increase their hours of work and put a greater effort into work (e.g., due to decreasing fertility, husbands doing more work at home, cheaper services or public policies) we can expect a swing in the direction of high investment occupations.

What if men reduce their average market hours? A reduction used for leisure, e.g., extended vacations, may make it possible to add extra effort during market hours or during certain periods of time, thus preserving "male" occupational choices. A reduction used for childcare or other non-market work on the other hand is likely to change occupational choice in a female direction.

The division of labor theory also explains wage differentials between men and women and between male and female occupations by reference to differences in human capital investments. Thus, the method of reducing wage differentials by gender is to encourage women to invest more in education and on-the-job-training, partly through entering male-dominated occupations that are assumed to provide such investments. Narrowing wage differentials are then expected to concur with falling occupational segregation as a result of human capital investment by gender becoming more equalized as well as by a reduced supply of labor to female occupations and an increased supply of labor to male occupations.

Such a relationship between wage relations and segregation assumes, however, that women upon entry in male occupations and making the concurrent investments will be able to follow the same career as men and reach the same high wage levels. If women, are encouraged to enter male occupations through, for example, educational or labor market policies, but there is no concomitant change in family responsibilities by gender, the consequence may be increased wage differentials by sex within the occupation. Women may indeed be better off staying in female occupations.

What effects on occupational segregation could we expect if wage differentials by education or between occupations declined as a result of union or government wage policies? Or if tax policies further reduced the net pecuniary outcome of varying occupational choice? Gains of specialization in the household would be reduced and this would work in the direction of smaller gender differences in choice of occupation. On the other hand the net return on investment in human capital would also drop. Incentives to enter career occupations would fall. If women prefer the female occupations for any reason other than income – perhaps just because it may feel difficult psychologically to make a non-traditional choice – there is slight motivation to change course. Segregation will persist.

LABOR DEMAND THEORIES OF OCCUPATIONAL HIRING

Next we consider theories in which the major cause of occupational segregation is seen as generating from the decisions of those responsible for labor demand. Most of the theories covered are theories of discrimination.[25] However, we will look initially at the human capital theory from the employer's side of the market. With respect to the human capital investments that take place in the labor market, not only the worker but also the employer is a decision-maker.

Human capital investment – employer perspective

Investments in knowledge and skills in the labor market are assumed to be financed and rewarded through variations in the relation between an individual's earnings stream and productivity profile. The acquisition of general skills, useful with many employers, has to be paid for by the employee in accepting a wage lower than could be obtained in another job during a period of learning, in return for a higher wage after the skill is mastered. For specific skills, useful only with one firm or with a limited number of firms, the employer has to share the financing, since the employee has no guarantee of a return on such investments. The employee will be paid somewhat less than his/her alternative wage in other companies, but also somewhat more than his/her productivity in the particular firm may justify during the period of training. On the other hand the employer can keep the worker at the firm by paying better than other firms after training, even though the wage then will be less than the value of marginal productivity. Occupations are characterized by mixtures of human capital of varying degree of generality and specificity.

The employer wants to maximize the return on his/her investment. There is no reason for him/her to treat men and women differently unless there is something in their expected labor market behavior that differs. Assuming flexible wages, general training will be paid for by the employee, and be made available to anyone who desires it. In jobs with some degree of specific training, for which employers bear some of the cost, employers will, however, be concerned with the expected behavior of trainees. If women have shorter expected job tenure or are for other reasons less willing or able to make use of their investment than men, employers will be reluctant to hire women for such jobs. Thus, if the division of labor theory's description of the labor supply side of the market holds, its effects on occupational segregation will be amplified by employer investment behavior, even assuming non-discriminatory employers. As increasing labor force participation draws in more women with family responsibilities, the availability of on-the job training for women may decrease rather than increase. Further, any restrictions in the employer's opportunities to use wage adjustments to share investment costs and risks with the employee will make him/her more reluctant to invest in women.

Discrimination

Theories of discrimination assume that the supply and demand observed in the market and the resulting occupational and wage structure are affected by discrimination. Whereas the human capital theory analyzes segregation of people with unequal skills, discrimination theories analyze differentiation between people with equal productive capacities. Discrimination exists when equally able and qualified individuals (or potentially equally able and qualified) are treated differently solely on the basis of their sex (Blau and Ferber 1992). Some forms of discrimination have their direct effects on the supply side of the market as described in the discussion of sex role socialization, other forms work directly on the demand side, as will be discussed below. However, one must keep in mind that demand-side discrimination will have indirect effects on occupational choice by reducing the monetary and non-monetary benefits (alternatively raising the costs) of entering an occupation for the disadvantaged sex. Supply-side discrimination will have repercussions on occupational hiring and placement by influencing the human capital and productivity of potential applicants, thus reducing employers' demand for the disadvantaged and raising it for the advantaged group.

The simplest approach to discrimination ascribes the different treatment of men and women in the labor market to the preferences of employers, employees or customers.[26] If employers prefer male workers, they will employ women only if they can pay them less than men, even if women are equally qualified and potentially equally productive. In order to link taste discrimination to occupational segregation, we have to add the assumption that employers' preferences vary across occupations, in such a way that women are more acceptable in some occupations, e.g. as secretaries and nurses, than in others, e.g. as managers and technicians (or even preferred to men in some, as for work in the home). However, even such a model does not necessarily lead to occupational segregation. With flexible wages, as normally assumed in neoclassical models, women could always buy their way into male occupations by offering to work for less money.

Usually this is not a rational choice for women. "Wage discrimination" in relation to an occupational career involves more than not paying the same to men and women with equal qualifications. Women follow a different wage path than men as a result of being paid less, being denied on-the-job training, access to information channels, promotion, etc. Women are granted entry into the occupation only if they agree to work at a lower level and lower status than men. If the degree of discrimination varies between occupations, women will be interested in how well they will do in their life-cycle earnings path relative to men. Assume that there is competition between men and that men's wage path in the male occupation provides a normal return on their human capital. Then investment in this field will most likely not be worthwhile for women. They will do better in female fields, maybe even in household work. In what will appear as a "voluntary" choice, women will enter female occupations, where discrimination is less or non-existent.

Nevertheless, occupational segregation may not only be the result of discrimination, but can also under certain conditions be a means of discrimination. Any restrictions on wage discrimination such as equal pay regulations should make employers resort instead to discrimination in hiring or promotion which will increase occupational segregation. Social pressure to pay equal wages may make segregation a more acceptable, less apparent and less costly form of discrimination.

In addition the employer has to deal with the attitudes of other employees and customers. Even a sex-neutral, profit maximizing employer has to consider the effects that a mixed workplace or mixed occupations have on productivity. Such effects may be positive through higher creativity, less absence, or a better work environment, for example. They may also be negative through communication problems or outright discrimination. Again, to account for occupational segregation we have to assume tastes that vary across occupations. If coworkers dislike working with women in certain positions or occupations, they may demand a higher wage in order to accept the situation. Alternatively the negative attitudes may reduce their own productivity or have detrimental effects on women's productivity, if women do not receive accurate instruction and training, are excluded from informal networks or exposed to sexual harassment.[27] If customers prefer dealing with a specific sex, it will directly affect the productivity of that sex. Maybe even without realizing it, the employer will be the agent of discrimination and relegate women (or men) to acceptable jobs or let them bear the consequences of higher costs and lower productivity in the form of a lower wage.

A theory based on taste discrimination has the same weakness as one based on taste in occupational choice. It provides in itself no clues as to what characteristics differentiate various occupations and what are the attributes of male or female occupations. If there are sufficient female jobs in relation to female labor supply, occupational segregation need not lead to wage differentials between male and female sectors. The formation of tastes has to be explained outside the model: by psychology, history, socialization, etc. For an economist, a model that explains behavior based on economic motives, e.g. a profit motive, is more attractive. From that perspective reference to employee or customer taste provides more rational explanations of employer behavior than simply putting it down to the employer's own taste.

Other researchers go further and try to construct models to illustrate that a discriminating group can make monetary gains at the expense of those discriminated against. A common theme running through these theories is that a group of individuals colludes to establish monopoly (or monopsony) power in order to extract rents in their trading relations.[28]

In this view men are rent seekers, who jointly, formally or informally, through direct regulations and the establishment of social norms try to keep out the competition of women in order to uphold their own wages. Since women working for low wages within an occupation are a threat to men's own wages as well as to the status and image (masculinity) of their job, men cooperate with (male) employers to keep women out through occupational segregation. There are many methods besides direct discrimination within the occupation: recruitment channels, requirements with respect to hours of work, overtime or leaves, forming a masculine culture. Encouraging women's home responsibilities is part of the norm. A problem for these monopsony models, as for all similar models of collusion, is providing mechanisms for compliance with informal norms and rules. Socialization of boys and girls who internalize norms and values at an early age is one possible mechanism.[29]

The monopsony models have implications for the characteristics of women's jobs that are more distinct than the simple "taste" models. Women are segregated into low-wage, low productivity occupations, while men keep the "good" jobs to themselves. The result is similar to that described as the result of tastes in occupational choice in Figure 2.1. In this case, however, not only do women gather by choice into low-wage occupations, but their wages in these may be even further decreased as a result of the so-called "crowding" of women, due to restricted entry into male occupations.[30]

Discrimination can thus decrease women's wages in several ways: through direct wage discrimination, restricted entry to well-paid male occupations, unequal access to on-the-job training and promotion in male occupations, wage pressure in female occupations through crowding, and finally through the cumulative effects on future human capital accumulation.

Assuming labor market discrimination has a causal role in occupational segregation, what can we expect regarding occupational segregation as the labor force participation of women rises? In a world with discrimination, rising labor force participation for women is most likely to occur as the result of a growing demand and opportunities in occupations in which the discrimination of women is low or absent. If this is the case we can expect rising labor force participation alongside continued or increased occupational segregation.

Suppose however that the increase in labor force participation is the result of changes on the supply side (decreasing fertility, expanding education, subsidized childcare). What can we then expect? That depends upon what we assume about tastes. A few women in a male occupation may be considered acceptable, as they will not disturb the social codes within the occupation. A small group should also find it easier to find non-discriminating employers, as long as not every employer has the same taste. The aversion among employers or employees may grow as the number of potential women entrants rises, which will strengthen segregative forces. On the other hand, even if founded on tastes, the will of employers to segregate is related to the price of discrimination, which in this case is the loss associated with not employing low-price productive workers who could contribute to profits. As the share of women in general as well as the share of women with good educational credentials in the labor force grows, the employer will be confining his/her search for good workers to a progressively smaller share of the potentially competent workers. The rising price of discriminatory behavior should reduce the "consumption" of discrimination, by employers as well as customers and fellow employees (who may become aware of the negative effects of sorting out productive colleagues on company profits and growth and accompanying employee wage growth). Such costs are further added to in periods of labor shortage, when women are known to be allowed to enter new fields. Furthermore, we may expect customer discrimination to be reduced towards women (and maybe increase towards men) as women's incomes rise and their influence on consumption decisions grows, assuming that women prefer dealing with other women.

The system of social norms and sanctions enforcing the collusion among men should also lose its strength and slowly disintegrate as more women take up work, since men in their role as fathers and husbands will have a self-interest in women's pay. On the other hand we cannot expect such changes to take place without tension as individual men find themselves competing with women in the top professions. Women will question established norms and requirements: as long as these are not related to productivity – e.g. if part-time work can be combined with management positions without productivity loss – they should be abolished, thus making it easier for new women to enter.

This interpretation of discrimination models thus points to opposing forces at work with respect to occupational segregation, as labor force participation rates rise depending upon whether the growth in labor force participation is generated from the supply or the demand side of the market. Furthermore, when discrimination is at work any restrictions on wage flexibility will strengthen segregative forces.

TRANSACTION COST THEORIES OF OCCUPATIONAL MATCHING

During the past decades economists have paid increasing attention to methods and institutions in the labor market that deal with the problem of economizing on transaction costs: e.g., cost of information, contract and control. Such costs and the methods used by the market to decrease them have consequences on the employment structure and wage structure and likewise have implications for gender differentiation. So far gender differences have been extensively analyzed only within the context of models of imperfect information, but more recent models of efficiency wages and contract theory should be applicable to gender issues as well.[31]

Statistical discrimination – demand

Employers do not have full information about the future productive capacity of job seekers. As they screen applicants, they make use of various indicators thought to correlate with individual productivity: education, prior work experience, test scores, interviews and sometimes periods of short-term employment. Even when hiring is based on such credentials, mistakes are made in hiring, eliminating a person with high productivity and hiring someone with low productivity. Since there is always variability within the group, none of the indicators gives a perfect signal. To seek information and to screen are costly activities and employers have incentives to search for inexpensive information sources. An individual's sex is easily available information. If, due to expectations such as higher turnover, less effort and commitment, lower ambitions, less adaptation to the "culture" of the profession or production line, a smaller professional network and so on, the employer believes that sex is correlated with future achievements in the organization, he/she will want to use that information to supplement other data on the individual in the hiring, investment or promotion decisions. Statistical discrimination bases screening on the average productivity of groups with ascribed characteristics such as sex.[32]

Models of statistical discrimination are based on assumptions that there are supply-side differences in the labor market behavior of men and women. Explanations for these have to be found outside the model, socialization, division of labor in the family, etc. Without such differences the employer has nothing to gain from screening according to sex. However, if the information used by the employer is indeed correct, the screening method will contribute to the productivity of the organization, and its use is not dependent on any prejudice from any part. The model serves to illustrate the interaction between gender roles and the decisions by firms. As with other types of discrimination, there will be vicious circles with feedback effects on women's investment in human capital and labor market behavior so that employers' expectations will be fulfilled (Arrow 1973).

Statistical discrimination does not necessarily result in wage discrimination as usually measured since women are paid according to their average productivity. It does, however, contribute to occupational segregation and may result in crowding effects on wage levels. Statistical discrimination restricts opportunities for career-oriented women as well as other women. Employers treat all women within a given qualification group as if they have the characteristics of the average woman in that group. The profitability of doing so and thus the use of statistical discrimination will differ between occupations. It should be especially profitable for entry level screening in occupations with internal job ladders that involve extensive firm-specific training: i.e., the type of employer human capital investment decisions described above. Thus we can expect professionally educated women to be the ones particularly exposed to this type of discrimination.

How does the basis for statistical discrimination alter as more women enter the labor market? The economic value of employing statistical discrimination depends upon the variation in behavior within each group as compared to the difference between the groups in average behavior. Its continued profitability will depend upon what changes in the labor market behavior of women are implied by the rise in labor force participation rates. If the rise in labor force participation is the result of a growing proportion of women in full-time, year-round careers, with career ambitions and no labor force interruptions, the continued use of screening according to sex may prove costly for the employer. On the other hand, if the increase is the result of a new life style for a majority of women with a combination of work in the home and part-time market work and frequent use of extended periods of paid parental leave, statistical discrimination will continue to be cost efficient. It may even increase in occupations where this type of behavior is more costly than traditional labor force interruptions. In the latter case the employee leaves and can be replaced by another full-time worker. In the former case the woman returns with rusty knowledge and has to be given a part-time job.

The basis for statistical discrimination is also the difference in the average behavior of men and women. If women's entry is followed by some men starting to take their share of family responsibilities and parental leave, the foundation for such screening will be eroded and the tactic will become riskier for employers. Any reduction in the use of sex as a basis for statistical selection should be most noticeable among the professions, where it is most likely to have been extensively exercised.

Statistical discrimination – supply

Theories of statistical discrimination have been developed to analyze the behavior of employers. It is possible to picture similar processes on the supply side, although to my knowledge they have not been modeled. Young people making their occupational choice do not have full information about the costs and benefits of pursuing different careers. They too, try to economize on information costs and find inexpensive methods of acquiring information on which to base their decisions. One well-known method is to select occupations that are close in character to those of their parents. Another is to employ "gender discrimination" and select occupations in which most of the workers are the same sex as oneself. Similar to statistical discrimination on the demand side, the assumption is that such occupations will have on the average characteristics more suitable to the lifetime labor force behavior of one's own sex than the average characteristics of occupations dominated by the other sex. This illustrates the importance of female role models and mentors as carriers of information in occupational choice.

Contract theory and efficiency wages

The relation between an employer and a worker is complicated and full of conflicting interests. The employee wants to earn as much as possible, work as leisurely as possible, change jobs at will and on the other hand be protected from wage reductions, layoffs and unemployment. The employer wants the employee to use as much as possible of his/her productive capacity, wants to pay as low a wage as possible, and wants to lay off and find equally productive workers whenever the business cycle goes up or down. The market solutions to these conflicting interests are more complicated than simply flexible wages. The basic reasons are costs of finding information, carrying out transactions and writing up contracts covering all future contingencies. Methods and institutions to solve such problems are the object of study in new labor market theories using contract theory, transaction cost theory and efficiency wage theory. Models in this area are of recent date and have not been applied to gender issues to any great extent.[33]

The theories are aimed at explaining peculiarities in the labor market such as wages rising with seniority, wages above market clearing levels, unemployment, etc. Efficiency wage models describe mechanisms that can be used to induce workers to work at their greatest efficiency. Assumptions are that wages and wage structure affect behavior and productivity, i.e., productivity is not exogenously given. According to the theory, employers may find it profitable to pay wages in excess of those that would immediately clear the market. Several reasons for this have been suggested. An employer who pays above market wages would reduce labor turnover, deter shirking at work, attract good workers to the firm, and increase loyalty and good performance within the company since the workers feel well and fairly treated. Other models focus on the wage profile typical of career occupations with an internal mobility ladder, which relates wage level to seniority within the firm, even if productivity does not follow seniority. This wage structure, with low wages at the beginning of working life and high wages at the end, is interpreted as an implicit contract between employer and employee formulated so as to generate behavior that is of mutual benefit.

In my interpretation all efficiency wage theories suggest the same mechanisms of occupational segregation. Gender roles in the family result in different labor market behavior by men and women with respect to labor force interruptions, part-time work and the commitment to market work. While there is variation within the group of women in the extent of this behavior, depending upon their education, family status, etc., there are still differences between men and women at each level of qualification. These average differences are known to employers, but they can identify a career-motivated woman only at a high cost. Thus they employ statistical discrimination and employ fewer women in certain occupations and more in others for reasons suggested by the models, e.g., because women are riskier investments than men or because they are not as easily or cheaply motivated and monitored by wage incentives. Women are placed in those jobs where their expected behavior will inflict the least cost on employers. From the perspective of these models we can alternatively characterize the situation as being one in which the wage structure, incentive structure and control system are designed differently in women's jobs than in men's jobs. Job structure and job characteristics are not exogenously given, but the organization within the firm and character given to jobs are part of the employer's profit maximizing behavior and are designed according to expected employee behavior. Thus men and women have to be separated into different types of jobs.

Since the sex composition of occupations in this case is related to statistical discrimination, the comments above about the relation between rising labor force participation and occupational segregation hold. In order for statistical discrimination to be profitable for employers there must be differences between men and women in their reaction to wage incentives. If occupational segregation is to change, it depends upon what alteration in behavior is signified by a rise in labor force participation rates.

INSTITUTIONAL THEORIES

The institutionalist school emphasizes constraints on individual choice in the form of institutions, laws, social norms, customs and tradition.[34] Wages are determined by administrative procedures and customs within the company rather than by competitive forces. An individual's behavior, ability and knowledge, rather than being the reasons for individuals selecting or being recruited to different positions, are the result of their adjustment within a given job. Wages and productivity are thus related to a certain position instead of to the individual. Internal labor markets are important. They have career ladders that vary in length and in the wage path attached to each one. Competition for the starting positions of the different careers occurs at the entry level.

These theories view occupational segregation as the result of employment adjusting to given wage relations. The lack of competition within the firms leaves plenty of room for discrimination. Internal labor markets are designed to reduce staff turnover, develop skills and encourage productivity. Statistical discrimination is employed at the entry positions in a manner similar to what has been described above.[35] Women are assigned to the short job ladders, with little wage growth and little learning on the job.

There is a variety of theories within the institutionalist school, which will not be treated individually here. It is difficult, however, to see anything in these theories that would argue for falling levels of segregation in connection with rising labor force participation rates for women. Discrimination of various kinds has a prominent role within the various theories and the arguments given in connection with various discrimination theories apply.

OCCUPATIONAL SEGREGATION AND LABOR FORCE PARTICIPATION

Let me try to summarize what we have learned about the relationship between rising labor force participation rates and changes in occupational segregation from this survey of various economic theories. Initially I pointed out the importance of integrating work at home in the analysis of occupational segregation. Several authors on occupational segregation bring up the point that the organization of work and structuring of jobs are endogenous in the labor market, but forget to mention that this includes the transfer of work between the home and the market as well.

The rise in the labor force participation of women involves a reorganization of work. Work tasks such as childcare and care of the elderly are now partly carried out in the market instead of in the home. This can be looked upon in two ways from the perspective of segregation. Both men and women today work in the market sector as well as the household sector. In that sense there has been a great reduction of segregation. On the other hand, many women moving into the market have taken up jobs in healthcare, social care and education, producing services similar to those produced at home. This signifies a persistence of segregation. Measuring occupational segregation in the conventional way, within the labor market, a persisting occupational segregation concomitant with rising labor force participation rates should not be surprising.

Keeping the focus on segregation between work in the home and market work, it is clear that there is still a division of time between men and women, such that women devote a larger share of their time, energy and concentration to home work and men a larger share to market work (Jonung and Persson 1993). According to the supply-side theories, women's allocation of time to work in the home should make them select occupations compatible with that work. We thus expect women to enter the labor market in greater numbers as demand rises and opportunities open up in "female" occupations or as conditions in occupations change to give them the characteristics desired by women working both in the home and in the market, e.g. part-time jobs. In Sweden the rapid rise in labor force participation rates has coincided with the expansion of the public sector and a growth in part-time jobs. The present rising rates of participation in other European countries occur as the service sector expands.

The rising labor force participation rates have led to a change in the composition of the labor force, with a larger proportion of women who combine work in the market with work at home. A focus on the importance of labor force interruptions for women's occupational choices in theoretical and empirical work may have led to neglecting the fact that as labor force interruptions decline, there will remain a similar influence on occupational choice from the desire to find jobs that make it convenient simultaneously to earn money and raise children.

Human capital theory seems to predict a reduction in occupational segregation as more women work in the labor market. But the change from work in the home to market occupations is in itself a decrease in segregation. The theory has to be interpreted to predict falling occupational segregation within the labor market at stable labor force participation rates as women within the labor force choose to increase their time and effort in market work. But will this take place in all areas? Human capital theory can only account for integration within areas requiring a significant investment in education or on-the-job training. The segregation within other jobs has to be explained by other theories and here changes are more difficult to predict. As the labor market gets more integrated, we should expect integration to take place primarily within professional occupations where also the pecuniary gains are the largest. Studies of the European experience (Jonung 1993; Rubery and Fagan 1993) verify that this is also what is taking place in practice: integration can be seen in the professions, while blue-collar and service work remain segregated.

According to discrimination theory, women will enter the labor market only if job opportunities expand within female areas or the barriers to male occupations are reduced: for example, in a period of shortage of labor. Rising labor force participation and rising occupational segregation are thus not inconsistent with such theories. On the other hand the costs of adhering to discriminatory tastes or upholding a male monopoly agreement should rise as more women enter the labor force. Statistical discrimination will remain in force as long as the average labor market behavior among women differ from those of men, or the variability within the female group is larger than among male workers. As women's behavior approaches men's, however, certain occupations may be the first to open up to women, while others may remain male preserves.

OCCUPATIONAL SEGREGATION AND WAGE DIFFERENTIALS

Different occupations have different wage levels and wage profiles according to age and experience. Wages in women's jobs tend to be lower than for men's and have a less steep wage profile. A human capital explanation would be that the characteristics of individuals – age, education, experience, family responsibilities – differ. Another explanation is equalizing wage differences on the basis of the physical and psychological attributes of a job. But even in studies that try to standardize for these factors, it is found that the proportion of women in an occupation contributes to a reduction in wage.[36]

Discrimination contributes to a reduction of women's wages in several ways, some of which are the result of segregation. First, there is the direct effect of wage discrimination. Second, there is the direct effect of segregation as women are kept from entering well-paid male occupations. A result of this is the indirect effect of not gaining access to on-the-job training opportunities. Discrimination through segregation contributes to crowding, the result of which is wage differentials such as those referred to above, which cannot be explained by human capital or job attributes. Finally, the cumulative effects of wage discrimination and hiring discrimination on women's occupational choice and human capital accumulation further contributes to occupational segregation and crowding effects on wages.

Can small wage differentials be expected to be related to low levels of segregation? This depends upon the size of wage differentials according to sex within occupations in relation to the differential between occupations. As women enter male occupations we should expect women's wages to rise both as a result of the access to male occupations and as a consequence of reduced crowding in female occupations. This is the great advantage of integration. It can be expected to improve wage conditions of all women in the labor market.[37]

However, this assumes that women can reach the high wage levels in the male occupations. If there is discrimination within the occupation, or if women, due to home responsibilities, cannot meet the demands of the highly compensated jobs, they may do better in a female occupation. Even if the average wage in male occupations is higher, the average wage for a woman in the labor force entering a male occupation may not be. This was suggested as the reason for women choosing female jobs in the first place.

Overall wage differentials between men and women are related to four factors. The first is the wage differential within occupations. The second is the wage differentials between occupations. The third is the occupational distribution of men and women. The fourth is the ranking of male and female occupations within the wage structure. Blau and Kahn (1992) showed that the overall wage differentials according to sex in various countries differ not only because men and women are differently distributed across the wage hierarchy, but also because the wage increases associated with each step vary depending upon the wage policy of the country. High levels of segregation are thus compatible with small, overall wage differentials if there is a general leveling of wages in a society.

As pointed out in connection with the discussion of several of the models, a leveling of wages administered through government or union policy may in fact contribute to segregation. According to discrimination theories, reduced opportunities for wage discrimination increase hiring discrimination and segregation. According to supply-side theories, there are effects on both the employees and the employers. Smaller wage differentials reduce monetary incentives for women to enter non-traditional jobs. If women prefer female jobs for reasons other than the wage – maybe just because of the trouble of choosing in a non-traditional way – the motives for shifting direction are minor. Employers become more careful in hiring and investing in women, and women's opportunities to buy their way into occupations with firm-specific training are reduced.

An additional factor affecting mainly women in demanding professional work in societies with equalized wages (often in addition to high marginal taxes and social security payments) is that the purchase of services to substitute work in the home becomes very expensive. The possibilities for highly educated women to compete with men on equal terms are then restricted.[38]

CONCLUSIONS

This chapter is a survey of economic theories of occupational segregation, focusing on the mechanisms of change in occupational segregation, in particular on the relationship between changing labor force participation, changing wage differentials by sex and occupational segregation. An attempt has been made to shed light on the apparent paradox that rising labor force participation rates across the Western nations do not seem to have led to a corresponding reduction in occupational segregation. It was found that from a theoretical perspective these developments are not inconsistent, whether one supports human capital theories or discrimination theories. Instead it is quite reasonable to expect stable or even increasing occupational segregation as labor force participation rates of women are rising and wage differentials by gender are falling.

If this is the correct empirical relationship it has important policy implications. As we are striving for increased participation of women in the labor force, reduced wage differentials and occupational integration, we may be trying to achieve goals that are at least temporarily incompatible.

Lately many writers have emphasized the importance of feedback effects in understanding gender differentials. In analyzing the change over time we have to consider the interdependencies between supply, demand and the wage and thus between increases in labor force participation, the structure of demand, reduced wage differentials within and between occupations and occupational segregation. The aim has been to contribute to such a discussion. To gain a fuller understanding of changes over time it is argued that work in the home as an occupation must be given a more integrated role in the analysis. This will also illustrate that occupational structures are not independent of the sex composition of the labor force.

The meaning and consequences of occupational segregation may be different even if the overall measured level is the same. Theories show that there may be segregation even if there is no discrimination, as well as discrimination that does not result in segregation. The interpretation of occupational segregation is quite different if it is the result of efficient individual choices by well-informed individuals, or the result of a multitude of constraints on individual choice. Further, empirically it has been found that there are great differences between countries in the economic outcome of occupational divisions by gender.

Theories of occupational segregation are often put forward one at a time or compared as if they were mutually exclusive. Also, they are presented as if one theory were valid for the entire labor market. In fact, most theories are interrelated and rest on ad hoc assumptions related to other theories. Moreover, the processes described by different theories often reinforce each other and thus are complementary rather than mutually exclusive.[39] It is necessary to use several theories to explain the extensive segregation by gender as well as the changes in occupational segregation that have taken place over time. If different theories are valid for different occupations, this explains the divergent trend in occupational segregation within different parts of the occupational structure that has been found in empirical studies (Jonung 1993; Rubery and Fagan 1993). In particular it is necessary to differentiate between occupations requiring a varying degree of education, skill, training and labor force attachment. Human capital theory can apply only to certain areas of the labor market. In future studies more attention has to be paid to the changing pattern of occupational segregation over time. Which are the individual occupations that contribute to change, why do they change, and what are the consequences for the wage and working conditions for men and women in those occupations?

ACKNOWLEDGMENT

Economic support from the Institute for Future Studies, Stockholm, Sweden is gratefully acknowledged.

NOTES

1 This is a shorter and revised version of an article earlier published as Jonung (1996).

2 For example, in *Employment in Europe* (ECC 1993: 145), it is stated: "The result of the past decade is a kind of paradox . . . at a time when the extent of men's and women's involvement in the labor market has become more similar, inequalities in employment still linger on. They show themselves in the maintenance of a marked segregation in the kind of work done as well as by an expansion of jobs performed predominantly by women." Hakim (1992: 130) writes regarding the situation in Britain: "Arguably, the 1970s and 1980s were relatively favorable to women's labor force participation and we should expect a decline in occupational segregation, concentrated particularly in the late 1970s and early 1980s when change was most pronounced and rapid." The first sentence in the introduction to Rubery and Fagan (1993) reads: "The increasing participation of European women in the labor market might be expected to lead to integration and equality and away from gender segregation and inequality." Another example is found under the entry for occupational segregation in the *Palgrave Dictionary of Economics*: "The persistence of segregation by gender is seen as surprising in light of the marked increase in women's labor force participation rate in the post-World War Two period" (Strober 1987).

3 The dissimilarity index is calculated as

$$D_t = \frac{1}{2} \sum_{i=1}^{n} |m_{it} - f_{it}|,$$

where m_{it} and f_{it} designate the percentage share of the male and female labor force respectively employed in occupation i in year t.

4 Other overviews of theories of occupational segregation are for example Blau (1984), which focuses on economic theories, and Reskin and Hartman (1986: Chapter 3) which has a broader perspective and extensively discusses cultural,

social, economic and institutional processes that foster segregation. Textbooks such as Blau and Ferber (1992) and Jacobsen (1994) include lengthy chapters on occupational segregation. England (1992: Chapter 2) surveys economic theories of wage differentials and occupational segregation. My survey differs from earlier articles in the focus on change in segregation over time.

5 The definition and measurement problems discussed in this section are more fully treated in Jonung (1996).

6 Grossbard-Schechtman (1993) names this occupational option "spousal labor," benefits accruing to the spouse who pays through sharing his/her income.

7 Theories excluded are Marxist theories. For an overview, see England (1992: 91–8); for theories of patriarchy, see Hartman (1976); for queue theories, see Strober (1984), Strober and Catanzarite (1994) or Reskin and Roos (1990). There is also a great number of sociological and psychological theories of occupational segregation; see Reskin and Hartman (1986) and England (1992).

8 In this chapter I do not distinguish between sex, as the biological term, and gender, as the social term. The empirical problem we are studying is the composition of occupations by individuals categorized by sex. This is explained by theories describing how gender traits relevant for labor market outcome may develop. See Jacobsen (1994: 6).

9 There is no clear definition of what constitutes a female-dominated, male-dominated or integrated occupation. If we are studying the occupational segregation within the labor force, any empirical definition should relate to the female proportion within the labor force.

10 See some basic textbooks such as Ehrenberg and Smith (1982), Elliott (1991). When occupation is mentioned it is usually in the context of human capital theory; see, e.g. Joll *et al.* (1983).

11 While there have been several empirical studies of occupational segregation in Europe (see Rubery and Fagan 1993), theoretical work on segregation emanates almost exclusively from the USA, hence the American bias in this survey.

12 Killingsworth (1987, 1990) has strongly argued for the importance of including tastes in the analysis of occupational segregation and wage differentials. An empirical study of the influence of preferences on job choice is Filer (1986).

13 Nor is there a clue as to how to distinguish occupations.

14 In fact in this case we are in practice dealing with only one occupation.

15 The only explanation is again simply to refer to preferences. Different jobs offer different combinations of income and working conditions. Men prefer income, women prefer "other things in life," i.e., women are willing to give up income for other values in life.

16 For a summary of such research see Jacobsen (1994: Chapter 1). See also Hakim (1996) for a presentation of Goldberg's psycho-physiological theory relating the effects of male hormones to the sex differences in vertical distribution in society.

17 Marini and Brinton (1984) survey the influence of socialization on occupational choice. Corcoran and Courant (1985) discuss how socialization can be modeled and empirically tested. Perlman and Pike (1994) claim that social conditioning and pre-market discrimination are the major factors behind occupational segregation.

18 Even if social norms, traditions and habits were once efficient, since they normally change only slowly, they may survive as outdated and inefficient for a significant amount of time under new economic circumstances, and thus be experienced as a social discrimination.

19 I do not discuss here the theory of marriage, which relies strongly on the gains of specialization described below (Becker 1991). Gains of specialization, however,

can be obtained equally well or better through the market, so marriage has to amount to more than simply this. See also Blau and Ferber (1992: 41–3)

20 The idea of a common utility function for the family has been questioned by a number of researchers and alternative models based on transactions costs and bargaining have been developed. See the chapters in the accompanying volume to this book (Persson and Jonung 1997).

21 While this model emphasizes advantages of specialization, it is not difficult to find disadvantages of specialization as well (see Blau and Ferber 1992: 43–8).

22 Blaug (1980) criticizes the "new home economics" on the basis that it does not lead to clear, testable implications unless it is complemented with ad hoc assumptions, for example, about the productivity differences between members of a family.

23 That includes what commodities are produced at home: e.g. cleaning, where family members' time is substitutable, or leisure activities, where members' time is most likely complementary.

24 Jonung and Persson (1993) demonstrate that the high labor force participation rates in Sweden have come about largely as the result of a growth of part-time work and generous parental leaves. Hakim (1996) argues that in Great Britain there have been no changes in full-time female employment over the past 150 years.

25 There is a large number of theories of discrimination. For surveys see Lundahl and Wadensjö (1984), Sloane (1985), Cain (1986). Many theories have focused on race rather than sex, and most theories have been more interested in spelling out implications for wage differentials than for occupational segregation.

26 The classic reference here is Becker's (1957) analysis of race discrimination.

27 The effects of coworker discrimination has been analyzed by Bergmann and Darity (1981), Bergmann (1986), Bergmann (1989).

28 A neoclassical monopoly model is Madden (1973). Theories of patriarchy can also be interpreted as monopoly models, Hartman (1976), and queue theories also rely on the existence of monopoly power, Reskin and Roos (1990), Strober (1984), Strober and Catanzarite (1994). See also the chapter by Johnson and Stafford in this book.

29 There is another type of monopsony model describing how a single buyer can divide the workforce and pay women lower wages if their supply is less elastic than men's labor supply. However, such a model cannot explain the market-wide, extensive, occupational segregation. It is a better description of how a buyer in a local area can exploit women by paying lower wages, as a result of restricted occupational opportunities.

30 This is what is known as the "crowding hypothesis" of the effects of the use of occupational segregation as a discriminatory method (Bergmann 1974). The crowding hypothesis forms the basis for the application of comparable worth (England 1992).

31 See, for example, the discussion in England (1992) and Jacobsen (1994).

32 Statistical discrimination can also arise if one group shows greater variance in productivity or if the reliability with which productivity can be predicted differs between groups. If employers are men it is easy to imagine that they are more confident in their judgment about the productive capacity of men than of women after a test or an interview. It should be the other way around with female employers.

33 A textbook presentation of several of the new ideas is found in Chapters 10–12 in Elliott (1991). Their application to gender issues is discussed in England (1992).

34 For a survey of the institutionalist theories, see Taubman and Wachter (1986).

35 Some theories picture the entry competition as a queue, with women at the end of the line. Only under certain conditions (such as obtaining higher qualifications than the men in the queue) may women move ahead (Reskin and Roos 1990; Strober and Catanzarite 1994).

36 For a summary of such research, see Sorensen (1994). For a similar Swedish study, see le Grand (1991).

37 See Chapter 3 by Johnson and Stafford in this volume which through a general equilibrium model illustrates how the reduction of occupational exclusion affects the relative wages of men and women.

38 The chapter by Påhlsson in the accompanying volume to this book, Persson and Jonung (1997), analyzes this problem.

39 This point is emphasized by authors of other surveys, e.g. Blau (1984), England (1992) and in the entries by Blau (1987) and Strober (1987) in the *Palgrave Dictionary of Economics*. See also Blau and Ferber (1992: 217–18) on feedback effects.

REFERENCES

Arrow, K. (1973) "The theory of discrimination," in O. Ashenfelter and A. Rees (eds) *Discrimination in Labor Markets,* Princeton: Princeton University Press

Becker, G. (1957) *The Economics of Discrimination,* Chicago: University of Chicago Press.

—— (1965) "A theory of the allocation of time," *Economic Journal* 75: 493–515.

—— (1985) "Human capital, effort and the sexual division of labor," *Journal of Labor Economics* 3, 1, 2: 33–58

—— (1991) *A Treatise on the Family,* 2nd ed., Cambridge: Harvard University Press.

Beckmann, P. (ed.), (1996) *Gender Specific Occupational Segregation,* Beiträge zur Arbeitsmarkt- und Berufsforschung No. 188, Nürnberg: Federal Employment Services (IAB).

Bergmann, B. (1974) "Occupational segregation, wages and profits when employers discriminate by race or sex," *Eastern Economic Journal,* 1: 103–10.

—— (1986) *The Economic Emergence of Women,* New York: Basic Books.

—— (1989) "Does the labor market for women need fixing?," *Journal of Economic Perspectives* 3, 1: 43–60.

Bergmann, B. and Darity, W.(1981) "Social relations in the workplace and employee discrimination," Proceeding of the Industrial Research Association: 155–62.

Blau, F. D. (1984) "Occupational segregation and labor market discrimination," in B. Reskin (ed.) *Sex Segregation in the Work Place: Trends, Explanations, Remedies,* Washington: National Academy Press: 117–43.

Blau, F. D. (1987) "Gender," in Eatwell *et al. The New Palgrave: A Dictionary of Economics,* London: Macmillan: 492–97.

Blau, F. D. and Ferber, M. A. (1992) *The Economics of Women, Men and Work,* Englewood Cliffs NJ: Prentice Hall.

Blau, F. and Kahn, L. M. (1992) "The gender earnings gap: learning from international comparisons," *American Economic Review* 82, 2: 533–8.

Blaug, M. (1980) *The Methodology of Economics,* Cambridge: Cambridge University Press.

Cain, G. (1986) "The economic analysis of labor market discrimination: a survey" in O. Ashenfelter and R. Layard (eds) *Handbook of Labor Economics I,* Amsterdam: North Holland: 693–785.

Corcoran, M. and Courant, P. (1985) "Sex role socialization and labor market outcomes," *American Economic Review* 75, 2: 275–8.

Eatwell, J., Milgate, M. and Newman, P. (1987) *The New Palgrave: A Dictionary of Economics*, London: Macmillan.

ECC (1993) *Employment in Europe* Luxembourg: Commission of the European Communities.

Ehrenberg, R. G. and Smith, R. S. (1982) *Modern Labor Economics*, Glenview IL: Scott, Foresman and Company.

Elliott, R.F. (1991) *Labor Economics. A Comparative Text*, London: McGraw-Hill.

England, P. (1992) *Comparable Worth. Theories and Evidence*, New York: De Gruyter.

Filer, R. (1986) "The role of personality and tastes in determining occupational structure," *Industrial and Labor Relations Review* 39, 3: 412–24.

Grossbard-Shechtman, S. (1993) *On the Economics of Marriage: A Theory of Marriage, Labor and Divorce*, Oxford: Westview Press.

Hakim, C. (1992) "Explaining trends in occupational segregation: the measurement, causes and consequences of the sexual division of labor," *European Sociological Review* 8, 2: 127–52.

—— (1996) *Key Issues in Women's Work: Female Heterogeneity and the Polarisation of Women's Employment*, London: Athlone Press.

Hartman, H. I. (1976) "Capitalism, patriarchy and job segregation by sex," *Signs*, 1: 3, 2: 137–69.

Jacobsen, J. (1994) *The Economics of Gender*, Cambridge: Blackwell.

Joll, C., McKenna, C., McNabb, R. and Shorey, J. (1983) *Developments in Labor Market Analysis*, London: George, Allen and Unwin.

Jonung, C. (1993) "Yrkessegregeringen på arbetsmarknaden" (Occupational segregation in the labor market) in *Kvinnors arbetsmarknad – 1990-talet – återtågets årtionde?*, Ds 1993: 8, Swedish Department of Labor.

—— (1996) "Economic theories of occupational segregation by sex – implications for change over time" in P. Beckman (ed.) *Gender Specific Occupational Segregation*, Beiträge zur Arbeitsmarkt- und Berufsforschung No. 188, Nürnberg: Federal Employment Services (IAB): 16–54.

Jonung, C. and Persson, I. (1993) "Women and market work: the misleading tale of participation rates in international comparisons," *Work, Employment and Society* 7: 259–74.

Killingsworth, M. R. (1987) "Heterogeneous preferences, compensating wage differentials, and comparable worth," *Quarterly Journal of Economics* 102: 727–42.

—— (1990) *The Economics of Comparable Worth*, Kalamazoo, Michigan: W.E. Upjohn Institute for Employment Research.

le Grand, C. (1991) "Explaining the male–female wage gap: job segregation and solidarity wage bargaining in Sweden," *Acta Sociologica* 34, 4.

Lundahl, M. and Wadensjö, E. (1984) *Unequal Treatment: A Study in the Neo-Classical Theory of Discrimination*, London: Croom, Helm.

Madden, J. (1973) *The Economics of Sex Discrimination*, Lexington, Mass: D.C. Heath.

Marini, M.M. and Brinton, M.C. (1984) "Sex stereotyping in occupational socialization", in B. Reskin (ed.) *Sex Segregation in the Work Place: Trends, Explanations, Remedies*, Washington DC: National Academy Press: 192–232.

Mincer, J. and Polachek, S. (1974) "Family investments in human capital: earnings of women," *Journal of Political Economy* 82, 2, 2: 76–108.

Perlman, R. and Pike, M. (1994), *Sex Discrimination in the Labor Market. The Case for Comparable Worth*, Manchester: Manchester University Press.

Persson, I. and Jonung, C. (1997) *Economics of the Family and Family Policy*, London: Routledge.

Phelps, E. (1972) "The statistical theory of racism and sexism," *American Economic Review* 62, 4: 659–61.

Polocheck, S. (1981) "Occupational self-selection: a human capital approach to sex differences in occupational structure," *Review of Economics and Statistics* 63, 1: 60–69.

Reskin, B. F. (ed.) (1984) *Sex Segregation in the Work Place: Trends, Explanations, Remedies*, Washington DC: National Academy Press.

Reskin, B. F. and Hartman, H.I. (1986) *Women's Work, Men's Work: Sex Segregation on the Job*, Washington DC: National Academy Press.

Reskin, B.F. and Roos, P. (1990) *Job Queues, Gender Queues: Explaining Women's Inroads into Male Occupations*, Philadelphia: Temple University Press.

Rubery, J. and Fagan, C. (1993) *Occupational Segregation of Women and Men in the European Community*, Luxembourg: Commission of European Communities.

Sloane, P. (1985) "Discrimination in the labor market," in Carlin *et al.* (eds) *Surveys in Economics*, London: Longman.

Sorensen, E. (1994) *Comparable Worth: Is it a Worthy Policy?*, Princeton NJ: Princeton University Press.

Strober, M. (1984) "Toward a general theory of occupational sex segregation: the case of public school teaching," in B. F. Reskin (ed.) *Sex Segregation in the Work Place: Trends, Explanations, Remedies*, Washington DC: National Academy Press: 144–56.

—— (1987) "Occupational segregation," in Eatwell *et al.* (eds) *The New Palgrave: A Dictionary of Economics*, London: Macmillan: 691–3.

Strober, M. and Catanzarite, L. (1994) "The relative attractiveness theory of occupational segregation by gender," in P. Beckman and Engelbrech (eds) *Arbeitsmarkt für Frauen 200 – Ein Schritt vor oder ein Schritt zurück?*, Nürnberg: Federal Employment Services: 116–34.

Taubman, P. and Wachter, M.L. (1986) "Segmented labor markets," in O. Ashenfelter and R. Layard (eds) *Handbook of Labor Economics II*, Amsterdam: North Holland: 1183–217.

Zellner, H. (1975) "The determinants of occupational segregation," in C. Lloyd (ed.) *Sex, Discrimination and the Division of Labor*, New York: Columbia University Press: 125–45.

3

ALTERNATIVE APPROACHES TO OCCUPATIONAL EXCLUSION

George E. Johnson and Frank P. Stafford

THE CONCEPT OF OCCUPATIONAL EXCLUSION

This chapter concerns the stylized empirical fact, which appears to apply to virtually all societies in all recorded history, that men and women tend to perform different functions in the labor market. We call this phenomenon "occupational exclusion," although it is more often referred to as "occupational segregation" and, occasionally, as "occupational dissimilarity."

The extent of occupational exclusion in a society at a moment in time is usually characterized by an index of occupational dissimilarity. This takes the form:

$$D = \sum_j |wt_{mj} - wt_{fj}| / 2 \qquad (3.1)$$

where wt_{gj} is the fraction of each gender (m for men and f for women) employed in occupation j. The value of D can range in principle from zero (men and women have identical occupational distributions) to one (men and women never work in the same occupations). In much of the social science literature on gender differences in labor market outcomes the value of D is the principal focus of attention.[1] There is a presumption in much of the literature that occupational exclusion is the problem that women around the world face in the labor market. By extension, the achievement of gender earnings equality in a society would, in the popular view, require a very large decrease in the value of D, possibly to 0.[2]

Our interest is with the questions of why occupational exclusion exists in the first place and what its existence implies about the gender distribution of earnings. To answer the first question, we set out a comprehensive model in which there are four distinct potential reasons why men and women may have different occupational distributions. Two of these reasons involve forms of discrimination, which means that women tend to be excluded from men's occupations. The other two reasons involve women's non-pecuniary preferences regarding different occupations and their relative abilities in different jobs compared to men, which suggest that women tend to exclude themselves from certain occupations. Most reasonable people would agree that discriminatory exclusion is not fair (and should, perhaps, be subject to societal policing) but that self-exclusion is not intrinsically unfair.

The chapter starts by identifying potential sources of occupational exclusion. The basic model is set out in the next section, and its major implications are examined in the section that follows. A major puzzle in this topic concerns why, historically, men would set up institutional arrangements that result in a suboptimal allocation of tasks to women, and this is explored next. A concluding section discusses some of the empirical and policy issues associated with exclusion.

SOURCES OF EXCLUSION

The potential sources of occupational exclusion can be illustrated by a very simple model of the labor market. There are four sets of explanations (which are by no means mutually exclusive) of why men and women have different occupational distributions. These are as follows:

1 Differences by gender in preferences for different jobs.
2 Differences in the relative ability of men and women to perform different jobs.
3 Differences between jobs in the degree to which employers practice direct discrimination against women.
4 Institutional discrimination (legal or otherwise) that restricts women from working in "non-traditional" jobs.

Each of these explanations has somewhat different implications,[3] and, although it is easier to identify the causes of occupational exclusion theoretically than empirically, it is useful to examine the alternative explanations and their implications carefully.

To begin the discussion let us illustrate how the effects of (4) institutional discrimination and (2) relative ability could operate with a simple geometric model. In Figure 3.1 we illustrate two occupations, the output of which is the production of A and B. Occupation A is non-market output and B is market output. The production possibility frontier (ppf) for women is W-W and for men it is M-M. This could be thought of as the representative female or male agent.[4] The ppfs suggest that men are more able to perform market work, but this is not necessary to the argument that follows. The ppfs could be congruent, implying equal relative ability.

Without exclusion men would spend more time in market work and less time in housework than women would (men at point m, women at point f on their respective ppfs). There would be an (implicit) price ratio defining the terms of trade (the inverse of the slope of f-f, where the slope of f-f = the slope of m-m). Suppose there were institutional restrictions that reduced the hours per woman devoted to market work. This would lead to an equilibrium with less market work for them, with women "crowded into"

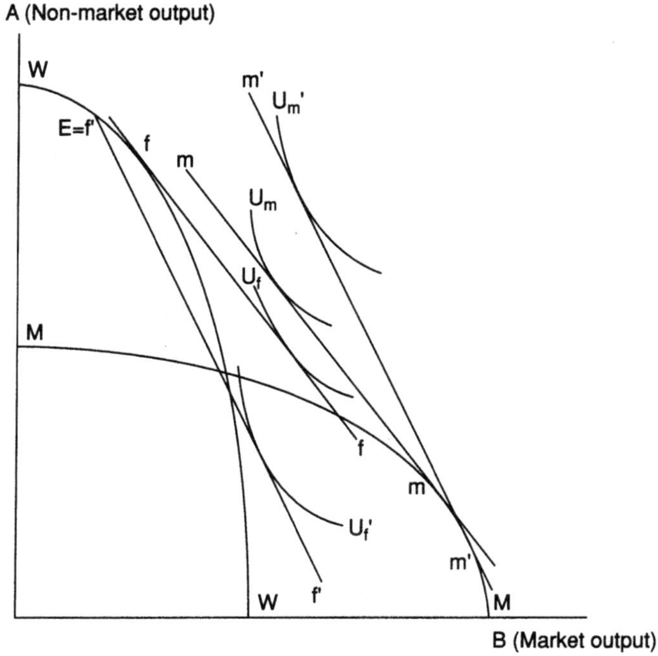

Figure 3.1 Gains and losses from exclusion

the housework occupation (at E = f′). This would drive down the relative price of housework, and in response men would increase their specialization in the market occupation and move to the point on their ppf tangent to m′m′. In the process men's utility would rise (from U_m to U_m'), but women's utility would fall by a larger amount (from U_f to U_f'). If the institutional restrictions were to persist there would be a net utility loss. Note that if the restrictions were too great, women would have some incentive to become economically independent from men (i.e., to operate at a point on their ppf, W-W, tangent to their indifference curve).

Another illustration of the role of exclusion is suggested by Figure 3.2. Here we have an initial equilibrium as in Figure 3.1, absent the institutional restrictions. Now, the relative ability of women in the production of good B changes. That is, suppose there were a skill-biased technical change which allowed women to become much better at market production changing their ppf to WW′, a case which seems empirically plausible for industrial society as modern production methods evolved. This increase in the aggregate share of production in the B good reduces its price and reduces men's well-being to U_m'. Women are better off (moving from U_f to U_f') since they have improved their relative ability to produce B and still hold a strong absolute advantage in the production of A, a good with a rising price.

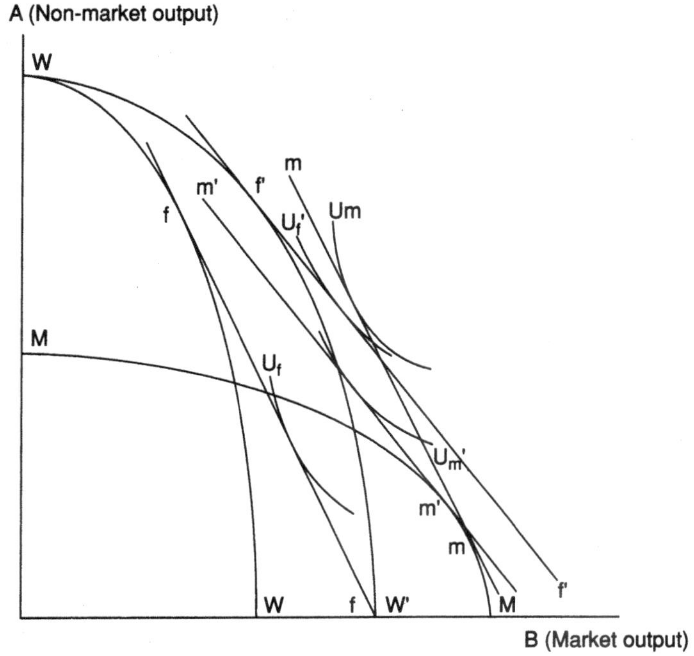

Figure 3.2 Gains and losses if technology changes favor women

Industrial history provides evidence of protective legislation limiting women's activities in the market sector (Goldin 1990; Pott-Buter 1993) when such technology shifts occurred. In this interpretation occupational exclusion via legislation (Figure 3.1) was sought by men for relief of losses which would have occurred from the changes portrayed in Figure 3.2. As will be shown below in a somewhat different approach, if women had improved in the production of A (or men improved in their respective specialty, the production of B), both men and women would realize economic gains.

AN ALGEBRAIC MODEL

Here we turn to a simple algebraic model, which is somewhat different from the previous geometry. This allows us to illustrate more formally all four exclusion sources above, and demonstrate the impact of changes on D. There is a single final good produced by two occupations, which have as their output intermediate goods. For simplicity, suppose that there are two jobs in the economy: job 1 and job 2, which are primarily (but not necessarily exclusively) staffed respectively, by men and women. The representative firm in the economy uses one unit of capital and hires men and women to perform jobs 1 and 2. Output per (identical) firm in the economy (q) is a function of the flow of services of the two types of labor, that is:

$$\frac{Y}{K} = q = \phi\left(\frac{G(N_1,N_2)}{K}\right) \tag{3.2}$$

where N_1 and N_2 are the effective aggregate flows of services in the two occupations ("men's jobs" and "women's jobs" respectively), K is the number of firms (equal to the stock of capital in the economy), and q is output per firm (equal to aggregate output, Y, divided by K).

The aggregate number of workers of each gender (g = m, f) in each job (j = 1, 2) is L_{gj}. All women are assumed to be λ_j as productive as all men in job j, and women have a comparative advantage in job 2 if $\lambda_2 > \lambda_1$, i.e., they are better relative to men in job 2 than in job 1. It then follows that the total flow of labor services in each job is:

$$N_j = L_{mj} + \lambda_j L_{fj} \tag{3.3}$$

Further, it is assumed that there is full employment of the (fixed) aggregate labor force of each gender, or:

$$L_g = L_{g1} + L_{g2} \tag{3.4}$$

This implicitly assumes that the real wage rates of both genders in both jobs are flexible.

The real rate of perceived profit (both financial and psychic) of the typical firm per unit of time is:

$$\pi_p = \frac{Y}{K} - W_{m1}L_{m1} - \frac{W_{f1}}{1-\delta_1} L_{f1} - W_{m2}L_{m2} - \frac{W_{f2}}{1-\delta_2} L_{f2} - fc \tag{3.5}$$

where the W_{gj}s are the market-determined real wage rates by gender by job and fc is annual fixed cost per firm. δ_1 and δ_2 are exogenous discrimination coefficients that, if positive, are the same for every potential firm in the economy.[5] $\delta_1 > 0$, for example, means that each firm must be compensated by $\delta_1/(1-\delta_1)$ for each dollar it pays women in job 1.

Maximization of perceived profit by firms under conditions of (more or less) perfect competition implies that men will receive their marginal product in each of the two jobs. Thus, in the long run[6] observed male wage rates are:

$$W_{m1} = \frac{\delta Y}{\delta N_{m1}} = G_1 \qquad W_{m2} = G_2 \tag{3.6}$$

For women, on the other hand, the model recognizes the possibility that wages might be less than their marginal product in one or both of the two jobs, and females wage rates are given by:

$$W_{f1} = (1 - \delta_1)\,\lambda_1 G_1 \qquad W_{f2} = (1 - \delta_2)\,\lambda_2 G_2 \tag{3.7}$$

To complete the model, we must specify the supply of labor by gender to each occupation. The desired supply of labor of each gender in job 1 relative to that in job 2 depends on the relevant relative wage, W_{g1}/W_{g2}, and the distribution of preferences for the two jobs. The actual relative supply of labor for each gender is assumed to be:

$$\frac{L_{g1}}{L_{g2}} = X_g \theta_g \psi_g \left(\frac{W_{g1}}{W_{g2}}\right) \qquad (3.8)$$

where θ_g is an exogenous taste parameter and $\epsilon_g = (W_{g1}/W_{g2})\psi_g'/\psi$ is the relative wage elasticity of occupational labor supply. The parameter X_g represents the effect of institutional restrictions on relative occupational supply. An increase in θ_f, for example, implies that, holding W_{f1}/W_{f2} constant, some women want to transfer from traditionally female to traditionally male jobs. In the absence of any external restrictions on the entry of either gender into either job, both X_gs would equal one, and observed relative supplies would reflect market choices (although possibly affected by employer discrimination, the δ_js). If, however, women's entry into occupation 1 was restricted by law or some other institutional constraints,[7] X_f will be less than one and fewer women (none in the case of an absolute prohibition, $X_f = 0$) will enter occupation 1 than desire to do so.[8] Similarly, external restrictions on the entry of men into occupation 2 would be represented by $X_m > 1$.

Although the model is very simplified (there is only one skill level and two occupations), it leads to some useful insights about occupational exclusion. First, the wage rates in job 1 relative to job 2 for men and women are given by

$$\frac{W_{m1}}{W_{m2}} = \frac{G_1}{G_2} \quad \frac{W_{f1}}{W_{f2}} = \frac{1 - \delta_1\lambda_1 G_1}{1 - \delta_2\lambda_2 G_2} \qquad (3.9)$$

As a general rule, this relative wage (the reward for holding a man's job/the penalty for holding a woman's job) is greater for men than for women, a finding quite frequently observed in the literature (Johnson and Solon 1986). In terms of the model, this arises due to (a) women having a comparative advantage in job 2 ($\lambda_2 > \lambda_1$) and/or (b) women being subject to greater employment discrimination in job 1 than in job 2 ($\delta_1 > \delta_2$).

Second, the proportion of all workers of each gender in occupation 1 is:

$$P_{g1} = \frac{L_{g1}}{L_g} = \frac{X_g\theta_g\psi_g\left(\frac{W_{g1}}{W_{g2}}\right)}{1 + X_g\theta_g\psi_g\left(\frac{W_{g1}}{W_{g2}}\right)} \qquad (3.10)$$

Since $P_m > P_f$, the Index of Occupational Dissimilarity for the model is $D = P_m - P_f$. D is the greater the lower are the values of X_f and θ_f (the more women are restricted from job 1 and the lower are their relative preferences for that occupation). By (3.9), D also rises as λ_2 increases relative to λ_1 (i.e. the higher is women's comparative advantage in job 2) and as δ_1 increases relative to δ_2 (i.e. the stronger is the discrimination of women in job 1 relative to in job 2).

Notice that women's tastes and institutional restrictions against the entry of women into job 1, respectively the θ_f and X_f parameters, have essentially the same effect on D and the other endogenous variables of the model. Similarly, the parameters λ_1 and δ_1 have essentially the same effect (but in opposite directions) on outcomes. If one observed, for example, both that women earned much less than men in job 1 and were relatively under-represented in that occupation (i.e., P_m was much larger than P_f), one could argue that women chose not to enter job 1 because (a) they were, on average, better at job 2; (b) they were discriminated against more in job 1. The observation that, relative occupational wages held constant, women are less likely to be employed in job 1 is similarly consistent with the explanations that (i) women prefer, ceteris paribus, to work in job 2; (ii) many women were not permitted to enter job 1 although they wanted to.

COMPARATIVE STATICS OF THE MODEL

The comparative statics of the model are fairly straightforward – although all of the endogenous variables are determined simultaneously by the exogenous variables (in particular, the values of λ_1, λ_2, δ_1, δ_2, θ_f, and X_f). The initial effects of changes in any one of the exogenous variables can be understood in terms of the geometric depiction of the model in Figure 3.3. A decrease in either θ_f (i.e. women getting less taste for "male" jobs) or X_f (i.e. an increase in institutional restrictions) causes a leftward shift in women's relative supply curve (as shown in Figure 3.3). This causes a reduction in L_{f1} and an increase in L_{f2}, which increases the value of G_1/G_2, shifting the relative demand functions for both men and women to the right (although by less than the initial leftward shift in women's relative supply curve). After all adjustment has occurred, the wage rates in job 1 are higher and the wage

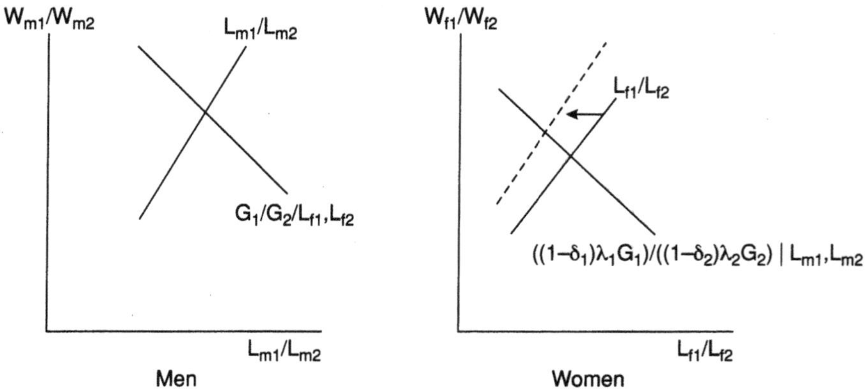

Figure 3.3 Equilibrium of the aggregate labor market with occupational choice and gender differences in tastes, abilities, and discrimination

rates in job 2 are lower. Given that men have a higher fraction in job 1 than do women, men's average wages rise and women's average wages fall due to the decrease in θ_f and/or X_f.

A somewhat similar story can be told about the effect of an increase in employer discrimination against women in job 1 (the δ_1 parameter). This causes the relative demand curve for women to shift to the left, implying a transfer of women from job 1 to job 2. This, in turn, causes the relative demand function for men to shift to the right and W_{m1} to rise. Again given that men are more highly represented in the traditionally male occupation, men's wages rise as a result of employer discrimination against women.

To illustrate some of the distributional implications of the model, consider the case in which the relative occupational supply elasticity for both men and women is zero; i.e., most men and fewer women are employed in job 1 no matter what is the value of the relative occupational wage. The average wages of men and women (assuming, for expositional simplicity, zero employment discrimination) are given by:

$$W_m = G_1 \frac{L_{m1}}{L_m} + G_2 \frac{L_{m2}}{L_m} \quad (3.11)$$

and

$$W_f = \lambda_1 G_1 \frac{L_{f1}}{L_f} + \lambda_2 G_2 \frac{L_{f2}}{L_f} \quad (3.12)$$

We will consider one change, a shift of one woman from job 2 to job 1 ($\Delta L_{f1} = -\Delta L_{f2} = 1$), i.e., a reduction in the extent of occupational exclusion. The total wage bill of men is $Z_m = G_1 L_{m1} + G_2 L_{m2}$ and the total wage bill of women is $Z_f = \lambda_1 G_1 L_{f1} + \lambda_2 G_2 L_{f2}$. The shift of one woman changes the marginal products of the two occupations. The wages in the two occupations adjust accordingly. The changes in the total wage bills of men and women due to this are:

$$\Delta Z_m = -\frac{s_2 - s_1}{\sigma}\left[(1-\beta)W_{f1} + \beta W_{f2}\right] \quad (3.13)$$

and

$$\Delta Z_f = W_{f1} - W_{f2} + \frac{s_2 - s_1}{\sigma}\left[(1-\beta)W_{f1} + \beta W_{f2}\right] \quad (3.14)$$

where $s_1 = \lambda_1 L_{f1}/N_1$ and $s_2 = \lambda_2 L_{f2}/N_2$ are the shares of the effective supplies of the two occupations that are accounted for by women, β is job 1's share of the total wage bill, and σ is the elasticity of substitution between the two occupations. Since $s_1 > s_2$, the average wage of men falls due to the shift in the occupational supply of women. The aggregate earnings of women rises by the increase in the aggregate wage bill ($W_{f1} - W_{f2}$) plus the amount by which men's aggregate wages fall.

A similar analysis can be performed concerning changes in λ_1 and λ_2. As women get more efficient in men's jobs ($\Delta\lambda_1 > 0$), G_1 falls such that men's average wage falls. On the other hand, as women get better at women's jobs ($\Delta\lambda_2 > 0$), men gain – possibly (depending on the value of σ) proportionately more than women gain.[9]

In other words, from the point of view of their own wage earnings, men (women) benefit from women (men) improving their skills in jobs that are not competitive with the jobs that men (women) traditionally perform. However, men lose when women improve their performance and move into traditionally male jobs.

MODELS OF SELF-INTERESTED EXPLOITATION

An interesting question raised by the model concerns why men, most of whom participate in opposite-sex marriages, would care about the distribution of total family earnings, in our notation W_m+W_f. Since the total consumption of the family, say c_m+c_f, is equal to total earnings, it might seem reasonable to assume that men, as well as women, would favor a legal environment and social mores such that total family earnings were maximized. This is equivalent to providing both women and men with whatever opportunities are necessary to earn the highest possible wage rates (adjusting, of course, for nonpecuniary preferences).

There is, however, ample historical evidence, alluded to above, that men – especially prior to the twentieth century when they had a monopoly on political power – have engaged in practices to restrict the entry of women into traditionally male occupations. It is also common in pre-industrial societies for men (the tribal elders) to assign tasks inefficiently such that the marginal product of men is higher than that of women (see, e.g., Udry 1994).

To look at this issue in more detail, consider a simple model of intra-family bargaining over the allocation of total family earnings to different forms of consumption.[10] The utility of both the husband ($g = m$) and the wife ($g = f$) is given by:

$$u_g = \gamma c_g, \text{ if remain married}$$

$$u_g = W_g, \text{ if separate / divorce,}$$

where $\gamma > 1$ reflects the gains due to marriage (or, generally, cohabitation) through increased efficiency of consumption and c_g is the level of consumption of each partner in marriage. The family budget constraint is $W_m + W_f = c_m + c_f$, and the couple must somehow decide on the allocation of family income between c_m and c_f. If the couple separates or divorces, the utility level of each partner is W_g. The Nash solution of this bargaining problem is the values of c_m and c_f that maximize:

$$\Omega = (\gamma c_m - W_m)^{\mu} (\gamma c_f - W_f)^{1-\mu} \qquad (3.16)$$

subject to the family budget constraint. μ is the fraction of family bargaining power possessed by males. W_m and W_f are the "threat points" of, respectively, the husband and wife in the family bargaining process (i.e., their utility if they break off negotiations and walk out the door).

The solution utility levels from the intra-family bargaining process are:

$$u_m = [1 + \mu(\gamma - 1)]W_m + \mu(\gamma - 1)\, W_f \qquad (3.17)$$

for men and

$$u_f = [1 - \mu(\gamma - 1)]W_m + [1 + (1 - \mu)(\gamma - 1)]W_f \qquad (3.18)$$

for women. Assuming that women have some power in the intra-family bargaining process (μ>0), a rise in W_f increases men's utility, but the same size rise in W_m causes a larger increase in men's utility. An analogous conclusion applies to the effect of changes in the two wage rates on the utility of wives.

Now consider the broader question of the selection of tasks to which men and women will be assigned. For simplicity, assume that the aggregate production function is Cobb–Douglas in the J tasks that technology requires to be performed, each of which is, without loss of generality, equally important in the production process. If this is the case the aggregate production function may be written as:

$$Y = J\prod_{j=1}^{J} e_j^{1/J} \qquad (3.19)$$

where e_j is the amount of labor assigned in the jth task. (Again for expositional convenience, we assume that there are no productivity differences between men and women as well as no differences in the nonpecuniary attributes of the different tasks.) The first βJ tasks are assigned to men, the remaining $(1 - \beta)$J tasks to women. Thus the amount of labor in the jth task is $e_j = L_m/\beta J$ for each "men's task" and $e_j = L_f/(1 - \beta)J$ for each "women's task." Substituting these quantities into (3.19), the aggregate production function becomes:

$$Y = \beta^{-\beta}(1 - \beta)^{-(1-\beta)}L_m^{\beta}L_f^{1-\beta} \qquad (3.20)$$

The value of β that maximizes aggregate output is found by differentiating Y with respect to β, and the value of the share parameter consistent with the maximization of Y is

$$\beta^* = \frac{L_m}{L_m + L_f} \qquad (3.21)$$

In other words, the share of tasks allocated to males should be equal to their population proportion. If β is set above or below β^*, the economy would be operating inefficiently in the sense that output would be lower than it could be with the same labor input.

With competitive pricing, the wage rates of men and women are:

$$W_m = \beta \frac{Y}{L_m} \tag{3.22}$$

and

$$W_f = (1 - \beta) \frac{Y}{L_f} \tag{3.23}$$

Notice that if $\beta = \beta^*$ in (3.21), $W_m = W_f$.[11] We can now consider the "optimal" value of β from the point of view of each gender. It is convenient to recognize that men and women are of (approximately) equal numbers in the population (and the workforce), i.e., $L_m = L_f = L/2$. Substitution of (3.22) and (3.23) into (3.17) gives the utility level of each male in the society, and this is given by:

$$u_m = [\beta + \mu(\gamma - 1)] \frac{2Y}{L} \tag{3.24}$$

Similarly, the utility level for women is:

$$u_f = [1 - \beta + (1 - \mu)(\gamma - 1)] \frac{2Y}{L} \tag{3.25}$$

If men could collectively set the value of β that maximized u_m, they would choose the fraction of jobs assigned to men such that:

$$\frac{du_m}{d\beta} = \frac{1}{L_m} \left[Y + (\beta + \mu(\gamma - 1))\frac{dY}{d\beta}\right] = 0 \tag{3.26}$$

Men's optimum β is greater than β^*, for at $\beta = \beta^*$ the value of $dY/d\beta = 0$ so that $du_m/d\beta > 0$.

This result is shown geometrically in Figure 3.4. The value of total family earnings (as well as Y) is maximized at the efficient value of β, β^*. Men's earnings, W_m, are maximized at $\beta = \beta'$. Men's utility is maximized at a value of β that is greater than β^* and, given that $\mu > 0$ (men have some power in the family bargaining process), less than β'. A similar theoretical argument can be made with respect to the value of β that women would want to be in effect. Women's optimal β is, of course, less than β^*.

To get an idea of the potential quantitative magnitudes of the effects of this form of exclusion, we calculated the value of β that maximizes u_m for a range of values of μ, the male intra-family bargaining power parameter. These results are reported in Table 3.1, all with the assumption that the value of the gains-to-marriage parameter, γ, is 1.5. The parameter values were chosen such that at $\beta = \beta^*$ the values of W_m and W_f are both equal to one.

The value of β that maximizes W_m is 0.782, which is the optimal β for men only if they have no bargaining power within the family (μ=0). As seen

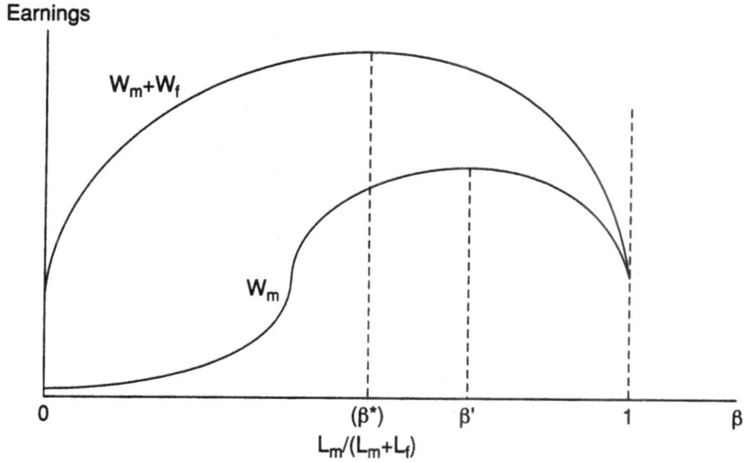

Figure 3.4 Effect of fraction of tasks allocated to men on total family earnings ($W_m + W_f$) and male earnings (W_m)

Table 3.1 Optimal value of β from the point of view of males for different values of μ ($L_m = L_f$; $\gamma = 1.5$)

μ^a	$\beta=\beta^*$ β^m	W_m	W_f	u_m	u_f	*% loss*
0	0.500	1.000	1.000	1.00	2.00	
	0.782	1.321	0.368	1.32	1.21	15.5
0.25	0.500	1.000	1.000	1.25	1.75	
	0.760	1.319	0.416	1.54	1.07	13.2
0.50	0.500	1.000	1.000	1.50	1.50	
	0.734	1.310	0.475	1.76	0.92	10.7
0.75	0.500	1.000	1.000	1.75	1.25	
	0.715	1.300	0.530	1.98	0.75	9.1
1.0	0.500	1.000	1.000	2.00	1.00	
	0.697	1.287	0.560	2.21	0.56	7.7

[a] For each value of μ in the table, the first row indicates the values for $\beta = \beta^*$ and the second row for β^m, i.e. the optimal β for males.

in Table 3.1, the male wage rate rises from 1 to 1.321 while the female wage rate falls from 1 to 0.368. The percentage loss reported in the last column of Table 3.1 refers to the percentage reduction of Y from its efficient value with $\beta = \beta^*$, in this case the loss is 15.5 percent.

The value of β that maximizes u_m, which is reported in the second column of Table 3.1 decreases with the assumed value of μ. This is due to the fact that as men move toward the position of being able to expropriate 100 percent of the gains from marriage they have slightly less incentive to maximize their own wages at the expense of women's wages.

FURTHER APPLICATIONS OF THE MODEL

The modeling framework set out in this chapter may be used for several empirical purposes. In an earlier paper (Johnson and Stafford 1995) we applied the model to two sets of questions involving the joint determination of male and female wage rates in the USA. The first question is: how much of a reduction in occupational exclusion would have been necessary for the achievement of gender wage equality? To provide a range of answers to this question we constructed a model in which there are two basic skill levels (non-college and college-plus labor) and three sets of jobs within each skill level (primarily female, "mixed," and primarily male jobs). The answer to the question was fairly sensitive to the assumed value of the elasticity of intra-factor substitution (σ in our model above), but it was fairly insensitive to the assumed attribution of the initial gender differential to differences in average productivity (λ_j above) versus employer labor market discrimination (δ_j above). For example, for less than college workers, the proportion of women in men's, mixed, and women's jobs in 1989 were, respectively, 0.21, 0.25, and 0.54, compared to 0.74, 0.19, and 0.07 for men. Gender wage equality in 1989 would have required that (i) $\lambda_j \rightarrow 1$ and/or $\delta_j \rightarrow 0$ and (ii) a change of women's occupational distribution to 0.34, 0.25, and 0.41 (plus or minus, depending on the assumptions).

The important point is that, whereas a shift of some women into traditionally male occupations is necessary for gender wage equality, it is not necessary for occupational exclusion to disappear completely (i.e. for D to go to zero). On the other hand, it is still true that the achievement of gender wage equality requires a significant shift in women's occupational distribution. The realization of condition (i) above (equal productivity and/or zero discrimination) is a necessary but not sufficient condition for gender wage equality.

A second question that can be addressed in the context of the model is the potential effect of a reduction in occupational exclusion on men's earnings. During the 1980s (and since) in the USA, women's wages have been rising at about 1 percent per year faster than men's wages. During this time there has also been a (slow but steady) reduction in the observed degree of occupational exclusion – especially among those at the high end of the educational distribution. Using the same model that was used for the first question, we conclude that this reduction in exclusion did indeed have a negative impact on men's earnings but that the magnitude of this reduction was quite small. Furthermore, other changes involving women in the labor market (in particular, increases in the productivity of women in traditionally female occupations) increased men's real earnings. On balance, developments related to women in the labor market were approximately neutral with respect to men's earnings.

Because of intra-country differences in social institutions, applications of the model to other countries (that collect the requisite data) would be interesting. For example, for the typical Western European country at the present time the model would have to be modified to reflect labor market rigidities that cause high unemployment (and high wages for those who are employed). Applications of the model to developing economies would also probably require additional modifications.

NOTES

1 See Jacobs and Lim (1992) for extensive international comparisons of the value of D.

2 Bergmann (1986), for example, entitles one of the chapters of her engaging book "Sex Segregation: The Root Cause of Women's Disadvantage."

3 Blau and Ferber (1992: Chapter 6, 7) discuss a similar set of reasons for gender differences in occupational attachment, referring to (i) and (ii) as supply side and (iii) and (iv) as demand side explanations. See also the discussion by Christina Jonung in Chapter 2.

4 The model is analogous to trade theory models of trade between two countries.

5 This assumption is extremely strong and, as has been noted in the literature (e.g., Goldberg 1982 and Lazear and Rosen 1990), not very defensible for long run analysis. Given free entry and product market competition, entrepreneurs or managers who do not have to be compensated for hiring women will emerge and drive discriminatory employers into bankruptcy. However, the above specification is maintained to illustrate what much of the literature assumes to be a major cause of occupational exclusion. The possible universality of discriminatory preferences has been argued as depending on social custom (Akerlof 1985).

6 We arbitrarily specify that ϕ is defined such that ϕ' is equal to one in long run equilibrium.

7 These would include trade union policy and informational barriers; see Phelps (1972) and Waldman (1984).

8 The value of X_f would result from the "protective" labor legislation that was very prevalent in the USA and Western Europe in the late nineteenth and early twentieth centuries. See Goldin (1990: Chapter 7) and Pott-Buter (1993: Chapter 8) on historical aspects of protective labor legislation. The motivation behind such legislation was apparently a combination of a sincere concern for the welfare of women and a wish to protect male workers from competition. An interesting set of complications arises from questions associated with why – in the absence of legal or institutional restrictions – a particular occupation becomes predominantly male or female in the first place. For an interesting analysis of one job (bank tellers), see Strober and Arnold (1987). Their framework suggests an additional interpretation of X_f (societal discrimination).

9 This result is analogous to models of international trade equilibrium that recognize competitiveness among nations. For example, developed countries gain when developing countries become more efficient at producing what they have traditionally specialized in, but developed countries lose when the developing countries adopt new technology and produce goods that were formerly produced only by the developed countries. See Johnson and Stafford (1995) and Gomery (1994) for models that focus on this issue.

10 For different applications of models of this sort see Manser and Brown (1980), McElroy and Horney (1981), and Wells and Maher (1996).

11 If women were λ as productive as men (in all tasks), the β that maximizes Y is $\beta^* = L_m/(L_m+\lambda L_f)$, at which point $W_f = \lambda W_m$.

REFERENCES

Akerlof, George (1985) "Discriminatory status based wages among tradition-oriented, stochastically trading coconut producers," *Journal of Political Economy* 92: 265–76.

Becker, Gary (1993) "Nobel lecture: the economic way of looking at behavior," *Journal of Political Economy* 101.

—— (1957) *The Economics of Discrimination*, Chicago: University of Chicago Press.

Beller, Andrea (1982) "Occupational discrimination by sex: determinants and changes," *Journal of Human Resources* 17.

Bergmann, Barbara (1974) "Occupational segregation, wages and profits when employers discriminate by race and sex," *Eastern Economic Journal* 1.

—— (1986) *The Economic Emergence of Women*, New York: Basic Books.

Blakemore, Arthur and Low, Stuart (1984) "Sex differences in occupational selection: the case of college majors," *Review of Economics and Statistics* 66.

Blau, Francine and Ferber, Marianne (1992) *The Economics of Women, Men, and Work*, 2nd ed., Englewood Cliffs: Prentice-Hall.

Blau, Francine and Kahn, Lawrence (1994) "The impact of wage structure on trends in U.S. gender wage differentials: 1975–87," NBER Working Paper No. 4748.

Bound, John and Johnson, George (1992) "Changes in the structure of wages in the 1980's: an evaluation of alternative explanations," *American Economic Review* 82.

Brown, Charles and Corcoran, Mary (1994) "Sex-based differences in school content and the male–female wage gap," mimeo, University of Michigan.

Cain, Glen (1986) "The economic analysis of labor market discrimination: a survey," in O. Ashenfelter and R. Layard (eds) *Handbook of Labor Economics*, vol. I, Amsterdam: North-Holland.

Carlin, Paul S. (1991) "Intra-family bargaining and time allocation," *Research in Population Economics* 7, Greenwich, Connecticut: JAI Press.

Corcoran, Mary and Courant, Paul (1987) "Sex-role socialization, screening by sex, and women's work: a reformulation of neoclassical and structural models of wage discrimination and job segregation," mimeo, University of Michigan, IPPS Discussion Paper No. 275.

England, Paula (1982) "The failure of human capital theory to explain occupational sex segregation," *Journal of Human Resources* 17.

Goldberg, Matthew (1982) "Discrimination, nepotism, and long run wage differentials," *Quarterly Journal of Economics* 97, 2, May: 307–19.

Goldin, Claudia (1990) *Understanding the Gender Gap: An Economic History of American Women*, New York: Oxford University Press.

Gomery, Ralph (1994) "A Ricardo model with economies of scale," *Journal of Economic Theory* 62.

Groshen, Erica (1991) "The structure of the female/male wage differential," *Journal of Human Resources* 26.

Gunderson, Morley (1989) "Male–female wage differentials and policy responses," *Journal of Economic Literature* 27.

Hill, Martha and Juster, F. Thomas (1985) "Constraints and complementarities in time use," in F. T. Juster and F.P. Stafford (eds) *Time, Goods, and Well-Being*, Ann Arbor: Institute for Social Research, University of Michigan.

Jacobs, Jerry (1985) "Sex segregation in American higher education," in L. Larwood A. Stromberg and B. Gutek (eds) *Women and Work: An Annual Review 1*, Beverly Hills: Sage.

—— (1989) "Long-term trends in occupational segregation by sex," *American Journal of Sociology* 95.

Jacobs, Jerry and Lim, Suet (1992) "Trends in occupational and industrial sex segregation in 56 countries, 1960–1980," *Work and Occupations* 19, November.

Johnson, George and Solon, Gary (1986) "Estimates of the direct effect of comparable worth policy," *American Economic Review* 76.
Johnson, George and Stafford, Frank (1993) "Real wages and international competition," *American Economic Review* 83.
—— (1995) "A model of occupational choice with distributions of relative abilities and tastes," mimeo, University of Michigan.
—— (1996) "Occupational exclusion and the distribution of earnings," mimeo, University of Michigan.
Jonung, Christina (1993) "Occupational segregation by sex in the Swedish labor market, 1960–1990," paper presented at the European Association of Labour Economists, University of Limburg, The Netherlands.
Juhn, Chinhui and Kim, Daeil (1994) "The effects of rising female labor supply on male wages," mimeo, University of Houston, December .
Katz, Lawrence and Murphy, Kevin (1992) "Changes in relative wages 1963–1987: supply and demand factors," *Quarterly Journal of Economics* 107.
Killingsworth, Mark (1987) "Heterogeneous preferences, compensating wage differentials, and comparable worth," *Quarterly Journal of Economics* 102.
Lazear, Edward P. and Rosen, Sherwin (1990) "Male–female wage differentials in job ladders," *Journal of Labor Economics* 8, 1, January: S106–23.
McElroy, Marjorie and Horney, Mary Jean (1981) "Nash-bargained household decisions: toward a generalization of the theory of demand," *International Economic Review* 22.
Macpherson, David and Hirsch, Barry (1995) "Wage and gender composition: why do women's jobs pay less?," *Journal of Labor Economics* 13.
Manser, Marilyn and Brown, Murray (1980) "Marriage and household decision-making," *International Economic Review* 21.
Milward, N. and Woodland, S. (1995) "Gender segregation and male/female wage differences," Centre for Economic Performance, London School of Economics, Discussion Paper No. 220.
Murphy, Kevin and Welch, Finis (1992) "The structure of wages," *Quarterly Journal of Economics* 107.
O'Neill, June and Polachek, Solomon (1993) "Why the gender gap narrowed in the 1980's," *Journal of Labor Economics* 11.
Phelps, Edmund S. (1972) "The statistical theory of racism and sexism," *American Economic Review* 62.
Polachek, Solomon (1978) "Sex Differences in College Major," *Industrial and Labor Relations Review* 33.
Pott-Buter, Hettie (1993) *Facts and Fairy Tales about Female Labor, Family and Fertility: A Seven-country Comparison, 1850–1990*, Amsterdam: Amsterdam University Press.
Sen, Amartya (1989) "Women's survival as a development problem," *Bulletin of the American Academy of Arts and Sciences* 43.
Smith, James and Ward, Michael (1989) "Women in the labor market and in the family," *Journal of Economic Perspectives* 3.
Sorenson, Elaine (1991) *Exploring the Reasons Behind the Narrowing Gender Gap in Earnings*, Urban Institute Report 91-2, Urban Institute Press.
—— (1990) "The crowding hypothesis and comparable worth," *Journal of Human Resources* 25.
Strober, Myra and Arnold, Carolyn (1987) "The dynamics of occupational segregation among bank tellers," in C. Brown and J. Peckman (eds) *Gender in the Workplace*, Washington DC: Brookings Institution.
Topel, Robert (1994) "Regional labor markets and the determinants of wage inequality," *American Economic Review* 84.

Udry, Christopher (1994) "Gender, agricultural productivity, and the theory of the household," mimeo, Tinbergen Institute.

US Department of Labor (1991) *A Report on the Glass Ceiling Initiative*, Washington DC: US Dept of Labor.

Waldman, Michael (1984) "Job assignments, signaling and efficiency," *Rand Journal of Economics* 15.

Welch, Finis (1976) "Employment quotas for minorities," *Journal of Political Economy* 84.

Wells, Robin and Maher, Maria (1996) "Time and surplus allocation within marriage," Working Paper, Graduate School of Business, Stanford University.

Wood, Robert, Corcoran, Mary and Courant, Paul (1993) "Pay differences among the highly paid: the male–female earnings gap in lawyers' salaries," *Journal of Labor Economics* 11.

Part II

GENDER ROLES, TIME ALLOCATION AND WAGES

4

PATTERNS OF TIME USE IN FRANCE AND SWEDEN

Dominique Anxo and Lennart Flood

INTRODUCTION

For an economist the study of household time use is analogous to the study of market work. For instance, in most empirical work on labor supply, all time not spent on market work is considered as non-productive and denoted as leisure. Based on time-use data from Sweden and France, this should then imply that less than 15 percent of household time use has a relevant economic implication.

In this chapter we take a different view and study the allocation of time in several activities. Furthermore we study similarities and differences in time-use patterns between France and Sweden. The main objective of the chapter is to analyze and compare the gender allocation of time in these countries. Even if time use data have been rarely used by economists, there is a rich and heterogeneous literature regarding time-use and country comparison: e.g., Szalai (1973). For a recent survey of time-use studies, see Juster and Stafford (1991).

This chapter is structured in the following manner. After an outline of the main characteristics of the two labor markets, a description of the French and Swedish time-use surveys is provided. Special attention is given to a comparison of the methods used in the collection of time-use data. Next, the broad patterns of time use are presented, followed by a closer inspection of some interesting activities. Time use will also be classified by working status and number of children. The chapter concludes with a summary.

LABOR MARKETS IN FRANCE AND SWEDEN – A GENDER PERSPECTIVE

From a gender perspective labor markets in France and Sweden show both similarities and dissimilarities. In Sweden about 82 percent of women are in the labor force, a level nearly as high as that for men (86 percent), while France exhibits a lower participation rate for both genders (51 percent for women versus 75 percent for men). In both countries, the labor force participation rates of men and women have shown a clear tendency to converge, but this trend is more pronounced in Sweden. Further, the common increase of the labor force during the period is essentially due to the rise in female participation. The activity rate for Swedish males has stagnated while in France it has fallen. This decline in the male participation rate, partially offset by the increase in female activity, is mainly due to the reduction of the length of working life (due to early retirement schemes) a tendency which is more marked in France than in Sweden.

The age profile of female participation has also undergone a similar evolution in the two countries, moving from a typical bimodal distribution in the 1960s, where women dropped out of the labor force after marriage or at the first pregnancy, toward profiles similar to those of men in the 1980s where the interval of non-participation declined significantly. Despite similar trends reflecting more sustained commitments to the labor market and continuity of participation, it is worth noting that female labor force participation is still significantly higher in Sweden than in France.

The two countries also exhibit contrasting gender distributions of unemployment. In Sweden in the 1970s the female unemployment rate was slightly higher than the male one but there was a clear tendency toward convergence with equal rates at the end of the 1980s. In France, the gender difference is striking, with a trend toward an increasing gap between the sexes. Other divergencies in the two countries can be illustrated by the differences in working time and by the dispositions concerning legal leave from work.

In both countries, in the long run, average annual and weekly hours have shown a significant decline. In 1985, the weekly average working hours for a wage earner were about 36.2 hours (39.9 hours for men and 31.9 hours for women) in Sweden and 37.7 hours in France (39.8 hours for men and 35.5 hours for women). A large part of the differences between the two countries can be ascribed to the higher incidence of part-time work and absenteeism in Sweden. However, the gender differential in working time has declined in both countries. It is also worth noting that on average the gender gap in working hours is still higher in Sweden (8.4 hours) than in France (4.7 hours).

In Sweden part-time work[1] is a crucial component of women's working life. This work pattern has expanded during the 1970s and may explain a large part of the rise in female labor force participation (Sundström 1987). In 1985, about 45 percent of employed women worked part-time while in France the corresponding figure was only 25 percent. In both countries almost 90 percent of part-time workers are women.

Nevertheless, the nature of part-time work is very different in the two countries. While in Sweden there are considerable opportunities to change working time throughout the life cycle, in France, part-time work is frequently synonymous with job insecurity. In contrast to Sweden, the growth of part-time labor in France has occurred against the background of high unemployment, where women have been subject to employers' short-term employment adjustments. Hence, part-time work in France is often concentrated in sectors with high employment rotation and short-term contracts. On the other hand, in Sweden, the incidence of involuntary part-time has been low and the possibility of shifting from part-time to full-time employment has not met with major difficulties. Part-time work in Sweden must be considered more as an historical transition from married women's inactivity toward a strategy, largely initiated by the government, to strengthen women's labor market commitments. Actually, along with the various forms of legal absenteeism (as for instance parental leave, see below), part-time employment in Sweden constitutes a means to regulate and combine household and market work and promote a more equal gender division of labor.

The parental leave program, introduced in 1974 in Sweden, has obviously sustained the growth of female labor force participation and contributed to the above-mentioned changes in women's behavior in the labor market. The length of parental leave was initially 6 months and has been successively extended to 12 months in the 1980s with full subsequent job security. This program is highly flexible and gives opportunities to mothers and fathers to vary working hours until the children are 8 years old (the benefits can be used full-time or part-time; the working day can be reduced to 6 hours for one of the parents). The level of compensation is currently 75 percent of gross earnings (down from 90 percent) and the benefits can be shared by both parents. Households with no earnings before the child is born are only entitled to a flat daily rate. This provides a strong incentive to parents to work full-time prior to having children. This benefit system has had a great influence on working time patterns. Usually, Swedish women work full-time before childbirth, take parental leave, come back to work on a part-time basis afterwards and increase their working time as the children grow up.

In France women are entitled to maternity leave (3 months) but in 1977 the government introduced a program of parental leave. In contrast to the Swedish program, the French parental leave system does not give the right to monetary compensation. Furthermore, the system does not offer the same flexibility and the guarantee linked to previous employment is weaker.

Regarding childcare in France, as in Sweden, the public childcare system has improved substantially during the last three decades, even though the coverage is still not sufficient. In Sweden the number of places in community childcare centers or community sponsored daycare facilities increased from about 14 percent of children under 6 years old in the mid-1970s to about 45 percent in the mid-1980s. The proportion of total costs paid by the parents was about 10 percent in the mid-1980s. The Swedish system is specially designed to facilitate market work for parents. As in France, the daycare centers provide meals for the children and are open until 6pm.

In France about 94 percent of all children between 3 and 6 years old are covered by public daycare programs, free of charge for the parents. Contrary to Sweden, the mothers do not need to work to be eligible for a place for their children. Compulsory school begins when children are 6 years old, as compared to 7 years old in Sweden, but school is completed earlier in France. It is important to note that in 1985 about 60 percent of the children younger than 3 years old in France were outside the daycare system. Thus, it appears that daycare facilities in Sweden are more adapted to working life for parents with children under 3 years of age. Conversely, the coverage in France is higher than in Sweden after 3 years old, and thus, the opposite can be said.

The Swedish tax policy has also contributed to the sharp increase in female participation. The shift in Sweden in 1972 from family-based to individual income taxation has encouraged the labor force entry of wives. Conversely, in France the system of joint taxation has significantly increased the marginal tax rate of women and reduced their incentive to work. This difference in tax structure might explain part of the disparities in participation rates between the two countries.[2]

To sum up, we may conclude that in Sweden the taxation system, parental leave system, working time flexibility and to a lesser extent the increase in childcare facilities have accelerated female labor force growth and secured the position of women in the labor market. These institutional and societal differences explain a large part of the disparity between the two countries as far as the households' situation in the labor market is concerned.

In both France and Sweden, women's wages are lower than wages for men. In both countries a rise in women's wages over time has resulted in a reduction of the gender wage gap, although Sweden still seems to show a lower gender wage differential than France. In 1985 women's wages in Sweden were, on average, about 85 percent of men's wages, while in France the corresponding figure was about 75 percent.The faster growth in women's than in men's wages appears also to be one of the most important determinants of the increase in women's labor supply (see Riboud 1985; Gustafsson and Jacobsson 1985).

In spite of different institutional and economic frameworks in the labor market, both countries are nevertheless characterized by substantial gender differences in the distribution of employment and occupations. To a great extent, men and women are found in different areas of economic activity and in different occupations.

In France as in Sweden, the labor market is heavily segmented. Female employment is concentrated in the service sector (77 percent in France and 83 percent in Sweden) while men have a more even distribution between the service sector (52 percent in France and 51 percent in Sweden) and manufacturing industry (27 percent in France and 32 percent in Sweden). Moreover in both countries women are more concentrated in a limited number of occupations. In 1985, for instance, 10 percent of engineers and technicians were women in France, 18 percent in Sweden. Women dominate clerical work (75 percent in France, 82 percent in Sweden), teaching and healthcare. In Sweden, according to a survey by Statistics Sweden (SCB) carried out in

1982, 55 percent of women were concentrated among the fifteen most female-dominated occupations. At the same date, about 26 percent of men in France were employed within the twenty most male-dominated occupations while in Sweden the twelve most male-dominated occupations employed 30 percent of men.

The general overview above shows clearly that, from a gender perspective, the labor markets in France and Sweden present similarities and dissimilarities. In order to analyze the gender division of labor and hence describe activities other than market work, we now turn to a more detailed comparison based on time-use data. First, however, a short description of the two time-use surveys will be provided.

DESCRIPTION OF THE TWO TIME-USE SURVEYS

The Swedish and French surveys present many similarities. The samples used are representative of the whole population. The survey techniques used in the collection of time-use data conform to the mainstream methods. Time-use diaries have been organized in such a way that they provide a probability sample of all types of days and of the different seasons of the years. Another advantage is that the surveys are close in time, 1984 for the Swedish Survey and 1985–6 for France. Further, apart from a few minor problems, it was easy to construct similar time-use categories. In addition to the information on time use, both data sets also provide a rich set of socio-economic variables.

A common problem with time-use data is the presence of simultaneity in different activities. As an illustration, consider the situation where the respondent takes care of children and watches TV at the same time. Which activity should be classified as the primary one? This problem might have been handled differently in the two surveys, which can affect the reliability of the comparison.

Time-use data, in contrast to conventional economic statistics (e.g., labor force surveys), give very detailed and quite often also very different information. Before we turn to a discussion about time-use data, a simple illustration might be appropriate in order to realize the pros and cons of these data. In Carlin and Flood (1997) two measures of male hours of market work in Sweden 1984 are compared. The first is a standard measure, based on a survey question about average hours of work per week. This is a typical measure which has been used in numerous studies of labor supply. The second measures working hours through time-use questions.

Although these measures give approximately the same mean values, they imply completely different distributions. The distribution for the conventional measure of market work is characterized by a large degree of concentration around one peak of 40 hours/week. The distribution for the time-use measure of market work looks quite different and suggests much more variation in working hours. One way of describing these distributions is to regard the conventional measure as paid hours and time-use data as a measure of actual hours. Another characteristic of the time-use data is the large proportion of individuals who have not reported any work during the days of measurement. This is not surprising since the measure of market work is based on two interviews only. Thus the respondents might be employed full-time but for various reasons did not work during any of the days of measurement. The high degree of zeros is a problem that can be controlled for using appropriate statistical methods. However, the problem of lack of variation in the conventional survey data is more serious.

An interesting example of the consequences of using these two alternative measures in a labor supply study is given in Carlin and Flood (1997). If the survey information is used, small children had no effect on male hours of work. On the other hand, time-use data gave strong negative and statistically significant effects from small children on male market work. This result can be explained since males, in contrast to females, do not reduce their paid hours, although their actual hours might be reduced: they might have to stay at home for one day in order to take care of a sick child, they might have to leave their job earlier in order to pick up the child from the daycare center, etc. In order to find these effects, a measure of actual hours has to be used, and not a measure of paid or contracted hours. One way to measure actual hours is by a time-use study.

The Swedish HUS data

The HUS survey (Klevmarken and Olovsson 1993) is based on a probability sample of individuals aged 18–74. The households to which these individuals belonged made up the household sample. In each household with a couple who were married or living together, both partners were interviewed. In the 1984 survey, socio-economic information was gathered through a personal interview. In addition to this interview, two telephone interviews about time-use were conducted with each respondent. The total sample size was 2,495; of these 1,680 participated in both interviews and the rest participated in at least one of them.

The allocation of days to each household proceeded as follows: the study period was 15 February 1984 to 14 February 1985, with exceptions for certain days at Easter and Christmas. The remaining 347 days were divided into four subperiods:

1 Winter-Weekday.
2 Winter-Weekend (holiday).
3 Summer-Weekday.
4 Summer-Weekend (holiday).

The whole sample was then divided into two groups. Households belonging to the first group were designated a combination of winter-weekday and summer-weekend. That is, households in this group were interviewed the first time during a day which is classified as a winter-weekday and the second time during a summer-weekend. Households belonging to the other group were interviewed first during a winter-weekend day and second during a summer-weekday.

Within each category a day of measurement was selected at random. The individuals were interviewed by phone regarding their time-use during this day. In most of the cases the interviewers called them one day after the day of measurement and asked them about their time-use the day before. If it was not possible to get in touch with them on the day after the designated day it was acceptable to interview them two days after or in a few cases even with a lag of three days. Also, note that the spouses in a household had the same day of measurement.

The answers were given as open answers which were then coded into 72 different activities. For each activity a weighted mean value was calculated. In the usual case, when two interviews have been obtained, the mean value is defined as $t_i=5t_{iw}+2t_{ih}$ for i=1,2, . . ., 72 where indices w and h mean that the day of measurement is a weekday and a weekend (holiday) respectively. If a respondent participated during only one of the interviews, the value was defined as $t_i=5t_{iw}$ if the day of measurement was a weekday and as $t_i=2t_{ih}$ otherwise.

The analyses in this chapter are based on this synthetic measure of weekly time use. At the aggregate level six different activities have been defined:

- market work;
- household work;
- repair and maintenance;
- care and needs;
- leisure;
- travel.

Within each one of these broad categories several activities have been defined at an intermediate level. For most of the activities at the intermediate level a further disaggregation has also been made.

The French Time-Use Survey (Enquête sur les emplois du temps)

The French time-use survey, conducted by the French Bureau of Statistics (INSEE), is based on a random sample of the French population (1/200 of the total population). The sample unit is the household dwelling (15,150 households). Only the main residences have been included in the survey. Housing such as offices, institutions, etc., have thus been eliminated. The response rate of the survey was 66 percent. A probability sample of individuals was drawn from the household sample. The final number of individuals included in the time-use survey amounted to 16,047 aged 15 years and over. Each individual was interviewed once about his/her time use during a randomly selected day. In order to obtain a description of individual time use for the whole year, each month and each day was equally represented. The survey was conducted from the end of September 1985 up to the end of September 1986.

As regards the fieldwork, in the first stage, a personal interview was carried out by professional INSEE interviewers. Information was gathered on the type of housing and on household-related variables such as family composition and background, marital status, conditions during childhood, education, labor market experience, current employment and type of occupation, household and individual income, childcare, vacation home, domestic equipment, ownership of cars, boats and other durable goods.

In a second stage, one of the individuals belonging to the household was drawn at random in order to describe his/her time use. In each household with a couple (married or living together), both spouses were interviewed on the same day. The drawing method used makes it possible to take into consideration the selection bias due to different household size. As in the Swedish survey, the answers were given as open answers. The selected persons had to fill out a detailed description of his/her time use during a day. The following day the interviewers collected the information.

At the most disaggregated level the code book contains 199 activities. At the aggregate level the time use survey contains eight main categories of activities:

- physiological needs;
- market work;
- household work;
- care;
- social activities;
- active leisure;
- passive leisure;
- travel and commuting.

In this study we use a classification into 6 activities at the most aggregate level and into 25 activities at the intermediate level. The classification was first made according to HUS data and then we tried to match this classification using the INSEE data. Since the French time-use data were given at a very disaggregated level, the matching could be done without major problems. One exception relates to the activity "Breaks on main job." The definition of this activity is problematic both in the Swedish and French data. To illustrate, if the respondent went home during the lunch break and ate lunch, this is not coded as time spent on a break but rather as time spent having a meal at home. However, this problem seems much more acute in the French data. A lot of the respondents who reported time spent working did not report any time on a break. In order for us to make the data more comparable we decided to leave the Swedish data unaltered but have inflated the French break times.[3]

Main characteristics of the two samples

In Tables 4.1 and 4.2 some background variables have been listed based on the two samples. From this comparison interesting differences can be found. French males spend almost 32 hours/week on market work (remember that persons out of the labor force such as housewives, retired persons, etc. are included), compared to about 30 hours/week for Swedish males. These figures are based on normal working hours and not on information from the time use study. The labor force participation rate for males is rather similar: 74 percent and 76 percent respectively for France and Sweden. As expected, the rate of unemployment is higher in France; 8 percent versus only 3 percent in Sweden.

For the females the differences regarding these basic labor market statistics are larger. Swedish females spend more hours in the labor market, on average 21.5 hours/week, compared to 19.5 for French women. The data reported in Tables 4.1 and 4.2 confirm the results found in the labor force surveys. By international standards Swedish female labor force participation is very high, 70 percent, while the French is more in accordance with a

Table 4.1 Main characteristics of the French sample

Variables	*Men*			*Women*		
	Mean	*Min.*	*Max.*	*Mean*	*Min.*	*Max.*
Age (years)	41.90	18	75	42.92	18	75
Age 18–29	27%	0	1	26%	0	1
Age 30–54	48%	0	1	46%	0	1
Age 55–64	15%	0	1	16%	0	1
Age 65–74	10%	0	1	12%	0	1
Education level	1.34	1	3	1.31	1	3
Market work (hours/week)	31.98	0	130	19.49	0	96
Married	71%	0	1	67%	0	1
Participation rate	74%	0	1	53%	0	1
Unemployed	8%	0	1	10%	0	1
Household members	3.19	1	15	3.13	1	10
Number of children < 18	0.88	0	9	0.88	0	8
Size of home (m^2)	89.58	7	715	89.5	9	715
Freezer	46%	0	1	44%	0	1
Dishwasher	30%	0	1	29%	0	1
Washing machine	93%	0	1	94%	0	1
Dryer	4%	0	1	4%	0	1
TV	76%	0	1	76%	0	1
Car	90%	0	1	86%	0	1
Number of cars	1.29	0	5	1.22	0	5
Summer house	23%	0	1	23%	0	1
Big city	27%	0	1	26%	0	1
Medium city	28%	0	1	29%	0	1
Country	45%	0	1	45%	0	1

Source: INSEE (1985)

Table 4.2 Main characteristics of the Swedish sample

Variables	Men			Women		
	Mean	*Min.*	*Max.*	*Mean*	*Min.*	*Max.*
Age	44.26	19	75	43.73	18	75
Age 18–29	21%	0	1	22%	0	1
Age 30–54	50%	0	1	49%	0	1
Age 55–64	14%	0	1	17%	0	1
Age 65–74	15%	0	1	13%	0	1
Education level	1.32	1	3	1.27	1	3
Market work (hours/week)	30.38	0	130	21.50	0	96
Married	72%	0	1	73%	0	1
Participation rate	76%	0	1	70%	0	1
Unemployed	3%	0	1	4%	0	1
Household members	2.75	1	11	2.79	1	11
Number of children < 18	0.80	0	9	0.85	0	8
Size of home (m^2)	106.01	7	715	105.38	9	715
Freezer	87%	0	1	89%	0	1
Dishwasher	38%	0	1	37%	0	1
Washing machine	75%	0	1	75%	0	1
Dryer	37%	0	1	37%	0	1
TV	90%	0	1	93%	0	1
Car	84%	0	1	75%	0	1
Number of cars	1.07	0	11	0.95	0	7
Summer house	23%	0	1	22%	0	1
Big city	28%	0	1	27%	0	1
Medium city	50%	0	1	53%	0	1
Country	22%	0	1	20%	0	1

Source: HUS (1984)

European standard, 53 percent. The unemployment rate among the French women is quite high, 10 percent compared to only 4 percent for the Swedish women.

It is interesting to note that despite this huge difference in female participation rates, the difference in average working hours is not very large. The reason for this is that the majority of Swedish women work less than full time, while working French women usually do so full-time.

Education is measured as a categorical variable, where 1 stands for the lowest degree and 3 for the highest. The mean value is close for all groups, with the Swedish females slightly below the others. However, it is difficult to compare the level of education using a crude measure like this. As will be discussed later there is other evidence that the level of education is higher in France.

Other differences include the size of the house: in France the average size is about 90 m^2 and in Sweden 106 m^2. This is not surprising since housing is heavily subsidized in Sweden. In France, housing is less subsidized. The tax deductions for interest payments amount to a maximum of 25 percent.

Regarding disparity in household equipment, it appears that ownership of a freezer is much more common in Sweden. This is interesting since it indicates differences in purchasing behavior and food processing. Owning a dishwasher is somewhat more common in Sweden but owning a washing machine is more common in France. But ownership is not equivalent to having access to a machine; in Sweden it is quite common to have access to a special laundry room if you live in an apartment. There is a dramatic difference in ownership of a dryer. This appliance is almost non-existent in France, whereas 37 percent of the Swedish households reported ownership; a disparity that may be explained by differences in climate.

More Swedish than French households own a TV, although the figures are quite high in both countries. Finally, car ownership is more common in France while owning a summer house is equally common in both countries.

PATTERNS OF TIME USE COMPARED

Overall allocation of time

Figure 4.1 shows the distribution of total time (168 hours/week) between the six aggregate activities: market work, household work, repair and maintenance, care and needs, leisure and travel.

At this level of aggregation and for the whole sample it is striking to see how similar are the patterns of time use between the two countries. Males in both France and Sweden are highly specialized in the labor market and spend roughly the same proportion of time on household activities. It is also striking to see that women in both countries spend the same share of total time in the labor market and that they spend on average three times more time on household activities than men do. The main differences are in household work, which is higher in France than in Sweden, and women's leisure, which in France is much less than in Sweden. If we look at the total amount of time spent on work (market work, household work, repair and maintenance) we can observe that total work is roughly the same between genders and across countries. Total work amounts to 27 percent for the French males and 26 percent for the Swedish males. For women the corresponding figures are 29 percent and 27 percent. Nevertheless, even though the differences between countries and genders are small, the difference in the gender allocation of time between these three activities remains important. At this level of aggregation, the picture revealed is that of a traditional gender allocation of time in both countries.

It is striking that based on the whole sample the female time spent on the labor market is exactly the same in the two countries. On average the females spend only 11 percent of total time on market work. The males, of course, spend more time on market work, in France about 35.5 hours and

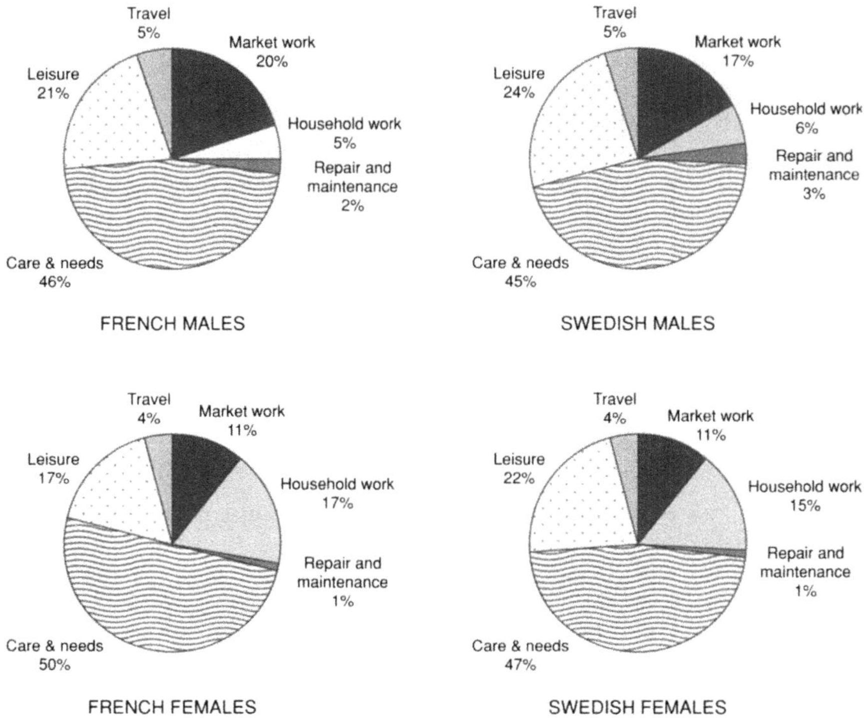

Figure 4.1 Overall allocation of time

in Sweden about 33 hours, but this is still only a minor part of total time (about 17–20 percent).

As far as the whole sample is concerned, females in both France and Sweden spend more time on household work than they do on market work, although the French females spend much more time than the Swedish ones, about 5 hours more per week. As expected, the males spend less time on household work than the females do, in fact, a lot less. Even if the Swedish males spend more time than the French males, the difference does not exceed one hour a week.

The amount of time allocated to repair and maintenance is quite small. As expected males spend more time than females doing this activity; further, this activity is more common in Sweden.

If the first three activities are again summed up we have a measure of total time spent on work, both market and non-market work. The French spend on average more time on household and market activities than the Swedes (about 3 hours more). The females in the two countries spend on average more time on market and household activities than their male counterparts. On average, the French females work around 5 hours a week more than the

French males, while the difference in Sweden is only 2 hours. The difference is highest between the French women and the Swedish men (6 hours more per week). It is also worth noting that the gender differences in time use within a country are greater than the differences in time use for the respective genders between the two countries.

The most time consuming activity is care and needs, not so very surprising as sleep is included in this activity. The French females spend a relatively large amount of time on this activity, about four and a half hours more than Swedish females. Bearing in mind the higher amount of hours spent by the French women on household work and on the labor market, it is not so surprising. The smallest amount of time spent on care and needs is by the Swedish males.

There are also large differences in time spent on leisure. If we rank from less to more the French females are followed by the French males and then by Swedish females and males. Swedish males spend 10 hours more per week on leisure than French females do.

Time spent on travel is about the same for each gender in the two countries. These activities take about 7 hours/week for the females and closer to 9 hours/week for the males. This gender difference is explained by differences in market work and hence differences in commuting.

The time-use patterns over the age groups show several interesting differences. For market work there is a strong reduction in the age group 55–64, for which early retirement or reduction in hours decrease working hours. The drop in hours is a bit higher in France, which is expected since early retirement was quite common in France at the beginning of the 1980s. Also, the legal retirement age is 60 years in France compared to 65 years in Sweden. Market work is rare in the oldest age group, with French males as the only exception, but they spend only roughly 6 hours/week on market work.

The reduction in market work from ages 30–54 to 55–64 has very different implications for males and females. The French females spend most time on total work irrespective of age and they are also the ones who spend most time on care and needs, with the only exception being French males in the age group 65–74. As time spent on market work drops the French females increase the time they spend on household work by about four and a half hours/week and Swedish females by about four hours/week. The French males spend about three hours more per week, whereas the Swedish males actually reduce their household work by about half an hour/week.

Market work

Figure 4.2 gives a detailed description of time allocated to market work. Since several figures will be presented with the same design, it is worthwhile to present it in detail.

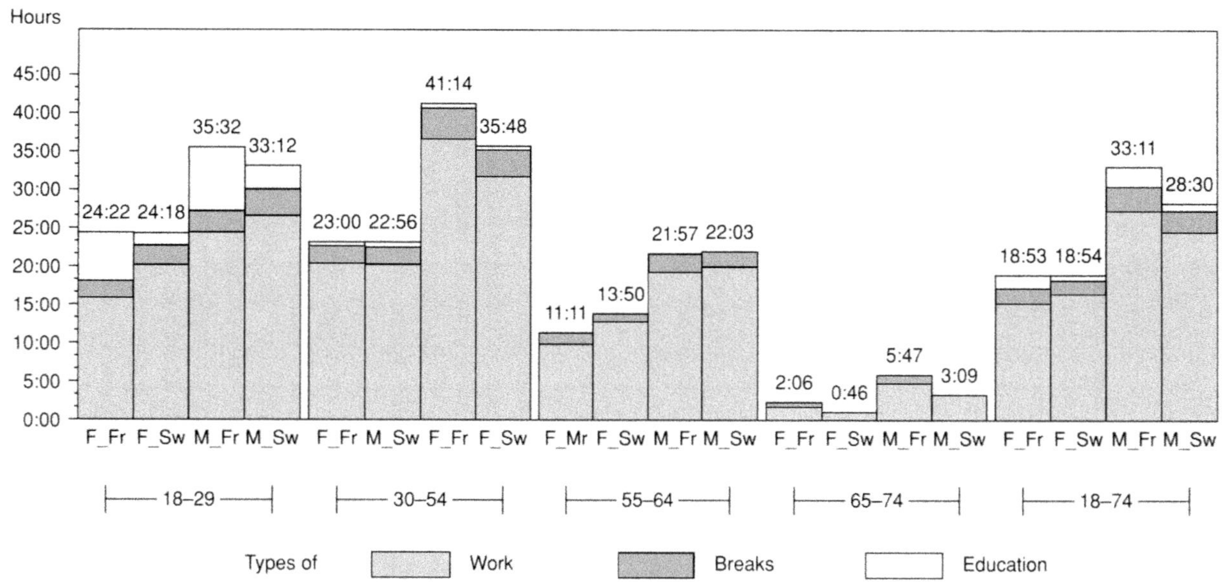

Figure 4.2 Time use in market work. Average hours/week for males and females at different ages

In Figure 4.2, as well as in Figure 4.3, we are looking at time-use in three dimensions, country, sex and age. The rightmost block of the figure presents time-use for the whole sample from 18–74 years of age. This block consists of four parts: first F_Fr, Female France, then F_Sw, Female Sweden then French and Swedish males respectively, M_Fr and M_Sw.

Market work is defined as consisting of three components: work, breaks and education. Of course, the major component is work. Looking at the whole age interval 18–74, it is seen that Swedish females work slightly more than the French ones, 16h 24m versus 15h 5m per week. Thus, despite the much higher participation rate in Sweden, the difference in hours is not substantial. The Swedish females have by any standard a very high participation rate but they do not work so many hours. The mean value for females who reported working hours from the time-use study are 39h 31m and 33h 16m for French and Swedish females, respectively.

For the youngest group the Swedish females work more, about 4h more per week, but the French females spend much more time on education, 6h 32m compared to only 1h 48m for Swedish females. This pattern is also repeated for the young males: the Swedes work 26h 30m and spend 3h 11m on education, the corresponding figures for the French are 24h 16m and 8h 18m. For the other age groups education drops to almost zero and for the age group 30–54 French men work substantially more than Swedish men, 5 hours more per week. However, due to early retirements, there is not much difference between the males in the age group 55–64 in the two countries.

To summarize, the main finding is that French males in active ages spend much more time on market work than Swedish males (14 percent more). For the youngest age group there are great differences in the time spent on education: on average, the French spend much more time on education. This difference might be ascribed to the large proportion of youth in France participating in labor market training schemes. An alternative explanation is the different situation of youths in the labor market in 1985 in the two countries.

Household work

As expected there are huge gender differences regarding time spent on household work. Based on the whole sample, Figure 4.3 shows that French females spend 29h 11m and French males only 8h 36m on household work. The corresponding figures for Sweden, 24h 18m and 9h 48m, indicate a somewhat smaller gender difference. Note that Swedish females spend less time on household work (almost 5 hours less per week) than French females.

Why do the French females spend so much more time on household work? It is interesting to study the decomposition of household work into the separate categories. Concentrating on females and the whole sample, it is seen from Figure 4.3 that the major difference is in the activity laundry. Swedish

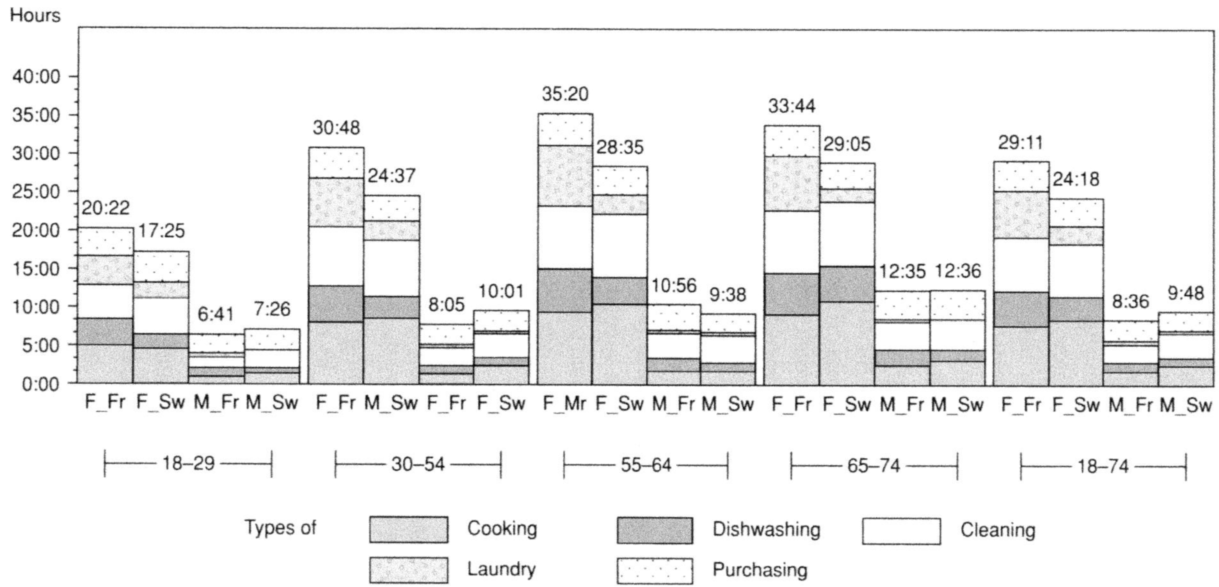

Figure 4.3 Time use in household work. Average hours/week for males and females at different ages

females spend 2h 15m per week compared to almost 6 hours per week for the French females. Thus the major reason why French females spend so much more time doing household work is that they spend a surprisingly large amount of time on laundry. There is also some difference in dish-washing: 4h 36m for the French versus 3 hours for the Swedes.

Thus, the question why do French females spend so much more time on household work is transformed into the question why do they spend so much time on laundry? It is interesting to compare ownership of washing machines and dryers, even if the percentage of French households who have reported that they own a washing machine is quite high: 93–94 percent compared to 75 percent for Sweden. This does not mean that 25 percent of the Swedish households do not have access to a washing machine, however. As mentioned above, in Sweden it is quite common that if you live in an apartment, you also have access to a well-equipped laundry room with washing machines and dryers. Comparing ownership of a dryer indicates an important difference, only 4 percent of the French households reported owning this appliance compared to 37 percent of the Swedish households. This might be one explanation but the major reason is probably cultural differences.

Laundry is interesting from a different perspective as well: no other activity displays such a huge gender difference. Looking at Figure 4.3, the small slice which represents time on laundry for the males is almost minuscule, while for the females it is a relatively large part of household work. For the whole sample French males spend 20 minutes/week on laundry compared to almost 6 hours/week for the females. The corresponding figures for Swedes are 12 minutes versus 2h 15m. Why is this activity done almost exclusively by females?

An additional piece of information is given by the number of individuals who actually reported doing an activity. Almost 64 percent of the French females in age group 18–74 reported doing laundry: that is, during a day selected at random, 64 percent of the females reported some time spent on laundry. The corresponding Swedish ratio is 46 percent. The ratios for the males are of course much smaller: only 10 percent for French men and 6 percent for Swedish men.

If we now consider the time spent doing an activity, given that one is doing it, huge differences can be found again. The average time spent doing laundry (given that time is reported on this activity) by the French females is 9h 20m and by the Swedish females 4h 54m. The corresponding figures for the French and Swedish males are actually exactly the same, namely 3h 11m. Thus the French females do laundry more frequently and they also spend more time on this activity when they are doing it. From a gender perspective there are also large differences in the allocation of time to other types of household work, perhaps with time devoted to shopping as the only exception.

Age has a major impact on the pattern of time use in household work. A major reason is that the elderly spend less time, as we have seen, on market work and also that the demand for household work changes over the life cycle. Younger people without children can reduce the amount of household work. French females in the youngest age group spend more than 10 hours less per week on household work compared to females in the next age group 30–54. The increase in household work from the youngest age group to the next is much higher for females than for males. The major change between these two age groups is that people get married and have children, though this does not have a very dramatic effect on the male time spent on household work. Although the gender difference is smaller in Sweden, the gender division of labor is still substantial.

It is also rather surprising that females spend most time on household work in the two older age groups, 55–64 and 65–74. Households in these age groups do not have small children. A large part of the time formerly spent on market work goes to household work: this is especially true for females.

Repair and maintenance

Although small in magnitude this activity has both an interesting economic implication and economic interpretation. It is not surprising that it is dominated by the males, but why do the Swedish males spend more time doing repair and maintenance than the French males? For the whole sample the Swedish males spent 5h 32m compared to 3h 42m for the French males. The major difference is in the time spent doing repair work on the house and also on durables: cars, boats, etc.

High marginal tax rates may create incentives for reducing market work which might stimulate individuals to take care of maintenance work themselves. It is certainly true that the marginal tax rates were quite high in Sweden in 1984, but that was also true for France. The income level at which this high marginal rate is enforced, however, is much higher than in Sweden. It is worth noting that about 50 percent of French households do not pay income tax.[4]

An alternative explanation might be in terms of alternative costs. In Sweden the supply of small service firms dealing with carpentry, painting, car repairs, etc., is much more limited, and these firms are probably more expensive (perhaps due to high taxes) than in France. The greater degree of competition in France reduces the prices. Also it makes sense to regard market work as a restriction, especially for males, since most prime age males work full-time and other activities can be regarded as a residual. The French males work more in the market and have less time to spend on other activities such as repair and maintenance.

The French males actually spend more time on gardening than the Swedes, but the difference is not very large, except at older ages. This activity has a lot of "leisure" character and the economic incentives are probably not very important. The females also spend relatively large amounts of time on gardening, though much less than the males. The Swedish females spend more time on repair and maintenance than do the French females. Time spent on this activity also increases with age as time devoted to market work drops.

Care and needs

Since sleep and rest are included in this activity it is not very surprising that it is the most time-consuming. Looking at the whole age interval, it is seen that the French females, who spend the most time on this activity, allocate almost 50 percent of their total time use to care and needs. The Swedish males, on the other hand, who spend the least time on this activity, allocate about 45 percent of their total time. Thus, despite the fact that this activity can be regarded as physiological needs, there are relatively large differences in time use. This is more striking if we just look at the activity of sleep and rest. Time spent on this ranges from a value of 62h 27m for French females to 57h 29m for Swedish males. Thus French females sleep about 5 hours more per week than Swedish males. On the whole, time spent on this activity is larger in France than in Sweden, the total difference is about 7.5 hours per week. This result is quite surprising since time spent on sleep and rest should reflect a physiological need and thus be rather constant from country to country.

Time spent sleeping also changes with age, and the patterns of variation are similar in both countries: starting with a rather high value for the youngest, dropping for the middle age groups and then rising again. Thus the time spent on sleep and rest seems to be rather elastic: the individuals adjust according to their situation. It is not easy to explain, however, why the French spend so much more time on sleeping. It might be argued that this is a result of a large amount of market work in France, but this is not quite in agreement with our data, which show that the differences get even larger for the oldest age group.

Childcare is concentrated to the two lower age groups and as expected there are large differences between men and women, though the differences are smaller in Sweden. For the age group 30–54 the difference between female and male time on childcare is about 3 hours in France and 2h 20m in Sweden. In this age group total time spent on childcare is 5h 39m in France and 8h 1m in Sweden.

Leisure

Time spent on leisure also varies greatly between countries. Looking at the whole sample, it is seen from Figure 4.4 that the Swedish men spend about 10 hours more per week on leisure than the French females. If leisure is considered as a positive activity, which it usually is, then the Swedish males

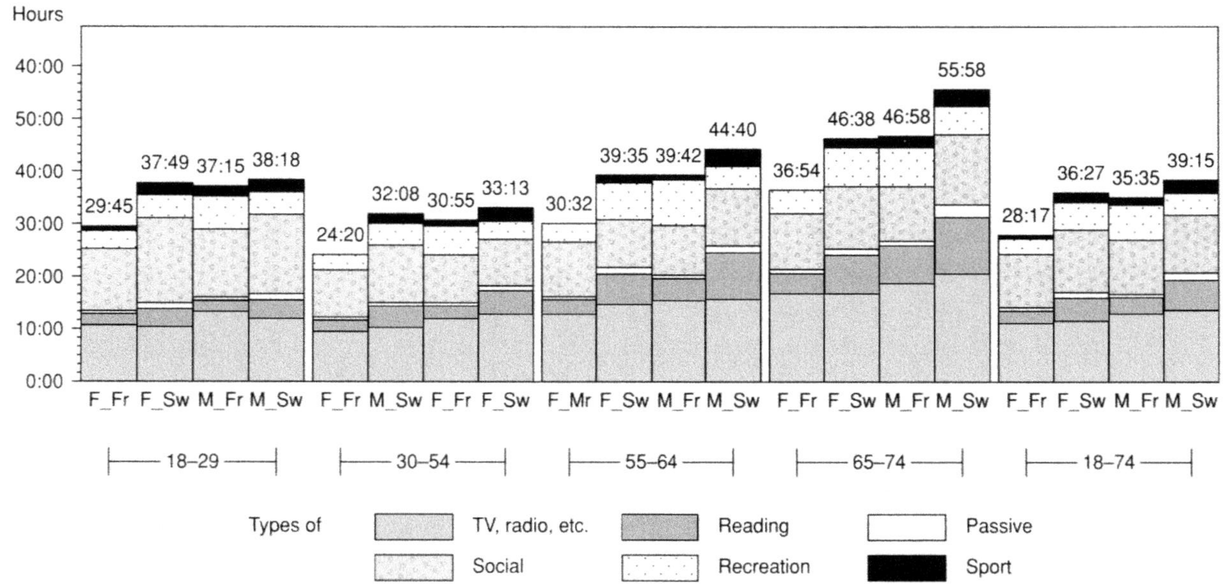

Figure 4.4 Time use in leisure. Average hours/week for males and females at different ages

can be ranked as the winners, followed by the Swedish females and then closely by the French males. The French females, however, may be called the losers. In all age groups the French females spend much less time on leisure than any other group.

TV takes a substantial amount of time. On average, for the whole sample, TV consumes 11h 15m for French females, 13h 31m for French males, 11h 55m for Swedish females, and 14h 13m for Swedish males. The time spent also increases strongly with age. For instance Swedish males aged 65–74 spend almost 21 hours/week on this activity. It is interesting to note that the Swedes spent so much time on TV despite the fact that broadcasting was rather limited in Sweden in 1984. At that time there were only two government controlled channels compared with three in France at the same time.

Indeed TV is one of the most time-consuming activities. For example, in the age group 30–54, only two activities at the intermediate level (sleep and rest and main job) are more time consuming than watching TV. It is interesting to compare time spent watching TV with time spent on childcare. Swedish females allocate about twice as much time to TV as to childcare. For French females the difference is slightly larger. The same comparison for the males reveals a huge difference. French males spend almost ten times more and Swedish males almost five times more time on TV than they do on childcare.

Time spent on reading shows a consistent pattern: for all ages the Swedes spend more time on this activity than the French. The time use in this activity also increases steadily with age. To some extent it might come as a surprise that the Swedes spend more time on social activities than the French do, but the differences are not so large. Recreation is a very heterogeneous activity. The French males spend a relatively large amount of time on this activity. The activity "sport" denotes active leisure, like sport activities and other outdoor pursuits, biking, walking, etc., and is also dominated by the Swedes. The time spent on sport by the French females is surprisingly little: 28 minutes/week compared to 1h 48m for Swedish females.

Travel time

The last aggregated activity is travel time. This takes a relatively large amount of time, for all age groups. The French females spend about 7 hours/week, Swedish females slightly more, 7h 20m, French males 8h 45m and finally Swedish males 8h 35m. Commuting is of course a large part of total travel time, although not the largest. In the age group 30–54 the French males spend the most time on commuting, 4h 8m, followed by Swedish males with 3h 14m. Both French and Swedish females spend approximately the same time on commuting, about 2 hours/week.

Time on care-related travel is essentially related to childcare, that is driving children to schools or daycare centers. This activity is larger in the youngest age groups. Travel time for other areas is dominated by travel time for shopping. Time spent on this activity can be quite large: young Swedish males spend 7h 22m on this activity.

So far we have only analyzed time-use at the individual level for all households, single as well as married. In order to study the allocation of time between the spouses, we will now concentrate on households with married or cohabiting couples. Further we will highlight the differences in time-use with respect to working status and number of children for this group of households.

FAMILY TIME USE

Allocation of time depending on working status

Figures 4.5 and 4.6 show the allocation of time given differences in working status. Here we limit our interest to households with married or cohabiting couples. A further limitation is that these figures are not based on a synthetic week but only on time-use for Monday to Friday: that is, working days.

In Figure 4.5 time use is given for households where only the husband works. This classification is based on whether any market work was reported during the time-use interview. It is not based on normal participation. What is interesting here is the household allocation of time given differences in time spent on market work. In Figure 4.6 the allocation of time is given for households where both spouses work full-time.

Looking at Figure 4.5 we see that Swedish males actually spend more time on market work than French males, though this might look contradictory to what was found above. The reason is that now we are concentrating on allocation of time during an ordinary work week, that is Monday to Friday, whereas earlier the whole week Monday–Sunday was used. This difference is explained by the fact that the French males work more on Saturdays than Swedish males.

Total time, that is the sum of male and female time, spent on household work for the whole sample 18–64 in French households is 33h 30m and in Swedish households 28h 35m. In France the males do 11 percent and in Sweden 14 percent of the total amount of household work. This rather unequal allocation between the genders can of course be explained by the fact that only the males in these families work in the market. However, it is interesting to compare this with Figure 4.6 where both the male and the female work full-time. As expected, there is a strong drop in the total time spent on household work. From Figure 4.6 it follows that for the ages 18–64 the French households now spend only 15h 23m and the Swedish 14h 3m on household work. Also, now the share done by French males is 26 percent and that by Swedish males, 30 percent.

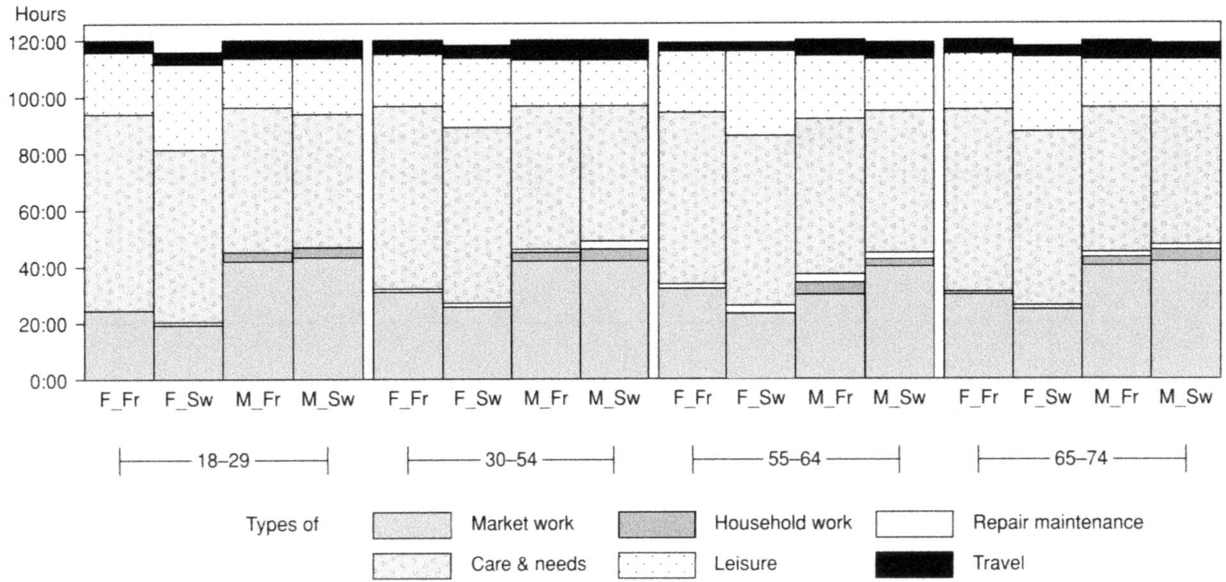

Figure 4.5 Overall allocation of time. Average hours/week for households where only the husband works

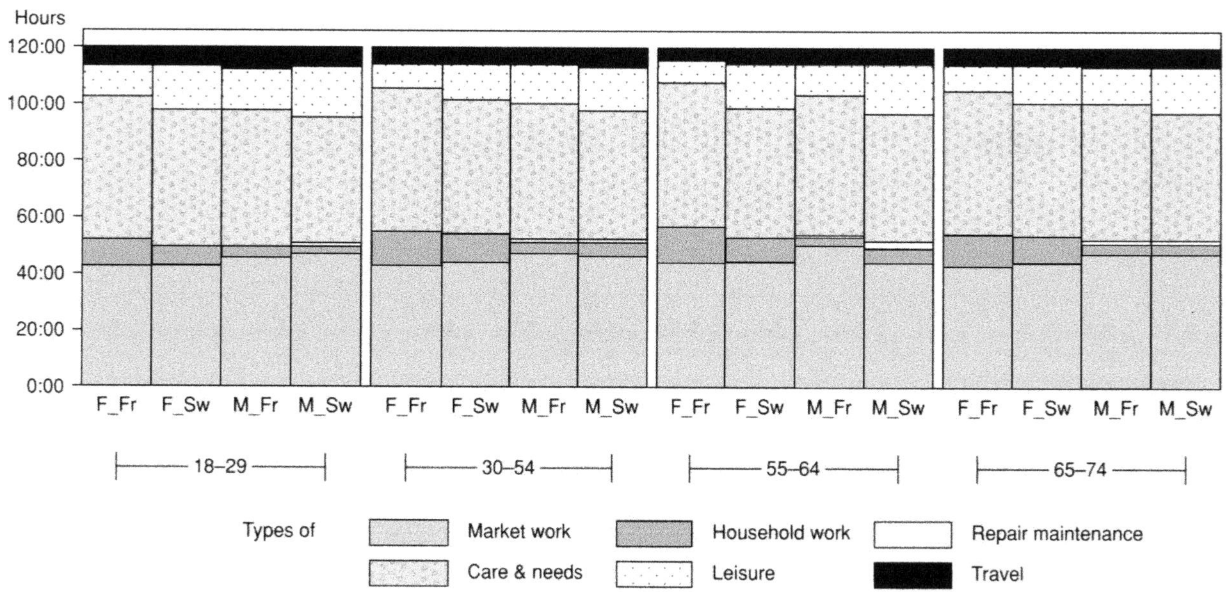

Figure 4.6 Overall allocation of time. Average hours/week for households where both spouses work full time

Analysis at a more detailed level shows that the female time spent on household work is strongly reduced for women working in the labor market. French females spend more time on household work than Swedish females regardless of working status and age. French females also increase their household work with age. French females in the age group 55–64 spend about 8 hours more than in the age group 18–29. In Sweden both males and females spend most time on household work in the age group 30–54. The time that males spend on household work is not affected much by changes in female working status, though the French males increase their household work by about an hour in that age group.

Thus to sum up, female time on household work varies a great deal depending on whether she works in the market or not, though male time use is hardly affected by women's market work.

Time spent on care and needs is strongly reduced when both spouses work full time. Based on the whole sample, French and Swedish females in households where only the male works in the market spend 64h 40m and 61h 40m respectively, while the corresponding figures for females in households where both spouses work full-time are 50h 19m and 47h 7m. Also the corresponding changes in male time-use are relatively large. All activities within care and needs are reduced but the strongest reduction is in childcare: this is because females with children are less likely to work full-time in the market than females without children. Again it is interesting to note the big variation in sleep and rest. Non-working French females in ages 30–54 spend about 4 hours more per week on sleep and rest than full-time female workers do. Also, French households spend more time sleeping and resting than Swedish households regardless of working status. For instance, in the age group 30–54 French households spend 84h 4m when the female is not working and 77h 29m if she is working. The corresponding Swedish figures are 79h 47m and 71h 37m. Thus the reduction is about the same but the level is much higher in France.

Time spent on leisure shows several interesting cross-country differences with respect to working status. The difference between the French and Swedish females is quite large. In the age group 18–29 the non-working Swedish females spend over 30 hours on leisure and the French females only 21h 43m. Despite this the French females spend more time on TV and radio. In fact this activity corresponds to almost half of their total leisure time. The time devoted to active leisure like recreation and sport is much larger among Swedish females. Of course time spent on leisure drops drastically when the females work. French working females in the age group 30–54 spend only 8h 37m on leisure compared to 12h 44m for Swedish females.

Allocation of time depending on number of children

In Figures 4.7 and 4.8 a comparison of time use is given depending on the number of children. Again only households with married or cohabiting couples are included, and they are classified according to whether they have no children or two children. First, a comparison based on the whole sample: average time in market work for females in households with no children is 24h 32m and 23h 21m in France and Sweden, respectively. The corresponding figures for the males are 39h 41m and 35h 45m. Now, if we compare this with the data for households with 2 children, we find that female working hours have been reduced to 20h 31m for France and 20h 53m for Sweden. However for the French males the time on market work has now increased to 43h 6m whereas the change for Swedish males is rather small.

The pattern of time use in the youngest age group is quite interesting. In this age group we have many households with small children and if there is a strong effect on time use from having children, we should find it in this group. As expected female time on market work is reduced as a result of children, but the reduction is much stronger in France, from 26h 1m to only 12h 25m. Looking at total time on market work the reduction for the French males from having children is quite small, only 12 minutes as compared to 1h 35m for the Swedish males. However, the largest effect for the males in households with two children is that time spent on education is essentially zero.

If we look only at time spent working, this occupies 31h 31m for French males and 28h 8m for the Swedish males in households with no children. The corresponding figures for males in households with two children are 33h 22m and 30h 22m. Thus children have an opposite effect on males and females: males with children actually spend more time working in the market than males without children.

Again, by looking at a more detailed level, we found (Anxo and Flood 1994) that children have a large impact on time use. In ages 18–29 French females with two children spend 30h 13m on household work compared to 20h 56m for females in the same age group with no children. Even for Swedish females there is a strong increase in household work as a result of children, though not quite as large as in France. The effect of children on male time use is that in France males with children actually spend less time on household work, from 8h 27m to 6h 44m, whereas the time spent by males in Sweden is increased, from 8h 53m to 10h 12m. An interesting result is the differences between age groups. Especially French females but also Swedish ones in the age group 30–54 spend much more time on household work than the group 18–29 does, given no children. Thus for ages 30–54 the increase in household work due to children is not very great: households in this age group have older children who are not so time consuming.

As discussed earlier, there is a dramatic difference in time spent on laundry between French and Swedish females. This difference is extremely large for households in the age group 18–29 with two children. On average in this group the French females spend 8h 25m compared to only 1h 15m for the Swedish females.

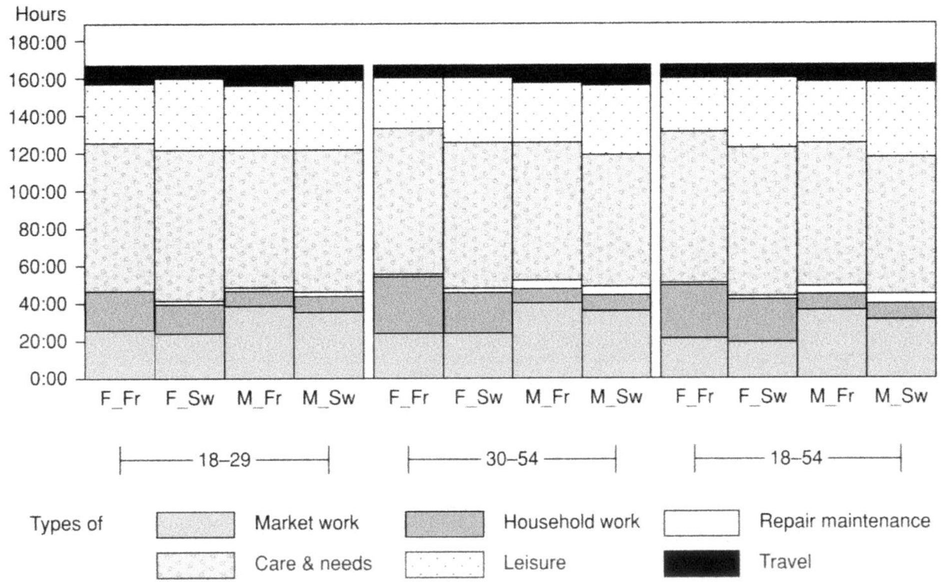

Figure 4.7 Overall allocation of time. Average hours/week for households with no children

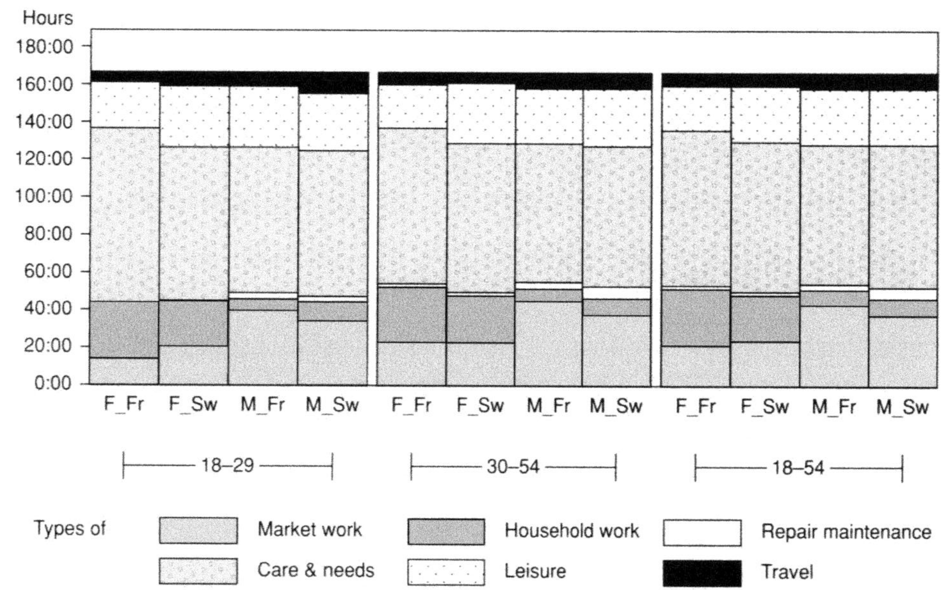

Figure 4.8 **Overall allocation of time. Average hours/week for households with two children**

SUMMARY

Despite important institutional and economic differences, the analysis of time use in France and Sweden reveals clearly that both countries are characterized by a rather traditional gender division of labor. Even though the level of gender specialization seems to be more pronounced in France than in Sweden, the gender division of labor is similar, with women and men highly specialized in typical activities. As far as the whole sample is concerned, males in both countries on average spend more time in the labor market than females. It is also worth noting that women in both countries on average spend the same amount of time in the labor market. However, this equality hides large disparities in labor force participation rates and incidence of part-time work. The labor market participation of Swedish women is higher than that of French women, but the French women work full-time to a greater degree; thus the two effects compensate each other. As regards the males, the French spend on average more time on market work than their Swedish counterparts, independent of age group. Even if the data analysis reveals that Swedish males spend on average more time on household work, the cross-country difference is surprisingly small. Generally, the Swedes spend (independent of age and working status) much more time on leisure than the French, the disparity being much more pronounced for women. As far as leisure is concerned, we thus found that French women are without doubt the losers, with up to 10 hours per week less leisure (depending on age group) than Swedish males.

Even if differences in level exist in the two countries, we found the same tendencies and an analogous pattern of time use when the different age groups are considered. Market work for males increases by age up to 55 years old and then decreases, while time spent on market work declines with age for women.

The inequality in the gender division of labor increases with age in both countries. Not surprisingly, and independent of the age group, women spend on average much more time on household activities than men. If French and Swedish women spend roughly the same time on the labor market, the time spent on household work differs notably between women in the two countries. Swedish females spend less time on household activities than their French counterparts and the difference increases with age. Thus the main difference between women in the two countries is not time spent on market work but on household activities and leisure. The cross-country difference between males, as far as household work is concerned, is much less than that for the females. The difference amounts to less than one hour per week for males between 18–29 years old and to about two hours for the age group 30–54 years old.

If we limit the analysis to households with married or cohabiting couples, some interesting observations can be made. With both spouses working full-time (16–64 years), the differences between Swedish and French males for time spent on household activities is reduced to 12 minutes a week. For the same category but now for the youngest age group (18–29 years), the Swedish males spend approximately one and a half hours less than the French males. When they work, the French women also spend much more time on the labor market than the Swedish females.

The time spent by females on household work is strongly reduced for women occupied in the labor market. French females spend more time in household activities than the Swedish females, however, regardless of working status and age. If women's time spent on household work varies a lot depending on whether they work in the market or not, the time spent on household work for males is nevertheless hardly affected by the labor market activity of their spouse.

In both countries children have a large impact on time use. The impact of children on women's market work is stronger in France than in Sweden. A larger proportion of French women withdraw from the labor market when they have children. Children also have an opposite effect on male and female allocation of time. There is a strong increase in women's household work as a result of children, the increase being larger in France. Conversely, the French males with children actually reduce their time spent on household activities, although the Swedish males increase it slightly. Women reduce their time spent on the labor market while males with children spend more time on the labor market than males without children. Therefore it is when the French and the Swedes get married and have children that the gender specialization is reinforced. Having children strengthens the unequal gender allocation of time in both countries.

NOTES

1 Part-time workers are defined as individuals who ordinarily work 1–34 hours/week.

2 However the work of Bourguignon (1985) seems to suggest that the French tax and benefit system had only a small effect on female participation.

3 This was done in the following simple way. If the respondent reported time on market work but break time less than 20 minutes, then time spent on the activity "lunch" and time spent on meals at a restaurant have been added to the activity "breaks on main and secondary job." Of course, this implies that the figures regarding the break activity should be treated with care.

4 By international standards, the French average tax rate is very low. According to Bourguignon (1988) the average income tax amounts to around 8 percent of full primary income in 1985 (6 percent for wage earner households with at least two persons). However, the fact that the average income tax was low did not prevent the French tax system from being, at this time, extremely progressive and consequently it may have had significant disincentive effects upon labor supply.

REFERENCES

Anxo, D. and Daune-Richard, A. M. (1991) "La place relative des hommes et des femmes sur le marché du travail: une comparison France-Suède," *Travail et Emploi* 47, 1.

Anxo, D. and Flood, L. (1994) "Patterns of time use in France and Sweden," Memorandum no. 205, Department of Economics, Goteborg University, Sweden.

Bourguignon, F. (1985) "Fiscalité, transferts et activités féminines," Centre d'Économie Quantitative et Comparative, Tiré à part no. 8304.

Bourguignon, F. (1988) "Labor supply and taxation in France," Document de travail, Paris: DELTA.

Carlin, P.S. and Flood, L.R. (1997) "Do children affect the labor supply of Swedish men?", *Labour Economics* 4,2.

Gustafsson, S. and Jacobsson, J. (1985) "Trends in female labour force participation in Sweden," *Journal of Labor Economics* 4, part 2.

Gustavsson, S. (1988) "Löneskillnader mellan kvinnor och män – gapet ökar igen," *Ekonomisk debatt* 8.

Gustavsson, S. and Stafford, F. (1988) "Day care subsidies and labor supply in Sweden," stencil, Stockholm: Arbetslivscentrum.

Jonung, C. (1984) "Patterns of occupational segregation by sex in the labor market," in G. Schmid and R. Weizel (eds) *Sex Discrimination and Equal Opportunity*, Aldershot: Gower.

—— (1989) "Jämställdhet på Arbetsmarknaden," in *Arbetsmarknad och Arbetsmarknadspolitik*, Arbetsmarknadsdepartementet, DS:44.

Juster, T.F and Stafford, F. P. (1991) "The allocation of time: empirical findings, behavioral models, and problems of measurement," *Journal of Economic Literature* XXIX: 471–522.

Klevmarken, N.A. and Olovsson, P. (1993) "Household market and nonmarket activities: procedures and codes 1984–1991," Stockholm: Industrial Institute for Economic and Social Research.

Mincer, J. (1985) "Inter-country comparisons of labor force trends and of related developments: an overview," *Journal of Labor Economics* 3, 1.

Persson, I. (1990) "The third dimension. Equal status between Swedish women and men," in I. Persson (ed.) *Generating Equality in the Welfare State, The Swedish Experience*, Oslo: Norwegian University Press.

Riboud, M. (1985) "An analysis of women's labor force participation in France: cross section estimates and time series evidence," *Journal of Labor Economics* 3, 1.

SCB (1963–1993) *Arbetskraftsundersökningarna, årsmedeltal*, Stockholm.

Sofer, C. (1983) "Emplois féminins et emplois masculin. Mesure de la ségrégation et évolution de la structure des emplois," *Annales de l'INSEE* 53, Paris.

Sundström, M. (1987) *A Study in the Growth of Part Time Work in Sweden*. Stockholm: Arbetslivscentrum.

Szalai, A. (1973) *The Use of Time*, The Hague: Muton.

5

COHORT EFFECTS ON THE GENDER WAGE GAP IN DENMARK

Michèle Naur and Nina Smith

INTRODUCTION

The gender wage gap in Denmark is small compared to most countries outside Scandinavia. On average, unskilled women workers earn about 90 percent of the level for unskilled male workers, while the figure for salaried female workers is lower, namely about 70 percent of the level for salaried male workers. During the 1960s and 1970s the Danish gender wage gap decreased, but this tendency stopped in the 1980s: since the mid-1980s the wage gap has been increasing slightly (see Rosholm and Smith 1996).

There are many explanations for this development. One is that public sector wage policies have reduced public sector wages compared to private sector wages. Since about 50 percent of the Danish female labor force is employed in the public sector, while this is the case for only 20 percent of the male labor force, a wage-twist policy of this kind tends to reduce female wages relatively to male wages (see Pedersen *et al.* 1990 and Rosholm and Smith 1996). Further, the wage formation process has changed considerably and has become much more decentralized, especially in the private sector, and the wage dispersion has increased slightly. Comparisons between countries have shown that the highest gender wage gap is found in the countries with the highest wage dispersion (see Blau and Kahn 1992).

Since the early 1960s the labor force participation rate of Danish women has steadily increased and is now close to that of Danish men. Thus, female employment experience has increased. The same holds for the educational level of women. The male workforce is still slightly more educated than the female workforce when measured by length of education, but the difference is decreasing. However, looking at industrial, educational or occupational categories, there are still very large differences between men and women in the labor market. The increase in female labor force participation rates in the 1960s and 1970s was accompanied by a dramatic increase in public sector employment (see Pedersen *et al.* 1995). During this period, the Danish welfare state took over many of the household tasks which women formerly carried out as unpaid work. Thus, women were employed in the educational sector as teachers, or they were involved in healthcare or care of children and the elderly: much of which the family undertook before the welfare state came into operation. To a large degree, the educational choice of young women is still directed towards public sector employment. Thus, looking at educational categories, there are considerable differences between men and women.

This type of sex segregation is often explained as the result of an optimal female job strategy, where women choose education and jobs in which the depreciation of human capital in periods out of the labor market is relatively small. This is mainly the case for care work, where a large share of the job includes tasks which were formerly undertaken by women at home (see Polachek 1980). Even though the labor force participation rate of women is high in Denmark, the "Polachek model" may be relevant, since the relatively favorable maternal and parental leave schemes in Denmark (as in other Scandinavian countries) result in a considerably lower employment frequency for women in the child-bearing and child-rearing ages.[1]

However, due to changing norms and the increasing relative level of female human capital variables, one might expect that the traditional allocation of time within the household has changed, and that the specialization in market work for the husband and in housework for the wife is less pronounced for younger generations of men and women. As an example, the part-time employment for men has increased slightly since the early 1980s, while the part-time employment for women has decreased sharply in Denmark. Further, the introduction of various parental leave schemes, partly as an extension of the maternal leave scheme, has induced some men to enter these schemes, even though the large majority of parents on parental leave are still women.[2] On the other hand, the introduction and extension of maternal and parental leave schemes may have unanticipated negative effects on the gender wage gap if women are considered as less stable workers because they use the leave schemes much more than men. This may increase statistical discrimination and may also increase occupational and sectoral segregation.[3]

The purpose of this chapter is to analyze the differences between cohorts of Danish women with respect to educational level, occupational attainment and earning capacity, and how these differences are reflected in the gender wage gap. During the 1980s the Danish labor market was characterized by a high level of unemployment with a temporary but strong cyclical upturn in the mid-1980s. However, the unemployment of women did not change much during this upturn, mainly because growth was limited to the private sector. The 1980s were also characterized by changes in the wage formation process, which implied a slightly larger wage dispersion and a change in the public–private relative wages, and by extensions of the maternal leave schemes. In the first part of the chapter we analyze whether three birth cohorts, aged 20–29 (cohort 1), 30–39 (cohort 2) and 40–49 (cohort 3) in 1980, had different experiences during the 1980s with respect to wages and the gender wage gap. Since the three cohorts are at different stages of their life cycles and labor market careers, they may be affected differently by a period with a permanently high level of unemployment, increasing wage dispersion and extensions of the maternal leave schemes.

In the second part of the chapter we analyze possible explanations of the gender gap in more detail. Based on the estimation of traditional human capital functions for men and women, we decompose the gender wage gap in order to analyze whether the effects of marital status and children vary between cohorts. Further, we examine whether younger cohorts of women receive higher returns on their investments in education and job training because they have fewer responsibilities at home, as the public sector has taken over much care work and there is a changed division of labor in the household.

We first describe the sample used in the analysis and the three cohorts. Then an empirical model for analyzing the gender wage gap is presented. The following section gives estimation results, and in a final section we present some conclusions based on the results of the analysis.

DATA

The sample used in this study is a subsample of a Danish longitudinal database which is a representative 5 percent sample of the Danish population. A description of the master sample, which stems from administrative registers, is given in Westergård-Nielsen (1988). The master sample was selected in 1980 as a random sample of the Danish population aged 18 and upwards. The sample also contains historical data (1976–9) on the individuals selected in 1980.

From the master sample three birth cohorts of men and women, representing 1 percent of the wage earners in each birth cohort, were selected in 1980. These individuals were observed each year through 1990: i.e., for eleven years. In order to secure representativity in the panel, the sample was supplemented with mainly younger birth cohorts during each of the years after 1980. Therefore, the panel sample is unbalanced. The three birth cohorts in the sample consist of individuals who were aged 20–29, 30–39, and 40–49 respectively in 1980. In Table 5.1 the number of observations in the three birth cohorts are shown for the years 1980 and 1990. The total number of individuals contained in the sample is 8,054 men and 7,059 women in 1980, and 7,382 men and 7,195 women in 1990.

The hourly wage rate is not observed directly, but is constructed as annual wage income divided by the number of working hours, which is calculated from the register on supplementary pension payment (ATP).[4]

We do not have exact information on periods out of the labor force prior to the sample period. But for each individual in the sample we have exact information on the accumulated employment experience since the start of

Table 5.1 Number of observations in the three birth cohorts

	Cohort 1 *20–29 years in 1980*		*Cohort 2* *30–39 years in 1980*		*Cohort 3* *40–49 years in 1980*	
	Men	*Women*	*Men*	*Women*	*Men*	*Women*
1980	2,932	2,617	3,066	2,700	2,056	1,742
1990	2,819	2,740	2,791	2,832	1,772	1,623

her/his labor market career. The experience variable measures the number of years during which the individual has been employed as a wage earner. The information on accumulated experience comes from the ATP register, which gives a relatively precise picture of the employment since the start of the career.[5] Periods out of the labor market or periods of part-time employment imply that no experience or less than full experience is accumulated.

In the sample we have information on the type of education. However, in the estimation of human capital functions we use only the number of years of formal education beyond the compulsory school age as an explanatory variable.

Marital status is measured by three indicator variables: "Married" takes the value 1 if the person is legally married. "Cohabitant" gets the value 1 if the person is living with a partner but not legally married. "Single" indicates that the person is neither married nor cohabiting. The number of children is indicated by the three dummy variables "no children," "1–2 children" and "3 or more children," which are given the value 1 if the person has no children, one or two children or more than two children, respectively. We have carried out experiments with various definitions of child variables, for instance more detailed indicators of the number of children, but this did not contribute significantly to the explanatory power.[6]

The variable "province" is given the value 1 if the person lives outside the Copenhagen metropolitan area. Finally, seven sectoral indicators (primary, manufacturing, construction, trade, private service, public sector, and no information) are included in the models in order to allow for changes in the distribution of men and women on sectoral categories, including shifts in the public and private sector employment.

Tables 5.A1 and 5.A2 in the Appendix show the mean values for the variables used in the estimation of wage functions for the three cohorts for the years 1980 and 1990, respectively.

THE THREE BIRTH COHORTS DURING THE 1980s

Table 5.2 shows the gender wage gap measured by the ratio of the average hourly female and male wage rates in 1990 and 1980 for several subgroups in the three birth cohorts. During the 1980s, the overall gender wage gap of wage earners in the three birth cohorts increased. The female–male wage ratio decreased from 0.82 in 1980 to 0.78 in 1990. The female–male wage ratio was 0.88 in cohort 1, 0.79 in cohort 2, and 0.78 in cohort 3 in 1980, while the figures had changed to 0.80, 0.76, and 0.79 in 1990. Thus, at the beginning of the 1980s cohort 1 had a relatively small gender wage gap but at the end of the period the gender wage gap was close to the level of cohort 3. It is remarkable that in 1990 the largest wage gap is found in cohort 2 rather than in cohort 3 which, based on the hypotheses put forward above, might be expected to have the largest gender wage gap.

A comparison of the gender wage gap in the three birth cohorts for the subgroups having 0, 1–2, and 3 or more children shows that the gap tends to increase with the number of children. The only exception is persons in cohort 1 who have three or more children compared with persons who have one or two children. The marital status also seems to affect the gender wage gap. The smallest gap is found in all three cohorts for single persons, while the largest gap is in the group of married men and women. There is no systematic tendency in Table 5.2 indicating that marriage has a more negative effect on the relative female wages in the older cohorts compared with younger cohorts. The female–male wage ratio is about 0.75 for married persons in all three birth cohorts.

The average gender wage gap in Table 5.2 shows the ratio between two averages, which may be highly dependent on the wage distributions. In general, the female wage distributions are more compressed than the comparable male ones (see Rosholm and Smith 1996). In order to analyze the relative position of female wages compared with male wages, the average percentile ranking of women if they were placed in the male wage distribution has been calculated for each cohort (see Blau 1992 or her chapter in this volume). The results are shown in Table 5.3.

The youngest cohort of women, cohort 1, aged 20–29, has the best relative position in 1980 at the start of the observation period: they have an average percentile of 35 in the male wage distribution, while this figure is

Table 5.2 The gender wage gap in the three birth cohorts,[a] 1990

	Cohort 1	*Cohort 2*	*Cohort 3*
0 children	0.90	0.86	0.83
1–2 children	0.76	0.75	0.79
3 or more children	0.81	0.74	0.73
Single	0.90	0.84	0.92
Cohabitant	0.83	0.77	0.77
Married	0.76	0.74	0.76
All 1990	0.80	0.76	0.79
All 1980	0.88	0.79	0.78

[a] Ratio between the average hourly female wage rate and the average hourly male wage rate in the group concerned.

Table 5.3 Average percentile ranking of women in the male wage distribution[a]

Year	*All*	*Cohort 1*	*Cohort 2*	*Cohort 3*
1980	29.0	34.9	25.4	25.5
1981	30.0	34.5	26.4	27.7
1982	32.2	35.4	29.4	30.9
1983	32.0	34.5	29.4	31.6
1984	31.7	34.7	29.7	29.7
1985	26.8	28.8	24.7	26.3
1986	25.6	26.6	24.1	25.3
1987	25.9	26.4	24.8	26.4
1988	25.9	25.9	24.8	26.7
1989	27.9	28.0	26.5	29.0
1990	28.4	28.3	26.9	29.9

[a] The male wage distribution has been subdivided into percentiles for each year, observing the highest and lowest wage level in each category. A percentile ranking in the male wage distribution is assigned to each woman's wage in the year concerned. The female mean of these percentiles is presented in the table.

25 for cohorts 2 and 3. The pattern changes during the 1980s, and the youngest cohort ends up having a relative position in the male wage distribution similar to that of the two older cohorts. This development may be the result of age-specific, time-specific, or cohort-specific factors. The age-specific factors might be that cohort 1 is observed during the period when family formation and childbirth usually take place. The deterioration of women's relative position in the male wage distribution in the youngest cohort may reflect the fact that family formation has a very different impact on men's and women's career profiles. Further, it is remarkable that cohort 2 rather than cohort 3 has the lowest percentile ranking all through the 1980s. The estimation of a statistical model in the next sections will clarify this issue further.

One of the time-specific factors which clearly affects the figures in Table 5.3 is the cyclical upturn in the mid-1980s, when private employment increased significantly and male unemployment rates fell, whereas the changes in female employment and unemployment were much more moderate. The wage increases during the mid-1980s were created mainly by wage drift, and the wage dispersion increased somewhat. Other empirical studies show that during the years 1984–6 the Danish gender wage gap increased (see Rosholm and Smith 1996). The figures in Table 5.3 clearly confirm these results. In 1982, the overall average percentile ranking of women in the three cohorts was 32.2 percent. This figure was reduced to 25.6 percent in 1986. Looking at each cohort separately, the drop in percentile ranking was much larger for cohort 1 than for the two older cohorts. Part of this large drop for cohort 1 may be attributed to the age-specific career effect mentioned above, but may also reflect the fact that the youngest cohort of women is more severely hit by the cyclical downturn than older women with a firmer attachment to the labor market.

In Table 5.4 the two human capital variables "accumulated experience" and "length of education" are shown for the three cohorts for the years 1980 and 1990. Since we use ten-year birth cohorts, the "accumulated experience" and "length of education" for cohort 2 in 1980 may be compared with the 1990 figures for cohort 1 because, in 1990, cohort 1 has reached the 1980 average age of cohort 2. The same is true for similar comparisons between cohorts 2 and 3.

The accumulated experience of men and women in the oldest cohort differs considerably. In 1980 the experience of men in cohort 3 was 22.8 years while the same figure for women was 13.4. Ten years later, men in cohort 3 had further accumulated 8.3 years of employment experience, while the women in this cohort had accumulated 6.1 years. Thus, the oldest cohort in the sample seems to follow the traditional pattern of time allocation between market work and home work. This pattern is less predominant in the younger cohorts. Comparing the accumulated experience of cohort 2 in 1990 with the same figures for cohort 3 in 1980, we find a much more even distribution of accumulated experience for men and women. In 1990, men in cohort 2 had accumulated 20.0 years of experience and women in this cohort 15.2 years. Thus, the gap between men and women in this cohort, aged 40–49 in 1990, was 4.8 years, while the same figure for cohort 3 was 9.4 years when they were aged 40–49 in 1980. For the youngest cohort, the differences in experience virtually disappear. In 1980, when the persons in this cohort were aged 20–29, the difference was close to zero. Ten years later, when the cohort was aged 30–39, and even though a considerable part of the childbirth and maternal leave periods must have been passed, the difference between men and women in terms of accumulated experience is only 1.2 years (see Table 5.4).

Table 5.4 Accumulated experience and the length of education for the three birth cohorts. Mean sample values (standard errors in parentheses)

		Cohort 1 20–29 *years in* 1980		*Cohort 2* 30–39 *years in* 1980		*Cohort 3* 40–49 *years in* 1980	
		Men	*Women*	*Men*	*Women*	*Men*	*Women*
Experience (years)	1980	4.3	4.1	11.6	8.6	22.8	13.4
		(2.3)	(2.5)	(4.9)	(4.0)	(5.8)	(4.6)
	1990	12.0	10.8	20.0	15.2	31.1	19.5
		(4.1)	(4.2)	(6.1)	(5.9)	(7.1)	(6.8)
Length of education (years)	1980	2.3	2.3	3.0	2.6	2.6	1.9
		(2.0)	(2.0)	(2.6)	(2.5)	(2.5)	(2.3)
	1990	3.2	3.1	3.1	2.7	2.7	2.1
		(2.6)	(2.6)	(2.7)	(2.6)	(2.6)	(2.5)

As to length of formal education it appears from Table 5.4 that in 1990, the oldest cohort had a lower educational level than the two younger cohorts. The gender gap with regard to educational level increases with age. In the oldest cohort, men had on average 0.6 years of education more than women in 1990. In cohort 2 this figure was 0.4, whereas there was practically no gap in the educational level in the youngest cohort in 1990.

Despite these tendencies towards a more equal distribution of formal qualifications, the horizontal segregation is considerable, as shown in Table 5.5. Women are concentrated in the public sector, while men are more evenly spread over the public and private sectors. The proportion of women employed in the public sector is only slightly lower for younger cohorts than for the oldest cohort. The calculations of the Duncan and Duncan index (DD) show that the three birth cohorts exhibit approximately the same level of horizontal segregation. The figures in Table 5.5 concern 1990, but the DD index for sectoral segregation was relatively stable during the 1980s.

Turning to occupational segregation, the variation across cohorts is slightly different. The Duncan and Duncan index in Table 5.6 shows that occupational segregation is lower for the youngest cohort than for the two older cohorts. This is mainly due to the fact that relatively more women in the younger birth cohorts manage to get higher ranking positions as salaried employees, fewer women there work as unskilled workers, and fewer women in the younger birth cohorts are categorized as "wage earners with no information on occupational group," which reflects that fewer women there have such a loose attachment to the labor market that they could not be placed in any occupational category. However, comparing the positions of men and women in 1980 with their positions ten years later in 1990, Table 5.6 illustrates that for cohort 1 the male–female gap in occupational position is widening greatly. During the period, the fraction of men employed as "salaried employees, high level" increased from 5 percent to 15 percent while for women the fraction increased only from 2 percent to 6 percent. In 1990,

Table 5.5 Horizontal segregation in the three birth cohorts, 1990

	Cohort 1		*Cohort 2*		*Cohort 3*	
	Men	*Women*	*Men*	*Women*	*Men*	*Women*
Public	0.23	0.55	0.28	0.56	0.29	0.59
Primary	0.02	0.00	0.01	0.00	0.01	0.01
Manufacturing	0.26	0.12	0.25	0.13	0.27	0.12
Construction	0.12	0.01	0.10	0.01	0.08	0.01
Trade	0.12	0.08	0.13	0.09	0.13	0.10
Other private service	0.25	0.21	0.23	0.18	0.22	0.16
No sector information	0.00	0.03	0.00	0.02	0.00	0.01
DD-index[a]	0.30		0.31		0.31	

[a] $DD = \Sigma_j \mid M_j - F_j \mid / 2$, where j indicates sector. M_j (F_j) is the relative frequency of men (women) in sector j.

Table 5.6 Occupational segregation in the three birth cohorts, 1980 and 1990

		Cohort 1		*Cohort 2*		*Cohort 3*	
		Men	*Women*	*Men*	*Women*	*Men*	*Women*
Salaried empl.,	1980	0.05	0.02	0.18	0.05	0.19	0.03
high level	1990	0.15	0.06	0.21	0.06	0.20	0.05
Salaried empl.,	1980	0.07	0.13	0.18	0.17	0.18	0.15
medium level	1990	0.15	0.22	0.21	0.19	0.19	0.17
Salaried empl., low	1990	0.23	0.48	0.17	0.44	0.13	0.36
level	1980	0.18	0.43	0.14	0.43	0.14	0.35
Skilled	1980	0.28	0.02	0.26	0.01	0.22	0.01
	1990	0.25	0.02	0.23	0.01	0.21	0.01
Unskilled	1980	0.30	0.29	0.20	0.29	0.26	0.36
	1990	0.24	0.25	0.20	0.28	0.25	0.37
No information on	1980	0.07	0.06	0.01	0.03	0.01	0.08
occupational group	1990	0.02	0.02	0.01	0.03	0.01	0.05
DD-Index[a]	1980	0.31		0.39		0.40	
	1990	0.33		0.37		0.35	

[a] $DD = \Sigma_j \mid M_j - F_j \mid / 2$, where j indicates sector. M_j (F_j) is the relative frequency of men (women) in sector j.

43 percent of the women in both the two younger birth cohorts were employed as "salaried employees, low level" which is a category consisting of low-paid occupations, mainly in the public sector.

To sum up, the overall picture of the three birth cohorts aged 20–29, 30–39, and 40–49 in 1980 is that there has been a gradual reduction of the differences between men and women when measured by formal qualifications like length of education and employment experience. The youngest cohort also exhibits less occupational segregation than the two older cohorts.

However, the family status of the three birth cohorts has changed. This is illustrated in Tables 5.7 and 5.8. The status "single" has become more widespread, and the proportion who are legally married has decreased substantially in the younger birth cohorts, because more and more mainly younger individuals cohabit rather than being legally married.

Table 5.7 Marital status in the three birth cohorts

		Cohort 1		*Cohort 2*		*Cohort 3*	
		Men	*Women*	*Men*	*Women*	*Men*	*Women*
Married (0/1)	1980	0.24	0.40	0.69	0.73	0.81	0.76
	1990	0.51	0.59	0.71	0.72	0.80	0.71
Cohabitant (0/1)	1980	0.42	0.34	0.13	0.09	0.06	0.05
	1990	0.24	0.21	0.12	0.09	0.07	0.06
Single (0/1)	1980	0.34	0.26	0.18	0.18	0.13	0.19
	1990	0.24	0.20	0.17	0.19	0.13	0.23

Table 5.8 Number of children[a] in the three birth cohorts

		Cohort 1		Cohort 2		Cohort 3	
		Men	Women	Men	Women	Men	Women
No children (0/1)	1980	0.78	0.54	0.32	0.15	0.31	0.36
	1990	0.44	0.19	0.20	0.09	0.26	0.31
1 or 2 children (0/1)	1980	0.22	0.45	0.56	0.68	0.55	0.57
	1990	0.48	0.68	0.61	0.67	0.59	0.59
3 or more children (0/1)	1980	0.01	0.02	0.12	0.16	0.13	0.07
	1990	0.08	0.14	0.19	0.23	0.15	0.10
Number of children	1980	0.32	0.67	1.34	1.67	1.31	1.05
	1990	1.06	1.55	1.66	1.92	1.42	1.19

[a] In 1980, "children" is defined as children below the age of 19, whereas in 1990 the definition is children below the age of 29.

Another demographic trend is the decrease in fertility and the postponement of birth. The youngest cohort of men and women had on the average 1.06 and 1.55 children in 1990. The corresponding figures were 1.34 and 1.67 for cohort 2 in 1980, when cohort 2 on average was the same age as cohort 1 in 1990. The proportion of cohort 1 who had no children in 1990 was 0.44 for men and 0.19 for women. For cohort 2, these figures were 0.32 and 0.15 in 1980.

EMPIRICAL MODEL

In this section a traditional human capital model is estimated in order to analyze and quantify the effects on the gender wage gap of changing family characteristics and human capital accumulation in the three birth cohorts.

Earlier studies of wage functions have found the existence of unobserved variables correlated with the included explanatory and dependent variables in the wage function (see, for example, Hausman and Taylor 1981). Depending on the number and quality of the explanatory variables, there may be unobservable variables such as motivation, ability, etc., which are correlated with the included explanatory variables. This may be of special interest when comparing male and female wage functions and evaluating discrimination, because the magnitude of the rate of return on included productivity characteristics plays an important role, and because the problem of unobserved variables may differ between men and women.

Since the sample used is a panel sample, we are able to deal with this problem by using an estimator proposed by Hausman and Taylor (1981). The estimator, which consists of several steps, is modified to allow for an unbalanced sample design, following the lines suggested by Greene (1990).[7] The basic model may be formulated as:

$$\ln W_{it} = \beta_0 + TD_t \beta_t + X_{it} \beta + Z_i \gamma + (\alpha_i + \epsilon_{it}) \quad (5.1)$$

where ln W_{it} is the log hourly wage rate for individual i observed at time t, TD_t is a time dummy, X_{it} is a vector of time varying explanatory variables, and Z_i is a vector of time invariant explanatory variables. Some of the X and Z variables are interacted with cohort indicators in order to allow for cohort specific effects of these explanatory variables.

The human capital model in (5.1) is estimated separately for men and women. One way of analyzing cohort differences might be to estimate separate wage functions for both genders and for the three birth cohorts. However, this strategy causes problems when interpreting potential differences in earnings profiles between the three birth cohorts because each cohort is observed in different segments in their earnings profile.[8] Instead, we have chosen to estimate one wage function which is common to all three birth cohorts, while cohort effects are allowed for through interactions with the variables length of education, child indicators, occupation and indicators of marital status. The variables not interacted with birth cohorts are (besides experience) an indicator for living outside the Copenhagen region and sectoral indicators. An F-test showed that interacting these variables with birth cohorts did not contribute significantly to the explanatory power of the model.

ESTIMATION RESULTS

Wage equations

The estimated wage equations are shown in Table 5.9. As found in other studies (see Rosholm and Smith 1996 and Asplund *et al.* 1996), the estimated return on educational investments is lower for women than for men in the two older cohorts whereas the opposite is the case for the youngest cohort. This result may confirm the hypothesis that younger cohorts of women receive a higher return on their educational investments than older women because the statistical discrimination of women is less pronounced in younger cohorts than in older cohorts. Alternatively, the explanation may be that the male spouses in younger cohorts do a larger share of the housework than the husbands in older cohorts. If so, we should expect a lower return on educational investments for younger than older cohorts of men. This expectation is in fact confirmed, since the highest estimated coefficient to the educational variable is found in the oldest cohort of men. An alternative explanation of this pattern might be changes in the demand for and supply of educated workers. However, the difference in the cohort pattern observed for men and women does not support this explanation.[9]

Estimations show that the wage profiles are relatively flat with a coefficient for the experience variable of only 0.6 percent for men and 0.8 percent for women. However, part of the steepness of the experience profile is picked up by the coefficients to the occupational variables and the cohort specific constant terms. As shown in Table 5.6, the occupational status changes considerably for the youngest cohort, especially for men, between 1980 and 1990. As an example, 5 percent of the men in cohort 1 were employed as "high level salaried workers" in 1980. In 1990 the figure was 15 percent. For women in cohort 1 the comparable figure was 2 percent in 1980 and 6 percent in 1990. Thus, the low "return" on experience in the youngest cohort is, to a certain extent, explained by a wage effect due to occupational mobility in the early part of the career, which is captured by the occupational indicators.

The sectoral dummies, representing six private sector industries, are all significantly positive for men, while for women in the private sector some indicators are insignificant and one indicator is significantly negative. Men in the public sector earn 9–10 percent less than men in the private sector (with the exception of men who are employed in the trade sector) while the comparable figure for women is 0–5 percent. Thus, the "penalty" for being employed in the public sector is much higher for men than for women. The same is true for the variable living in the province. Men living in the province earn 7.1 percent less than men in the Copenhagen metropolitan area, while the corresponding figure for women is only 4.8 percent.

Table 5.9 Estimated coefficients and standard errors

	Men		*Women*	
	Estimate	*Std error*	*Estimate*	*Std error*
Constant	3.927*	0.009	3.833*	0.011
Cohort 2	0.097*	0.012	0.075*	0.014
Cohort 3	0.017*	0.015	0.043*	0.014
Time indicator Year 1981	0.117*	0.003	0.113*	0.003
Time indicator Year 1982	0.256*	0.003	0.278*	0.004
Time indicator Year 1983	0.327*	0.003	0.351*	0.004
Time indicator Year 1984	0.376*	0.004	0.395*	0.004
Time indicator Year 1985	0.408*	0.004	0.376*	0.004
Time indicator Year 1986	0.461*	0.004	0.408*	0.005
Time indicator Year 1987	0.561*	0.005	0.513*	0.005
Time indicator Year 1988	0.626*	0.005	0.575*	0.006
Time indicator Year 1989	0.676*	0.006	0.636*	0.006
Time indicator Year 1990	0.714*	0.006	0.683*	0.007
Primary sector	0.076*	0.008	–0.245	0.015
Manufacturing	0.097*	0.004	0.050*	0.004
Construction	0.091*	0.004	0.045*	0.011
Trade	0.050*	0.004	–0.057*	0.005
Private service	0.082*	0.004	0.056*	0.004
No sector information	0.076*	0.010	0.154	0.011
Province	–0.071*	0.004	–0.048*	0.004
Cohabiting	0.002	0.003	–0.013*	0.004
Married	0.040*	0.005	0.006	0.005

Table 5.9 Continued

	Men		*Women*	
	Estimate	*Std error*	*Estimate*	*Std error*
Cohabiting Cohort 2	–0.001	0.006	0.003	0.008
Married Cohort 2	–0.030*	0.007	–0.014*	0.007
Cohabiting Cohort 3	0.005	0.009	0.001	0.011
Married Cohort 3	–0.017*	0.009	–0.026*	0.009
1 or 2 children	0.034	0.005	0.020	0.005
3 or more children	0.062	0.009	0.032	0.009
1 or 2 children Cohort 2	–0.047	0.008	–0.036	0.011
3 or more children Cohort 2	–0.058	0.013	–0.035	0.015
1 or 2 children Cohort 3	–0.094	0.019	–0.023	0.014
3 or more children Cohort 3	–0.085	0.022	–0.017	0.021
Salaried high level	0.096*	0.008	0.090*	0.011
Salaried medium level	0.058*	0.006	0.003	0.006
Skilled	0.020*	0.006	0.019	0.016
Unskilled	0.034*	0.006	0.017*	0.005
No information	0.047*	0.008	0.044*	0.010
Salaried high level Cohort 2	0.032*	0.011	0.076*	0.016
Salaried medium level Cohort 2	–0.003	0.010	0.066*	0.010
Skilled Cohort 2	–0.027*	0.010	–0.076*	0.026
Unskilled Cohort 2	–0.041*	0.010	–0.028*	0.008
No information Cohort 2	0.049*	0.019	–0.028	0.016
Salaried high level Cohort 3	0.071*	0.014	0.105*	0.020
Salaried medium level Cohort 3	0.014	0.012	0.082*	0.013
Skilled Cohort 3	–0.003	0.013	–0.058	0.037
Unskilled Cohort 3	–0.042*	0.012	–0.010	0.010
No information Cohort 3	–0.037	0.024	–0.022	0.016
Experience	0.006*	0.001	0.008*	0.001
Experience squared/100	0.000*	0.000	–0.000*	0.000
Length of education Cohort 1	0.024*	0.001	0.026*	0.001
Length of education Cohort 2	0.029*	0.002	0.017*	0.002
Length of education Cohort 3	0.037*	0.002	0.019*	0.002
R–square, step 2[a]	0.228		0.137	
R–square, step 4[a]	0.976		0.978	
No. observations	86,271		80,153	

* Significant at a 5% level.
[a] See Naur and Smith (1996).

During the period 1980–90, the hourly wages increased by 71 percent for men and 68 percent for women when controlling for changes in different characteristics. This should indicate a widening of the gender wage gap of about 3 percent during the period. The influence of the remaining variables may be difficult to interpret due to the large number of interaction terms. Therefore, we have chosen to analyze these variables by means of a traditional Oaxaca decomposition of the wage gap.

Decomposition of the wage gap

Denote the estimated row vectors of coefficients from the male and female regressions by β_m and β_f, and the row vectors of sample means $\bar{x}_m$ and $\bar{x}_f$, respectively.[10] Then the Oaxaca-decomposition (evaluated using "male" coefficients) may be written as follows:

$$\overline{\ln W_m} - \overline{\ln W_f} = \bar{x}_m \hat{\beta}'_m - \bar{x}_f \hat{\beta}'_f = (\bar{x}_m - \bar{x}_f)\hat{\beta}'_m + \bar{x}_f(\hat{\beta}_m - \hat{\beta}_f)' = C + D. \quad (5.2)$$

The first term (C) on the righthand side of (5.2) is the "characteristic component," which is the fraction of the wage gap explained by differences in human capital variables and other background characteristics. The second term (D) is the "coefficient component," which reflects the effect on the wage gap due to differences in estimated coefficients.

In order to analyze the factors behind the gender wage gap more thoroughly, we have also calculated the characteristic and coefficient components for each of the explanatory variables and for each cohort. The components for the ith cohort and the jth group of explanatory variables are calculated as follows:

$$C_{ij} = (\bar{x}_{mij} - \bar{x}_{fij})\hat{\beta}_{mij}' \quad (5.3a)$$

$$D_{ij} = \bar{x}_{fij}\,(\hat{\beta}_{mij} - \hat{\beta}_{fij})' \quad (5.3b)$$

where $\bar{x}_{mij}$ and $\bar{x}_{fij}$ are the vectors of cohort specific sample means for the jth group of explanatory variables, and $\hat{\beta}_{mij}$ and $\hat{\beta}_{mij}$ are the corresponding estimated vectors of coefficients. The results are shown in Tables 5.10 and 5.11.[11]

The contribution to the gender wage gap from gender differences in human capital, family background and other characteristics is shown in Table 5.10. These variables account for a total of 6.5 percentage points of the gender wage gap which, during the 1980s, amounted to an average of 21 percent for all three cohorts (16 percent for cohort 1; 25 percent for cohort 2; 21 percent for cohort 3). The characteristic component varies significantly across the cohorts, from only 2 percentage points in cohort 1 to 7 percentage points in cohort 2 and 13 percentage points in cohort 3. Contrary to a priori expectations, these cohort differences are not due to changing family background characteristics. The absolute size of the contribution from these variables is small for all three cohorts, and surprisingly the contribution from gender differences in the number of children and marriage is negative when significant.[12] The main differences between cohorts in the characteristic component stem from the human capital variables, education and experience. For the youngest cohort, gender differences in these variables do not significantly contribute to the wage gap, whereas the contributions to the oldest cohorts are significant and large (3.4 percentage points for cohort 2 and 8.2 percentage points for cohort 3). To a great degree, the experience component can be

Table 5.10 The contribution to the gender wage gap from differences in characteristics (C and C_{ij})[a] (standard errors in parentheses)

	All cohorts	*Cohort 1*	*Cohort 2*	*Cohort 3*
Children	–0.0041*	–0.0101*	0.0010	–0.0008
	(0.0007)	(0.0013)	(0.0010)	(0.0010)
Married	–0.0023*	–0.0053*	–0.0012*	–0.0012*
	(0.0004)	(0.0006)	(0.0003)	(0.0005)
Occupation	0.0168*	0.0079*	0.0155*	0.0323*
	(0.0014)	(0.0017)	(0.0024)	(0.0032)
Experience	0.0243*	0.0037*	0.0211*	0.0584*
	(0.0028)	(0.0004)	(0.0025)	(0.0068)
Education	0.0111*	0.0016	0.0127*	0.0231*
	(0.0004)	(0.0009)	(0.0007)	(0.0013)
Province	–0.0007	–0.0006	–0.0005*	–0.0012
	(0.0004)	(0.0004)	(0.0001)	(0.0007)
Sector	0.0269*	0.0270*	0.0267*	0.0271*
	(0.0009)	(0.0010)	(0.0010)	(0.0009)
Time	–0.0061*	–0.0044*	–0.0089*	–0.0037*
	(0.0000)	(0.0004)	(0.0008)	(0.0003)
Constant	–0.0009*[b]	0.0000	0.0000	0.0000
	(0.0002)	–	–	–
All	0.0650	0.0198	0.0664	0.1340
	(0.0033)	(0.0022)	(0.0037)	(0.0077)

[a] Note that $\Sigma_j C_{ij} = C_i$ and $\Sigma_j C_j = C$, while $C_j = \Sigma_i v_i C_{ij}$, where v_i is the relative frequency of cohort i in the total sample.

[b] Is not equal to zero because the relative distribution within the three cohorts differs between men and women.

* Significant at a 5% level.

regarded as measuring the indirect effect of family background, since women's lower level of experience reflects part-time jobs or periods out of the labor market due to childbirth and family obligations at home.

Family background may also affect the gender wage gap via differences in the occupational attainment of men and women. In line with the contribution from human capital variables, the characteristic component stemming from the occupational indicators increases significantly with cohort number, with 0.8 percentage points, 1.6 percentage points and 3.2 percentage points in cohort 1, 2, and 3, respectively.[13] Sectoral sex segregation accounts for 2.7 percentage points of the wage gap via the characteristic component.

The rest of the gender wage gap can be ascribed to differences in the estimated coefficients for men and women as shown in Table 5.11. In total, the coefficient component (D) contributes 14 percentage points to the gender wage gap for all three cohorts, ranging from 8 percentage points in cohort 3 to 14 percentage points in cohort 1 and 18 percentage points in cohort 2. The main contribution to the coefficient component stems from the constant term, especially for cohort 2.[14] The constant term for each cohort reflects the wage level in 1980 in that particular cohort for a single

Table 5.11 The contribution to the gender wage gap from differences in coefficients (D and D_{ij})[a] (standard errors in parentheses)

	All cohorts	*Cohort 1*	*Cohort 2*	*Cohort 3*
Children	–0.0059	0.0063	0.0030	–0.0378*
	(0.0056)	(0.0045)	(0.0105)	(0.0144)
Married	0.0263*	0.0182*	0.0289*	0.0349*
	(0.0054)	(0.0044)	(0.0104)	(0.0076)
Occupation	0.0058*	0.0118*	0.0035	–0.0001
	(0.0028)	(0.0034)	(0.0045)	(0.0071)
Experience	–0.0403*	–0.0209*	–0.0405*	–0.0692*
	(0.0114)	(0.0075)	(0.0121)	(0.0164)
Education	0.0237*	–0.0072	0.0381*	0.0486*
	(0.0034)	(0.0054)	(0.0060)	(0.0062)
Province	–0.0143	–0.0145*	–0.0142*	–0.0141*
	(0.0037)	(0.0038)	(0.0039)	(0.0038)
Sector	0.0326*	0.0338*	0.0319*	0.0317*
	(0.0019)	(0.0197)	(0.0018)	(0.0018)
Time	0.0175*	0.0179*	0.0174*	0.0171*
	(0.0051)	(0.0051)	(0.0051)	(0.0051)
Constant	0.0956*	0.0937*	0.1158*	0.0678*
	(0.0155)	(0.0143)	(0.0208)	(0.0234)
All	0.1410	0.1391	0.1839	0.0789
	(0.0161)	(0.0100)	(0.0201)	(0.0282)

[a] Note that $\Sigma_j D_{ij} = D_i$ and $\Sigma_j D_j = D$, while $D_j = \Sigma_i v_i D_{ij}$, where v_i is the relative frequency of cohort i in the total sample.
* Significant at a 5% level.

person without children who is employed in the public sector as a low-level salaried worker. Thus, the relatively high gender wage gap in cohort 2, discussed in connection with Tables 5.2 and 5.3, is due mainly to the relatively low wages of women as compared with men employed in the public sector as low-level salaried workers.

Looking at the coefficient components for children and marriage, the hypotheses about cohort differences in the effect of these variables are only partly confirmed. For the two younger cohorts, the coefficient component from the child variables is positive but insignificant, whereas it is significant and negative for cohort 3 (minus 4 percentage points), contrary to a priori expectations. On the other hand, the coefficient component from marriage increases with cohort number, but the differences between cohorts are not significant. The same tendency holds for education: the coefficient component is insignificant in cohort 1, but significantly positive in cohorts 2 and 3 (3.8 percentage points and 4.9 percentage points, respectively). Thus, with respect to education, the a priori hypotheses concerning cohort differences are confirmed for the coefficient as well as the characteristic components.

However, the picture is more puzzling with regard to the coefficient components for experience and occupation. Since the experience coefficient is estimated to be slightly higher for women than for men, the coefficient component for this variable is negative. This effect is not neutralized by the coefficient component of the occupational indicators. Except for cohort 1, we do not observe a significant positive contribution to the wage gap from a steeper earnings profile across occupational levels for men than for women. Even though part of the career effect on coefficients is probably transferred to the characteristic component due to occupational mobility, the total contribution to the gender wage gap from flatter earnings profiles for women seems to be small.[15] However, as described above, part of the effect from the constant term in Table 5.11 also reflects occupational differences, since the estimated components behind the wage gap are sensitive to the excluded categories of the categorical variables.[16]

The coefficient components for the variables "time," "sector," and "province" are the same size in the three cohorts, since these are not interacted with cohort indicators. On average, 3.3 percentage points of the gender wage gap is due to within sector differences between men and women in the wage they get.[17] The opposite effect is found for the regional variable: women who live outside Copenhagen are less "penalized" for not living in the metropolis than their male colleagues. The coefficients of the time indicators show that male wages increased about 3 percentage points more than female wages over the period studied (see Table 5.9). The coefficient component for the time variable indicates that on average this accounted for 1.8 percentage points of the wage gap during the 1980s.

CONCLUSION

During the 1980s, the gender wage gap increased slightly in Denmark. When controlling for changes in human capital variables and other background characteristics, the analysis in this chapter shows that from 1980 to 1990 male hourly wages increased 3 percent more than female hourly wages. The analysis is based on observations of three birth cohorts, aged 20–29, 30–39, and 40–49, respectively, in 1980. The analysis also shows that during the 1980s the development of the gender wage gap was very different in the three birth cohorts. The youngest cohort started with a very small gender wage gap in 1980 (12 percent) compared with the gap of the two older birth cohorts (21–22 percent). But ten years later, in 1990, the gender wage gap of the youngest birth cohort had increased to 20 percent, while it had decreased from 22 percent to 21 percent in the oldest cohort. In the "middle" cohort, the wage gap increased from 21 percent to 24 percent.

During the cyclical upturn in the mid-1980s, employment in the private sector increased dramatically and wage drift constituted the major part of the wage increases during this period. The female percentile ranking in the male wage distribution fell significantly during these years, but the drop was most pronounced in cohort 1. It is a puzzling to find that all through the

1980s the gender wage gap was largest in cohort 2. The women of cohort 2 also had the lowest percentile ranking in the male wage distribution. This cannot be explained by differences between the cohorts in number of children, human capital variables or other background characteristics. Estimation of human capital functions and decompositions of the gender wage gap show that in cohort 2 the difference in background characteristics between men and women accounts only for 7 percentage points of the gender wage gap, which amounted to 25 percent on average during the 1980s. For cohort 1 (the youngest cohort) the corresponding figure is 2 percentage points of an average wage gap of 16 percent, and for cohort 3 (the oldest cohort) it is 14 percentage points of an average wage gap of 21 percent. The main factor behind the high gender wage gap in cohort 2 is found in a very low wage rate observed for low-level salaried employees in the public sector, which is the largest occupational/sectoral group in cohort 2 (and cohort 1).

Contrary to a priori expectations, we do not observe that children account for a larger part of the gender wage gap in the two older cohorts than in the youngest cohort. The component reflecting gender differences in the coefficients for marriage and cohabitation increases with cohort number, in line with a priori expectations, but the differences across cohorts are not statistically significant. On the other hand, a lower level of education and a lower remuneration of educational investments in the oldest cohort account for a large part of the gender wage gap there, while these educational differences do not have any significant influence on the gender wage gap in the youngest cohort.

Thus, the main conclusion of this study is that even though the youngest cohort starts out with a lower gender wage gap in 1980, it ends up in 1990 with approximately the same gender wage gap as the older cohorts. But the explanations of the wage gap are different across cohorts. In the oldest cohort, lack of human capital is the major factor; in the youngest and the middle cohorts, sectoral and occupational wage differentials seem to be important. The Danish labor market is relatively segregated with a large number of women employed in the public sector and a large number of women working as unskilled or low-level salaried workers. Our findings indicate that children and family responsibilities do not show up directly as significant factors increasing the gender wage gap. They also do not reduce the human capital accumulation of women as much as earlier when measured by length of education and years of experience.

However, since the wage gap seems to be relatively stable across cohorts when family formation has taken place, the effect of family variables may still be important for the gender wage gap in the younger cohorts. In this study, we are not able to point out whether these effects work via demand factors, for instance because of a new type of statistical discrimination emerging as a result of extensions of maternal leave schemes, or whether the effects work via supply decisions concerning educational, sectoral and occupational choices made by the individual woman or man or within the families. These questions are left for future research.

ACKNOWLEDGMENTS

Thanks to Nabanita Datta Gupta, Peder Pedersen, Anette Borchorst, Richard Larsen and Jens Christian Petersen for many helpful comments on a previous version of this chapter.

NOTES

1 Most of the women on maternal leave or parental leave are registered as being in the labor force during their leave. Thus, the official labor force participation rate tends to be overvalued in Denmark as well as in other Scandinavian countries.

2 The maternal leave scheme was extended in 1980 from 3 months to 18 weeks, and in 1984 it was extended further to 28 weeks. The father may use the last 10 weeks instead of the mother, but this option has been used by only about 3 percent of fathers. In the early 1990s a new parental leave scheme was introduced which is also used mainly by women.

3 See Rosenfeld and Kalleberg (1991: 210).

4 Each wage earner aged 16–66 years employed by an employer for more than 9 hours a week is obliged by law to contribute to the ATP scheme. The contribution to ATP depends only on the degree of employment in each week. The share follows a stepwise function, where 0–9 hours/week implies 0 ATP contribution, 10–19 hours/week implies ⅓ of the full contribution, 20–29 hours/week implies ⅔ of the full contribution and more than 30 hours a week implies full ATP contribution. The hourly wage is calculated using this information together with information on standard working hours. Overtime work does not usually entail higher ATP contributions, which means that groups with extensive overtime work will have an upward-biased hourly wage rate. For more detailed information, see Westergård-Nielsen (1988).

5 As the ATP scheme was first established in 1964, employment experience acquired before 1964 has been calculated on the assumption that men worked full-time after entry into the labor market. The corresponding potential experience for women has been weighted using the aggregate employment frequency of women in different age groups. This pre-1964 employment experience variable has been added to the ATP employment information to obtain the experience variable.

6 The number of children includes children aged 18 or more, contrary to earlier analyses on the Danish longitudinal database, which includes annual information on number of children in different age categories, 0–2 years, 3–6 years, 7–14 years and 0–17 years. Based on this information for all of the years 1979–1990, we have estimated the number of children born in the families. For the oldest cohort we may still have underestimated the number of children if the individuals had children aged 18 or over before 1979.

7 See Rosholm and Smith (1996) and Naur and Smith (1996) for more information and application of this estimator on unbalanced data.

8 In a previous version of this chapter, six separate wage functions were estimated for men and women in the three cohorts.

9 The variation between cohorts might also be explained by variations in type of education. While male and female educational choices are very different, the

variation between cohorts is much less pronounced and thus changes in the type of education across cohorts cannot explain the observed differences in the return on educational investments.

10 For simplicity we do not distinguish between time-varying and time-invariant variables in (5.2). The constant term is included in the **x**- vector.

11 The calculation of standard errors on C_{ij} and D_{ij} is described in Naur and Smith (1996).

12 The absolute size and, in some cases, the sign of the components in Tables 5.10 and 5.11 depends on which weights are used in the Oaxaca decomposition (the indexation problem). However, as regards the contributions from the marriage and child variables, the signs of these components do not change if female coefficients are used as weights instead of the male coefficients.

13 As described earlier, the effect of differences in career profiles is reflected in the experience variable and the occupational indicators, and the division of the components in Tables 5.10 and 5.11 on these two variables is somewhat arbitrary.

14 Including the cohort specific effects for cohorts 2 and 3.

15 If the characteristic component for occupation and the coefficient components for occupation and experience are added, we get -0.1 percentage points, -2.1 percentage points, and -3.7 percentage points for cohorts 1, 2 and 3, respectively.

16 This is discussed further in Chapman and Mulvey (1986).

17 The size of the "sector" and "province" coefficient components is highly dependent on which sector indicator is excluded from the regression.

REFERENCES

Asplund, R., Barth, E., Smith, N. and Wadensjö, Eskil (1996) "The male–female wage gap in the Nordic countries," in N. Westergård-Nielsen (ed.), *Wage Differentials in the Nordic Labour Markets in the 1990s*, Amsterdam: North Holland, pp. 55–82.

Blau, F.D. and Kahn, L.M. (1992) "The gender earnings gap: learning from international evidence," *American Economic Review*, Papers and Proceedings 82, 2: 533–8.

Chapman, B.J. and Mulvey, C. (1986) "Sex differences in Australian wages," *The Journal of Industrial Relations*: 504–20.

Duncan, O.D. and Duncan, B. (1955) "A methodological analysis of segregation indices," *American Sociological Review* 20: 210–17.

Greene, William H. (1990) *Econometric Analysis*, London: Macmillan.

Hausman, J.A. and Taylor, W.E. (1981) "Panel data and unobservable individual effects," *Econometrica* 49, 6: 1377–98.

Heckman, J.J. (1979) "Sample selection bias as a specification error," *Econometrica* 47: 153–62.

Naur, M. and Smith, N. (1996) "Cohort effects on the gender wage gap in Denmark," *Studies in Labour Market Dynamics*, Working Paper 96:05, CLS, Aarhus: Aarhus University and Aarhus School of Business.

Oaxaca, R. (1973) "Sex discrimination in wages," in O. Ashenfelter and A. Rees *Discrimination in Labor Markets*, Princeton NJ: Princeton University Press.

Pedersen, P., Beyer Schmidt-Sørensen, J., Smith, N. and Westergård-Nielsen, N. (1990) "Wage differentials between the public and private sectors," *Journal of Public Economics* 41, 125–45.

Pedersen, L., Pedersen, P. J. and Smith, N. (1995) "The working and the non-working populations in the welfare state," in G. Viby-Mogensen (ed.) *Work Incentives in the Danish Welfare State*, Aarhus: Aarhus University Press.

Polachek, S. W. (1980) "Occupational self-selection: a human capital approach to sex differences in occupational structure," *The Review of Economics and Statistics*: 60–69.

Rosenfeld, R. and Kalleberg, A.L. (1991) "Gender inequality in the labour market," *Acta Sociologica* 34: 207–25.

Rosholm, M. and Smith, N. (1996) "The Danish gender wage gap in the 1980s: a panel data study," *Oxford Economic Journal.*

Westergård-Nielsen, N. (1988) "Timeløn, kompensationsgrad, erhvervserfaring og uddannelse," *Studies in Labour Market Dynamics*, Working Paper 88–3, Aarhus: Aarhus School of Business.

APPENDIX

Table 5.A1 Mean sample values, 1980

	Cohort 1		*Cohort 2*		*Cohort 3*	
	Men	*Women*	*Men*	*Women*	*Men*	*Women*
Hourly wage (DKK)	59.50	52.27	71.51	56.77	72.27	56.35
	(15.66)	(15.22)	(17.40)	(16.84)	(19.25)	(15.87)
Log (deflated wage)	4.05	3.92	4.24	4.00	4.25	4.00
	(0.25)	(0.26)	(0.24)	(0.27)	(0.26)	(0.26)
Experience (years)	4.28	4.08	11.57	8.64	22.79	13.41
	(2.26)	(4.47)	(4.86)	(3.96)	(5.83)	(4.63)
Experience squared/100	0.23	0.23	1.57	0.90	5.53	2.01
	(0.23)	(0.25)	(1.27)	(0.77)	(2.67)	(1.37)
Length of education (years)	2.34	2.33	3.04	2.58	2.55	1.91
	(2.01)	(2.02)	(2.62)	(2.50)	(2.53)	(2.32)
Married (0/1)	0.24	0.40	0.69	0.73	0.81	0.76
Cohabitant (0/1)	0.42	0.34	0.13	0.09	0.06	0.05
Single (0/1)	0.34	0.26	0.18	0.18	0.13	0.19
No children[a] (0/1)	0.78	0.54	0.32	0.15	0.31	0.36
1 or 2 children (0/1)	0.22	0.45	0.56	0.68	0.55	0.57
3 or more children (0/1)	0.01	0.02	0.12	0.16	0.13	0.07
Occupational status (0/1)						
Salaried empl., high level	0.05	0.02	0.18	0.05	0.19	0.03
Salaried empl., med. level	0.07	0.13	0.18	0.17	0.18	0.15
Salaried empl., low level	0.23	0.48	0.17	0.44	0.13	0.36
Skilled employment	0.28	0.02	0.26	0.01	0.22	0.01
Unskilled employment	0.30	0.29	0.20	0.29	0.26	0.36
Wage earner, no info.	0.07	0.06	0.01	0.03	0.01	0.08
Sectoral indicators (0/1)						
Public	0.22	0.48	0.24	0.56	0.24	0.54
Primary	0.04	0.01	0.01	0.01	0.01	0.01
Manufacturing	0.24	0.14	0.25	0.14	0.30	0.15
Construction	0.14	0.01	0.12	0.01	0.10	0.01
Trade	0.15	0.12	0.16	0.11	0.14	0.13
Private service	0.21	0.23	0.21	0.18	0.20	0.17
No sector information	0.00	0.00	0.00	0.00	0.00	0.00
No. of obser. 1980	2,932	2,617	3,066	2,700	2,056	1,742

[a] Here, "children" is defined as children below the age of 18.

Table 5.A2 Mean sample values 1990

	Cohort 1		Cohort 2		Cohort 3	
	Men	Women	Men	Women	Men	Women
Hourly wage (DKK)	144.66	116.08	155.53	118.44	147.26	115.88
	(50.60)	(39.14)	(62.71)	(39.48)	(62.97)	(43.41)
Log (deflated wage)	4.93	4.71	4.99	4.73	4.93	4.70
	(0.29)	(0.27)	(0.33)	(0.27)	(0.34)	(0.29)
Experience (years)	12.19	10.91	20.19	15.31	31.26	19.60
	(3.94)	(4.15)	(5.90)	(5.83)	(6.98)	(6.81)
Experience	1.64	1.36	4.42	2.68	10.26	4.30
squared/100	(0.91)	(0.91)	(2.37)	(1.81)	(4.19)	(2.77)
Length of education	3.22	3.16	3.14	2.74	2.66	2.12
(years)	(2.62)	(2.56)	(2.64)	(2.56)	(2.55)	(2.51)
Married (0/1)	0.52	0.59	0.71	0.72	0.80	0.71
Cohabitant (0/1)	0.24	0.21	0.12	0.09	0.07	0.06
Single (0/1)	0.24	0.20	0.17	0.19	0.13	0.23
No children[a] (0/1)	0.44	0.19	0.20	0.09	0.26	0.31
1 or 2 children (0/1)	0.48	0.68	0.61	0.67	0.59	0.59
3 or more children (0/1)	0.08	0.14	0.19	0.23	0.15	0.10
Occupational status (0/1)						
Salaried empl., high level	0.15	0.06	0.21	0.06	0.20	0.04
Salaried empl., med. level	0.15	0.21	0.21	0.19	0.19	0.17
Salaried empl., low level	0.18	0.43	0.14	0.43	0.14	0.36
Skilled employment	0.26	0.02	0.24	0.01	0.21	0.01
Unskilled employment	0.24	0.25	0.19	0.28	0.25	0.37
Wage earner, no info.	0.02	0.02	0.01	0.03	0.01	0.05
Sectoral indicators (0/1)						
Public	0.23	0.55	0.28	0.56	0.29	0.59
Primary	0.02	0.00	0.01	0.00	0.01	0.01
Manufacturing	0.26	0.12	0.25	0.13	0.27	0.12
Construction	0.12	0.01	0.10	0.01	0.08	0.01
Trade	0.12	0.08	0.13	0.09	0.13	0.10
Private service	0.25	0.21	0.23	0.18	0.22	0.16
No sector information	0.00	0.03	0.00	0.02	0.00	0.01
No. of obser. 1990	2,819	2,740	2,791	2,832	1,772	1,623

[a] Here, "children" is defined as children below the age of 28.

6

GENDER DIFFERENCES IN PAY AMONG YOUNG PROFESSIONALS IN SWEDEN

Maria Hemström

INTRODUCTION

Gender differences in pay are usually explained by gender-specific differences in human capital and/or effort allocated to market work. These explanations focus on the fact that women are expected to raise a family. They will consequently spend less time in the labor market and have, therefore, less incentives to invest in human capital. These arguments proceed from the assumption that no investments are yet undertaken. However, once they are the scenario changes: the higher the amount of investment, the larger the penalties for career interruptions and, hence, the lower the incentives to specialize in home production.

Accordingly, we would expect gender differences in pay to be negligible among young, highly educated professionals. They are not, however. Blau and Ferber (1990) focus on the expectations held by US business school seniors. They find that an anticipated female starting salary disadvantage of 3 percent is expected to increase to 28 percent during the first twenty years in the labor market. Wood *et al.* (1993) analyze pay differences among US law school graduates, and find a 7 percent female starting salary disadvantage that increases to 38 percent fifteen years out of law school. Similarly, Fornwall (1996a) analyzes the early labor market careers of young business administrators and economists in Sweden, and finds a 5 percent female starting salary disadvantage that increases to more than 12 percent during the first years in the labor market. Can this increasing wage gap be explained? This is the question on which this chapter focuses.

We use regressions separated by gender and focus on four issues:

1 The determinants of salaries and wage growth, i.e., earnings profiles.
2 To what extent the existing wage gap is explained by gender-specific differences in characteristics versus different returns to (seemingly) identical characteristics.

3 The determinants of self-reported discrimination and its correlation with earnings.
4 The determinants of wage expectations.

The results indicate that seemingly identical attributes yield different returns depending on gender. Experience and unemployment appear to have a large impact on the earnings profiles of men, but influence neither the earnings nor the wage growth of women. On the other hand, education seems to influence the earnings profiles of women, but it has no corresponding effect in the case of men. Only a small part of the salary gap is explained by gender-specific differences in characteristics.

The chapter is organized as follows. First a brief theoretical survey is given and then the dataset to be used is described. In the section that follows the determinants of earnings profiles are analyzed, as well as the extent to which the wage gap is explained by differences in characteristics versus different returns to identical characteristics. Then self-reported discrimination and expected wage growth are analyzed, before the chapter ends with a concluding discussion.

GENDER DIFFERENCES IN PAY: DIVISION OF WORK OR DISCRIMINATION?

Economic analysis explains gender differences in pay in terms of gender-specific differences in either characteristics or the returns to (seemingly) identical characteristics (Blinder 1973; Oaxaca 1973). Wage gaps caused by differences in characteristics – which make one gender more productive than the other – is referred to as the productivity gap. The remaining part is referred to as the residual or unexplained part of the earnings gap, the part also referred to as discrimination. A crucial ingredient for these definitions is the assumption that all aspects of worker productivity are observable and measurable. A major theme in the human capital explanation of gender differences in pay, however, is researchers' inability to identify, measure and check for all relevant aspects of worker productivity. Consequently, the decomposition presented above suffers from several, severe problems.

The literature on the economics of gender rests on the theory of the division of work within the family. Spouses are assumed to divide work between themselves and specialize – more or less – in either home market activities or market work. Why? Because of the advantages of specialization and the different skills and earning powers with which the different family members are endowed (Mincer and Polachek 1974), as well as the existence of increasing returns to investments in human capital (Becker 1985). Women are assumed to have an intrinsic comparative advantage not only in the production of children, but also in home activities (Becker 1981) and will thus specialize in home production, leaving the specialization in market work to the men.

This does not imply that women will not participate in the labor force, but the amount of time spent in the labor market will be lower, the labor force attachment weaker and the turnover higher for women than men. Their incentives to invest in human capital therefore decrease (Mincer 1962; Mincer and Polachek 1974; Polachek 1975; Goldin and Polachek 1987). Spells of labor force withdrawal further depreciate the human capital obtained by women (Mincer and Ofek 1982). On average, women will thus have less human capital and be less productive than men. Their hourly earnings will be lower and their earnings profiles flatter. But the resulting male–female wage gap is explicable: it is the part referred to as the productivity gap.

Specialization in household production has other implications. Once in the labor market, women will choose less demanding jobs with flexible hours. They will be absent due to other family members' illnesses and have less effort available for market work once there (Polachek 1975; Becker 1985). Thus, they will be less productive and earn less than men, even when investments in human capital and hours of work are held constant. The fact that (the more productive) men receive higher salaries is likely to be ascribed to discrimination, but it is not.

Closely related to issues concerning job attributes such as low requirements or flexible hours is the existence of compensating differentials (Rosen 1986), i.e., earnings differentials to compensate for unpleasant working conditions or more demanding work tasks. Differences in job attributes are difficult to quantify and measure, and compensating differentials are likely to be interpreted as discrimination. Differences in earnings despite equal productivity are not due to discrimination if these differences exist in order to compensate for differences in job characteristics.

Goldin and Polachek (1987) emphasize that the return to identical characteristics is likely to embody gender-specific differences, since identical attributes do not affect earnings the same way for men and women. That women receive a negative and men a positive return to marriage, for example, is not necessarily a token of discrimination, despite the fact that the unexplained part of the earnings gap thereby increases.

Given that discrimination exists, it can be divided into that which occurs in the labor market versus that which occurs outside. It is said to occur in the labor market if women are treated differently than men, other things equal, once there. Non-market discrimination, on the other hand, occurs before women enter the labor market.

Unequal pay for equal work is a straightforward example of discrimination occurring in the labor market. There are, however, less obvious examples as well. Lazear and Rosen (1990) argue that the threshold level of ability for promotion eligibility will be higher among women than men, given that firms base their decisions about promotions not only on the employees' ability but also on their probability of staying in the job. This proposition is also relevant with regard to firm-provided education and the value (on behalf of the firm) of different job assignments. Lundberg and Startz (1983) emphasize that firms act rationally by treating men and women differently, since they do not observe worker productivity but know that women are likely to have a lower labor force attachment than men.

Non-market discrimination is caused by gender-specific differences in upbringing, differences that induce girls to invest less than boys in human capital, with the result that adult women may be less productive than men (Blau and Ferber 1987). Closely related to non-market discrimination is the possible occurrence of feedback effects (see, for example, Gronau 1988; Neumark 1993). Perceived or expected discrimination might induce women to invest less in human capital, to withdraw from the labor force and specialize in household production.

Irrespective of the causes, however, both market and non-market discrimination will result in females, on average, being less productive than males. Consequently, women will be paid less than men. The resulting earnings gap can be explained by differences in productivity, but it is nevertheless due to discrimination.

The available measures of labor productivity are crude and imperfect. Resulting measures of discrimination are likely to overestimate the existence of discrimination in the labor market. On the other hand, discrimination due to feedback effects or discrimination occurring outside the labor market is likely to be underestimated by the definition of discrimination presented above and used by Oaxaca (1973) and Blinder (1973) in their decomposition of the earnings gap. With these shortcomings in mind, we shall proceed to a description of the data to be used in the following empirical analysis of existing gender wage differentials among young professionals in Sweden.

THE DATA

The dataset used in this study was collected through a survey conducted in 1992. This was directed towards former students of the BA program in business[1] at Uppsala University, who began their education in the autumn of 1983 or 1984 and entered the labor market a few years later. The data from this survey were matched with register data on taxable income and wealth in 1989 as well as the grades and exams from Uppsala University. The information thus obtained includes excellent controls for investments in human capital and work history prior to the survey. It does not include any information about family background, household responsibilities or preferences for different job attributes, however. The response rate amounted to 72 percent. Those who did not return the survey, as well as men working part-time and those with missing data on key variables, were excluded in the following analysis.[2]

Summary statistics are shown in Table 6.1. These indicate that measurable investments in human capital as well as the educational achievements

Table 6.1 Sample means[a]

	All Males	*All Females*
Family		
Married (%): – when entering the labor market	10.2	13.4
– after leaving the university	32.5	32.9
No. of children < 7: – when entering the labor market	0.11	0.02
– at the time of the 1992 survey	0.45	0.23
Education obtained at Uppsala University		
Education at the BA program in business (no. of months)	30.3	29.8
A PhD or MBA program was attended by (%)	2.3	1.7
Education other than the BA program in business (no. of months)	3.2	3.3
Educational achievements obtained at Uppsala University		
Educational speed (i.e. number of "points"/semester)	17.1	16.9
Graduated (% who got their degrees in business)	66.8	67.5
Firm-provided education		
Formal firm-provided education:		
– share (%) that attended such education	54.7	55.8
– no. of months spent in such education by these individuals	2.1	1.7
Labor force attachment		
Years of relevant labor market experience	3.5	3.3
Tenure	3.2	3.3
No. of employer changes	2.0	1.86
Unemployment: – share (%) unemployed	18.5	18.2
– no. of months spent in unemployment by these individuals	5.4	4.3
Career interruptions (no. of months)	19.3	26.1
Part-time work (%)	—	9.5
Overtime: – average number of hours/week	5.6	4.1
– entitled to overtime compensation (%)	51.3	62.8
Job settings at the time of the 1992 survey		
Working in the Stockholm area (%)	41.9	53.7
Working in the public sector (%)	13.2	26.0
Union membership (%) at the time of the 1992 survey	49.1	56.7
Self-reported discrimination (%)	6.4	32.0
Earnings		
Average monthly starting salary (SEK)	10,744	10,146
min	3,000	3,000
max	40,000	35,000
std dev	3,429	2,860
Average monthly 1992 salary (SEK)	19,232	16,189
min	5,000	3,000
max	50,000	27,000
std dev	5,845	3,614
Average expected monthly 1995 salary (SEK)	24,667	20,719
min	4,000	5,000
max	60,000	35,000
std dev	7,727	4,961
No. of obs	265	231

[a] These means are based on all survey replies except the five surveys returned by men who were working part-time in 1992. Earnings refer to the monthly salary, regardless of hours of work. The regressions presented use either the hourly salary (i.e. the monthly salary divided by hours of work) or the expected monthly 1995 salary as dependent variable.

and experience obtained were similar across gender. On average, approximately thirty (out of thirty-five) months were completed at the BA program in business and seventeen out of twenty stipulated points[3] were obtained each semester. Sixty-seven percent actually graduated from the program and approximately 55 percent had some kind of firm-provided education thereafter. Relevant experience, as well as tenure, amounted to slightly more than three years. Eighteen percent had been unemployed, on average for five months.

There were, however, some gender-specific differences in the family situation, job settings and opinions at the time of the 1992 survey. Although 40 percent, irrespective of gender, were married, men tended to have more children than women. Career interruptions were approximately six months longer among women than men. A larger share of the women were employed in the Stockholm area (54 versus 42 percent) and in the public sector (26 versus 13 percent). Women were entitled to overtime compensation to a higher extent than men (63 versus 51 percent), but men tended to have more weekly overtime than women (5.6 versus 4.1 hours/week). Thirty-two percent of the women versus 6 percent of the men reported that they had been exposed to discrimination at their place of work. Finally, the average starting salary and the 1992 salary amounted respectively to SEK10,744 and SEK19,232 in the case of men, versus SEK10,146 and SEK16,189 in the case of women.

EXPLORING THE GENDER WAGE DIFFERENTIAL

In this sample, men's starting salaries were 5 percent higher than women's. This wage gap increased in the years following the entrance to the labor market, and amounted to more than 12 percent at the time of the 1992 survey. Why were starting salaries and wage growth higher among men than women? To what extent were the existing wage gaps due to gender-specific differences in characteristics and to what extent were they caused by different returns to identical characteristics?

The determinants of earnings profiles

This section analyzes the determinants of starting and current salaries, as well as the wage growth experienced in between. We use OLS estimates of wage equations by gender.[4] The starting salary is defined as the (reported) monthly income at the respondent's first job after leaving the university, and the current salary is equal to the (reported) monthly salary at the time of the 1992 survey. Wage growth is defined as the difference between the current and starting salary (in logarithms). The dependent variables in the starting and the current salary equations are defined as hourly earnings: i.e., the monthly salary divided by hours of work.

What are the determinants of earnings profiles? Division of work within the family potentially influences the earnings received by men and women respectively. Such information is not available in our data, however. Instead, we use marital status[5] and children as proxies to account for the earnings effect of specialization within the family. Marriage is believed to make men more stable (Malkiel and Malkiel 1973) and to increase their productivity (Becker 1985). Marriage may also increase the earnings of men due to employer favoritism (Hill 1979) or selection into marriage based on unobservable characteristics (Becker 1981). The existence of a large, positive male marriage premium of between 10 and 40 percent is one of the most robust findings in empirical work on wage differentials (Korenman and Neumark 1991). According to Korenman and Neumark (1991: 293), the return to marriage appears gradually and not upon utterance of the words "I do" (Richardson 1995). However, estimates that the Swedish marriage premium is smaller and that it has been declining during the last decades due to, she argues, reforms intended to reduce the division of work within the family. She further finds no evidence that the marriage premium appears gradually. Her results indicate that the observed marriage premium is in part due to selection into marriage based on unobservable characteristics that make men more marketable in the marriage – as well as the labor – market.

Marriage, however, is usually not found to be correlated with higher earnings for women.[6] Children, on the other hand, tend to have a negative influence on the earnings received by women. This negative effect is reduced and sometimes eliminated when refined measures of labor force attachment are included in the wage equation (Hill 1979; Korenman and Neumark 1992a). This indicates that the female wage reduction due to children is primarily indirect, and works through the effect of children on experience, tenure and on-the-job training.[7] Refined measures of labor force attachment facilitate an analysis of the direct effects of children on earnings: i.e., the effect on effort and productivity once at work (Korenman and Neumark 1992a).

Our labor force attachment variables are constructed using retrospective work history questions. All variables refer to events that took place in the post-university period.[8] Relevant experience (and its square) represents years of experience with an (according to the respondent) educational relevant content.[9] Tenure equals years of employment at the respondent's 1992 employer. Number of employer changes and years spent in unemployment are self-explanatory. Also included in our set of labor force attachment variables are the weekly overtime[10] and a part-time dummy variable. We expect hours of work to affect the hourly earnings primarily through its correlation with work commitment and division of labor within the family. Years of career interruptions are also included. This is calculated as a residual,[11] and gives time spent without working, studying or being unemployed in the post-university period. It will be interpreted as parental leave in the following analysis.[12] The earnings effect of career interruptions has been thoroughly analyzed by Mincer and Ofek (1982), Corcoran and Duncan (1979) and Corcoran *et al.* (1983). They find substantial short-term wage losses, followed by a rapid wage rebound[13] (which reduces the long-term effects on wages to a minimum) associated with labor market withdrawals.

Years of experience are generally found to increase earnings. One obvious factor is on-the-job investments in human capital, i.e., skill acquisition and knowledge that increases worker productivity. The productivity aspect of experience is emphasized in our analysis by excluding irrelevant experience from our experience variable and, further, by including (in our set of independent variables) the amount of firm-provided education obtained and reported in the 1992 survey. Firm-provided education refers to shorter periods – weeks or months – of intensive formal, job-related education.[14] We expect such education to be positively related to earnings, either through its effects on worker productivity or due to selectivity bias: the provision of this type of education to employees with more inherent ability and/or higher work commitment.

These variables – firm-provided education and relevant experience – are likely to capture part of the productivity augmenting skills obtained at work. It is obvious, however, that post-school investments in human capital, acquired through experience, have dimensions that will not be controlled for. The value of experience, and hence its wage-earning effect, will therefore vary. There are reasons to believe that the returns to experience and tenure will be higher among males than females. Compare, for example, the results (concerning actual experience) presented by Mincer and Polachek (1974), Duncan and Hoffman (1979), Gronau (1988), and Löfström (1989).

According to human capital theory, a lower expected labor force participation provides disincentives to invest in human capital (e.g. Mincer 1962; Mincer and Polachek 1974; Polachek 1975; Goldin and Polachek 1987). Women in their late twenties who have not yet had children are likely (highly educated or not) to give birth, go on parental leave, work part-time to care for and be absent due to illness of their children within the foreseeable future. It could be argued that men, potential fathers-to-be, are as likely as women to take on the burden of parenting. Statistics show, however, that only 7 percent (RFV 1994: 15: 2) of the legally permitted parental leave[15] was de facto utilized by men in 1989–90.[16] The incentives to invest in human capital can thus be expected to be slightly lower among women than men, even in our self-selected sample of young professionals. It is further likely that employers (given the Lundberg–Startz and Lazear–Rosen arguments presented above) may hesitate to entrust their female employees with responsibility and valuable assignments. Consequently, we expect the value of (and, hence, the return to) experience and tenure to be lower among women than among men.

Human capital theory further predicts that education obtained in the pre-labor market period will be an important determinant of earnings profiles. The common denominator of our sample is the fact that they all began a BA program in business in the mid-1980s. Not all of them finished it, however. The amount of university education differs, as does that of additional education obtained at other programs or classes at the university. We use months at the BA program in business, years in other education at the university as well as a dummy variable that equals one if the respondent began a PhD or MBA program in order to account for differences in the amount of education obtained. Also included are university major dummy variables. The educational achievement variables include the educational speed, a graduation dummy and an interaction variable stating the educational speed of those who also graduated.[17] We expect more education and/or superior educational achievements to be associated with a steeper earnings profile – i.e., a low starting salary and rapid wage growth.[18]

An interaction variable (years of experience∗ln(starting salary)) is included to account for the possibility that lower starting salaries were associated with steeper earnings profiles. We finally include dummies for region, sector, the year of labor market entry, union membership and age in our analysis.

Empirical results

The results are shown in Table 6.2. The determinants of earnings profiles (the coefficients of the starting salary, wage growth and current salary equations) will be discussed simultaneously. On the basis of a standard Chow and t-test respectively, we conclude that the starting salary and current salary equations exhibit significant gender-specific differences.

According to our results, marital status does not influence the earnings profiles of either women or, more surprisingly, men. According to Richardson (1995), the male marriage premium in Sweden is due primarily to selection bias: i.e., selection into marriage based on unobservable characteristics. We are inclined to believe that our self-selected sample of highly educated males possesses characteristics such as ability and drive that make them more marketable in the labor market as well as the marriage market. This could explain why we find no return to marriage in our sample, even if it exists in society at large. The presence of children had no significant effect on the earnings profiles of either gender. This result was expected, given our refined measures of labor force participation.

Career interruptions – something closely related to issues concerning children – had no impact on the wage growth or current salaries obtained by either gender, according to our results. Mincer and Ofek (1982) as well as Corcoran *et al.* (1983) found substantial short-term and minor long-run wage losses associated with labor force withdrawals. According to these authors

Table 6.2 Salary and wage growth equations (OLS estimates)[a]

	Starting salary equations Dep. variable = ln (hourly starting salary)			*Wage growth equations Dep variable = ln (1992 hourly salary) − ln (hourly starting salary)*			*Current salary equations Dep variable = ln (1992 hourly salary)*		
	Males	*Females*	*t-statistics regarding gender differences*	*Males*	*Females*	*t-statistics regarding gender differences*	*Males*	*Females*	*t-statistics regarding gender differences*
Constant	3.89	3.32	2.002	0.414	0.687	−1.400	3.97	3.97	−6.871
	(17.87)	(18.24)		(3.08)	(4.87)		(15.96)	(28.6)	
Age at the point of time	0.004	0.011	−0.839	—	—	—	0.013	0.004	1.187
	(0.631)	(2.296)					(1.991)	(0.998)	
Family									
Married (1=yes) (at the point of time/during the current period)	−0.034	−0.113	0.837	0.062	0.024	0.544	−0.007	0.006	−0.253
	(−0.538)	(−1.617)		(1.195)	(0.511)		(−0.180)	(0.180)	
No. of children under the age of seven (at the point of time/born after leaving university)	0.069	0.099	−0.276	−0.052	0.011	−1.144	0.019	0.015	0.082
	(1.445)	(1.006)		(−1.513)	(0.237)		(0.704)	(0.437)	
Education obtained at Uppsala University									
Months at the BA program in business	−0.002	0.003	−0.823	—	—	—	−0.003	−0.001	−0.274
	(−0.398)	(0.797)					(−0.687)	(−0.563)	
A PhD or MBA program was begun after graduating from the BA program in business (1=yes)	−0.010	−0.115	3.455	—	—	—	−0.058	−0.005	−1.727
	(−0.419)	(−5.858)					(−2.488)	(−0.236)	
Years spent in other education at Uppsala University	−0.014	−0.082	1.484	—	—	—	−0.026	0.014	−0.961
	(−0.417)	(−2.545)					(−0.803)	(0.534)	
Educational achievements obtained at Uppsala University									
Graduated (1=a person completed the entire education in business)	−0.179	0.239	−2.199	—	—	—	−0.097	0.025	−0.725
	(−1.377)	(1.724)					(−0.753)	(0.233)	
Educational speed (i.e., number of "points"/semester)	−0.001	0.019	−2.064	—	—	—	−0.001	0.006	−0.829
	(−0.125)	(2.655)					(−0.213)	(1.030)	

Table 6.2 Continued

	Starting salary equations *Dep. variable = ln (hourly starting salary)*			*Wage growth equations* *Dep variable = ln (1992 hourly salary) − n (hourly starting salary)*			*Current salary equations* *Dep variable = ln (1992 hourly salary)*		
	Males	*Females*	*t-statistics regarding gender differences*	*Males*	*Females*	*t-statistics regarding gender differences*	*Males*	*Females*	*t-statistics regarding gender differences*
Educational speed of those who graduated (i.e. speed∗graduated)	0.011 (1.504)	–0.016 (–1.949)	2.457	—	—	—	0.006 (0.814)	–0.001 (–0.234)	0.761
Firm-provided education									
Years of formal firm provided education obtained after leaving university	—	—	—	0.312 (1.948)	0.356 (2.056)	–0.187	0.238 (1.867)	0.178 (1.291)	0.321
Labor Force Attachment									
Relevant experience obtained after leaving university	—	—	—	0.119 (2.558)	–0.041 (–1.059)	2.644	0.070 (1.667)	0.0007 (0.023)	1.358
Relevant experience squared	—	—	—	–0.012 (–1.702)	0.007 (1.107)	–2.059	–0.005 (–0.766)	0.005 (1.064)	–1.231
Tenure (=no. of years at the 1992 employment)	—	—	—	0.025 (2.178)	–0.006 (–0.432)	1.678	0.007 (0.843)	0.004 (0.539)	0.250
No. of job changes after university	—	—	—	0.010 (0.357)	–0.004 (–0.168)	0.375	0.019 (0.884)	0.049 (2.684)	–1.721
Unemployment (=no. of years after university)	—	—	—	–0.189 (–1.264)	–0.145 (–1.120)	–0.119	–0.216 (–1.842)	0.046 (0.490)	–1.740
Career interruptions (=no. of years after university)	—	—	—	–0.016 (–0.508)	–0.008 (–0.266)	–0.166	0.023 (0.945)	–0.003 (–0.123)	0.792
Part-time work (1=yes)	—	—	—	—	—	—	—	0.097 (1.789)	—
Overtime (hours/week)	—	—	—	—	—	—	0.014 (2.928)	0.016 (4.590)	–0.399
Job settings									
Working in the Stockholm area (1=yes)	—	—	—	—	—	—	0.138 (3.851)	0.110 (3.640)	0.590

Table 6.2 Continued

	Starting salary equations Dep. variable = ln (hourly starting salary)			*Wage growth equations Dep variable = ln (1992 hourly salary) – ln (hourly starting salary)*			*Current salary equations Dep variable = ln (1992 hourly salary)*		
	Males	*Females*	*t-statistics regarding gender differences*	*Males*	*Females*	*t-statistics regarding gender differences*	*Males*	*Females*	*t-statistics regarding gender differences*
Working in the public sector (1=yes)	—	—	—	—	—	—	–0.047 (–0.945)	–0.087 (–2.365)	0.643
Union membership (1=yes)	—	—	—	—	—	—	–0.051 (–1.387)	0.016 (0.588)	–1.460
Years of experience∗ln(starting salary)	—	—	—	–0.00004 (–2.134)	–0.000001 (–0.055)	–1.366	—	—	—
University major – dummy variables are included	Yes	Yes	—	—	—	—	Yes	Yes	—
Firm size — dummy variables are included	—	—	—	—	—	—	Yes	Yes	—
Year of labor market entry – dummy variables are included	Yes	Yes	—	Yes	Yes	—	—	—	—
R^2	0.170	0.285	—	0.246	0.270	—	0.336	0.331	—
F	3.390	5.046	—	6.095	6.329	—	4.631	4.141	—
Chow–test, p–value	0.01		—	0.25		—	0.05		—
Testing for normality Skewness	–0.505	0.169	—	0.675	0.366	—	0.855	0.128	—
Kurtosis	5.882	7.305	—	2.554	3.897	—	2.029	0.242	—
Wilk–Shapiro test, p-value	0.0001	0.0001	—	0.095	0.109	—	0.006	0.542	—
Testing for heteroskedasticity; Ramsey's RESET test, F–value	0.285	1.951	—	0.120	0.559	—	0.451	0.695	—
No. of observ.	222	194	—	220	203	—	195	179	—

[a] t-statistics regarding each separate parameter estimate are given in parentheses (below the relevant parameter estimate). t-statistics regarding the male–female differences in parameter estimates are given in separate columns. Ramsey's RESET test proceeds from regression $e_t = \alpha+\beta_1(yhat)^2+\beta_2(yhat)^3+\beta_3(yhat)^4$.

there are several reasons to expect career interruptions to have a negative influence on earnings:

1 Expected labor force withdrawals provide disincentives to invest in human capital in the pre-maternal period.[19]
2 Due to eroded human capital, wages tend to be lower at the return to than at the departure from the labor market.
3 There is no wage growth during career interruptions.

The first two reasons are likely to be of minor importance in our analysis, given the homogeneity of our highly educated sample and the fact that a majority of all Swedes return to their original jobs (and salaries) after a parental leave. Our results thus appear reasonable: they also resemble the ones presented by Gustafsson and Lantz (1985), who based their results on Swedish data.

Career interruptions, however, are but one of several labor force attachment indicators used in our analysis. Our results indicate that while men received a large[20] return to experience, women received no return at all. We expected the return to experience to be lower among women than men. We are, however, struck by the magnitude of the difference, given our self-selected sample of young professionals and the fact that our analysis controls for firm-provided education and reported, relevant experience.[21]

Our results suggest that the wage growth de facto experienced by women was provided mainly to those with more education: education beyond the one obtained at the BA program in business decreased starting salaries, but did not influence current salaries, thus indicating that women with more education chose jobs with a high degree of skill acquisition and, hence, a steeper earnings profile.[22] Time spent at the BA program in business had, on the other hand, no influence on either starting or current salaries. Educational speed, however, had a tiny impact, and having a degree had a large positive (but only marginally significant, t=1.724) impact on the starting salaries obtained by women. However, neither having finished a degree nor the speed in which it was done influenced the current salaries obtained by either gender. We suspect that these attributes acted as screening devices (see Spence 1974) when entering the labor market: once there, however, other factors appear to have determined the outcome.

Firm-provided education added significantly to the wage growth, but not to the current salaries obtained by women. Regressions (not shown) further indicate that such education received after the entrance into the labor market was associated with lower starting salaries, other things equal. This indicates that women deliberately accepted lower starting salaries in order to get access to on-the-job-training and a steeper earnings profile.[23] However, for men firm-provided education was not associated with lower starting salaries, but had a marginally significant impact on both wage growth and the current salaries.

There is no significant impact of the education and the educational achievements obtained at the university on the earnings received by men.[24, 25] These results are not in line with the human capital theory. It should be remembered, however, that these men all applied for and were accepted on the same educational program at the same point of time. Our results indicate that educational differences obtained in the pre-labor market period for such a homogeneous sample of men has no significant impact on the earnings received.

Tenure significantly increased the wage growth obtained by men, but had no further effect on the earnings of either sex. Changes of employment were associated with higher current salaries for women, but not for men. Periods of unemployment appear to decrease the current salaries received by men ($t=-1.84$), but had no corresponding effect in the case of women. Why? We suspect that women are affected more stochastically by unemployment than men, due to expectations about future labor force withdrawals. We believe further that employers are likely to view unemployment as a signal of low productivity,[26] particularly in the case of men. Previously unemployed men may therefore not be trusted with the most valuable assignments and will not gain access to the steepest earnings profiles.

According to our results, part-time work had no significant impact on the hourly 1992 salary.[27] There was, however, a tiny return to overtime, independent of gender. It could be argued that higher earnings are not caused by but result in overtime. Our results indicate that this argument is valid in the case of males, but not females. Regressions (not shown) indicate that the overtime worked in 1992 significantly increased the starting salaries received by males, but not females. However (also not shown), it significantly increased the wage growth experienced by women, but had no effect on the wage growth obtained by men.[28] Thus for women, the wage effect of working overtime appears after the entrance into the labor market: that is, not until their work commitment has been proven.

Finally, working in the Stockholm area increased earnings, age affected earnings marginally in only two cases and union membership did not affect earnings at all. Public sector work had a negative impact on the current salaries obtained by women, but no effect on the salaries received by men: results that resemble those presented by le Grand (1991) but contradict those shown by Zetterberg (1994).

In conclusion, our results give an impression of a labor market divided by gender, where men and women are assigned to play on different courts, guided by different rules and conditions. Characteristics that significantly influenced the earnings of women had no effect in the case of men and vice versa. We do not know, however, to what part the existing differentials in earnings are explained by gender-specific differences in characteristics and to what part it is left unexplained by our explanatory variables. This is the question to which we now turn.

Decomposing the wage gap

A 5 percent female starting salary disadvantage had increased to more than 12 percent in 1992, only a few years later. We use the method of decomposition initially suggested by Blinder (1973) and Oaxaca (1973) to analyze to what extent the existing salary disadvantages experienced by women are explained by gender-specific differences in characteristics and to what extent they are left unexplained by our explanatory variables.

The analysis proceeds from the OLS estimates presented in the previous section. Specifically, let $\ln W_m$ and $\ln W_f$ denote the natural logarithms of hourly mean earnings. Let X_m and X_f specify the mean values of the characteristics used as explanatory variables, and let β_m and β_f denote the slope coefficients of the male and female wage equations respectively. It is then true that:

$$\underset{\text{(i)}}{\ln W_m - \ln W_f} = \underset{\text{(ii)}}{\Sigma\hat{\beta}_m(X_m - X_f)} + \underset{\text{(iii)}}{\Sigma X_f(\hat{\beta}_m - \hat{\beta}_f)} \tag{6.1}$$

where (i) is the male–female differential in log earnings; (ii) is the part of the wage gap that is due to differences in mean values of the explanatory variables, i.e., characteristics; (iii) is the part of the wage gap that is due to different returns to (measurable and seemingly identical) characteristics. This latter part is often assumed to reflect discrimination.[29]

Before we go any further we wish again to stress the limitations associated with this method. Two elements are crucial for the Oaxaca–Blinder decomposition:

1 All productivity related aspects which affect earnings are included in the wage equations.
2 The slope coefficients used to decompose the wage gap have a significant impact on earnings.

Neither of these conditions is likely to be fulfilled. The fact that differences in the return to identical characteristics need not necessarily be due to discrimination (Goldin and Polachek 1987) as well as the argument that differences in characteristics can also be due to discrimination (Blinder 1973; Lazear and Rosen 1990; Blau and Ferber 1987) ought also to be mentioned. With these shortcomings in mind, we shall continue with our analysis. The results are shown in Table 6.3.

If women's characteristics were to equal men's, how much would the existing wage gaps decrease? Not much. Our results indicate that the starting salary gap would increase and that the current salary gap would decrease by approximately 3 percentage points, thus leaving women with a 7 percent starting salary and a 9 percent current salary disadvantage, other things equal. In other words, gender-specific differences in characteristics explain approximately one-fourth of the current salary gap, but nothing of the starting salary

Table 6.3 Decomposition of the salary disadvantage experienced by women[a]

	Gender specific differences in salaries	*Explained by differences in*	
		(1) characteristics, i.e. mean values	*(2) the return to different characteristics*
	$lnW_m - lnW_f$	$\hat{\beta}_m(X_m - X_f)$	$X_f(\hat{\beta}_m - \hat{\beta}_f)$
		$[\hat{\beta}_f(X_f - X_m)]$	$[X_m(\hat{\beta}_f - \hat{\beta}_m)]$
The starting salary equation	0.049	–0.019	0.068
		[–0.005]	[0.054]
The current salary equation	0.124	0.031	0.093
		[0.032]	[0.092]

[a] Part-time working men are excluded from the sample used in this chapter (see note 2), as is, consequently, the part-time dummy variable from the male current salary equation. The decomposition presented above assumes that the return to part-time work in the case of males equals the coefficient for the female part-time dummy variable.

gap. The rest is left unexplained, despite the homogeneous character of our sample and the excellent controls for worker qualifications and labor force attachment included in the analysis. We shall return to this issue in the last section of the chapter.

FEELING DISCRIMINATED AGAINST: A MATTER OF GENDER?[30]

A very large part of the salary disadvantage experienced by the women in our sample cannot be accounted for by gender-specific differences in characteristics. Some would argue that our alumni students were subject to discrimination, something we really know very little about. What we do know, however, is whether they reported that they felt discriminated at the time of the 1992 survey. Irrespective of gender, the respondents were requested to report whether they had been exposed to discrimination (regarding earnings or job assignments) at their place of work, due to their sex.

Every third woman (as compared to every sixteenth man) felt that she (he) had been discriminated at her (his) place of work, due to her (his) sex. Self-reported discrimination is not associated with the 1992 salary of either men or women, however, other things equal. Probit estimates indicate, among other things, that among women unemployment and career interruptions are associated with a higher propensity to feel discriminated against. We suspect that discrimination is due mainly to interruptions in market work and that it is reflected in restricted access to wage-increasing job assignments and, consequently, to valuable experience that yields a positive return.

WAGE EXPECTATIONS AND THEIR DETERMINANTS

The respondents were also requested to state their expected 1995 monthly income in the 1992 survey. The answers show that, on average and independent of sex, they expected their real monthly income to increase approximately 30 percent in the following three years. What were the determinants of the variation in these expectations?

Our empirical analysis indicates that for neither gender did the 1992 family situation, the previous experience or career interruptions influence the expected 1995 salary. Nor was there any visible impact of the education obtained at university. However, women with superior educational achievements had a larger expected future income than other women: again, there was no corresponding effect in the case of men. On the other hand, firm-provided education was vitally important, and previous unemployment devastating in the case of men only: neither had any significant impact on expected income in the case of women. The 1992 amount of overtime was positively associated with the expected 1995 income. We suspect that this mirrors the expected return to work commitment and division of labor within the family. Women employed in the public sector had lower income expectations than other women. No corresponding effect is evident in the case of men. Both men and women in the Stockholm area did, however, have a higher expected income than men and women elsewhere.

CONCLUDING DISCUSSION

Gender differences in pay are usually explained by gender-specific differences in human capital or work effort. Given an equal division of labor within families and an equivalent amount of human capital, we would expect gender differences in pay to be minor and consequently expect the wage gap between men and women in our sample of young Swedish professionals to be negligible. It is not, however.

A starting salary differential of less than 5 percent increased to more than 12 percent in just a few years. Only one-fourth of the current salary disadvantage, and nothing of the female starting salary disadvantage, is explained by gender-specific differences in characteristics, despite the refined measures of investments in human capital and labor force attachment included in our analysis. We do not know whether the unexplained part of the salary disadvantage experienced by women is due to discrimination or to our inability to account for all relevant aspects of worker productivity. What we do know, however, is that seemingly identical attributes yielded different returns depending on sex.

Men received a huge return to experience, women none. On the other hand, education influenced the starting salaries and wage growth received by women, whereas it had no corresponding effect in the case of men. We suspect that these differences are explained by gender-specific differences in childrearing responsibilities, and that children and career interruptions are very significant in determining the labor market outcome, despite the fact that neither marital status, children or career interruptions had any visible impact on the earnings profiles of either sex.

Some would argue that the division of labor within the family is less pronounced in Sweden than in many other countries (see Gustafsson 1981b: 10; Richardson 1995). The Swedish parental leave system facilitates combining market work and childrearing responsibilities and parents are also encouraged to share the burden of parenting. We are inclined, however, to believe that childrearing responsibilities bear more heavily on women than men,[31] even in our sample of young professionals. We further believe that childrearing responsibilities may have a negative effect on worker productivity.

Firms do not know in advance whether their employees will have children, and if so whether the employees themselves will take on the job of parenting. What they do know, however, is that their female employees are statistically more likely than their male counterparts to go on parental leave, work part-time and be absent due to childrearing responsibilities after giving birth.[32] This produces incentives to treat male and female employees differently (see Lundberg and Startz 1983; Lazear and Rosen 1990). Valuable job assignments and positions, incompatible with absenteeism, ought to be held by men while female employees ought to be easily replaceable. What if jobs are therefore divided into two categories? Less valuable and easily replaceable versus valuable and not easily replaceable jobs and positions; jobs with a flatter versus jobs with a steeper earnings profile; jobs held by women versus jobs held by men.[33] The result would be a dual labor market (Dickens and Lang 1985, 1988), and such a duality could explain why women receive no return to experience.[34]

An outcome like that would depend crucially on the expectations held by employers. This has two implications. First, once job assignments and responsibilities are segregated, women may voluntarily choose a less demanding job, as the more valuable jobs are incompatible with childrearing responsibilities (see Goldin and Polachek 1987). Second, why not exploit the parental leave system fully? The cost associated with doing this is paid in advance, irrespective of the outcome: career interruptions yield no further penalty. The expectations are thus likely to become self-fulfilling.

Is there no way for women to avoid such a scenario? We believe there is. Assume that women with more ability and/or work commitment, i.e., women with more education and superior educational achievements than other women, are less likely to exploit the parental leave system to its full extent. Assume further that this is recognized by employers who view more education and superior educational achievements as attributes held by more productive women, who are thereby detached from the negative presumptions concerning women at large. It is possible that this is the case and that more education and superior educational achievements increase women's access to valuable job assignments and, hence, to a steeper earnings profile.

It is further possible that unemployment has a similar, but opposite, effect in the case of men. Employers may suspect that men who were unemployed in the boom of the late 1980s have some unobservable, negative, productivity-related quality. If this is the case, these men will not be trusted with the most valuable assignments, nor will they gain access to the steepest earnings profiles.

In conclusion, our results indicate that men receive a higher return to experience than women, and that education and educational achievements are more important in the case of women than men. They give no clue to the reasons behind these results, however. Our discussion above is a mere hypothesis, a hypothesis that might explain the results obtained. If true, it indicates a substantial amount of statistical discrimination by employers. It should be obvious, however, that these kinds of expectations, whether true or not, are likely to be self-fulfilling, and that the average woman is likely to be less productive than the average man. The central tenet in this process is the preconceptions held by employers, beliefs that will remain until the job of parenting is equally distributed between mothers and fathers. A generous parental leave system is not an open sesame to decreasing gender differences in pay as long as employers know – or expect – that the parental leave system will be utilized more by women than by men.

ACKNOWLEDGMENTS

I am indebted to Bertil Holmlund and Per-Anders Edin for valuable help and comments. Helpful suggestions from participants at the 1995 Arne Ryde Symposium and the 1995 EALE conference are also acknowledged.

NOTES

1 A BA program in business includes three and a half years of education. The first two years offer a basic program that includes a variety of business-related subjects. In the last three semesters, the student specializes in one specific area.

2 See Fornwall (1996) for details on respondents and non-respondents. Five men (=1.9 percent) held part-time jobs at the time of the 1992 survey. Including them in the regression sample (and, consequently, the part-time dummy variable in the male current salary equation) increases the sample size of the current salary equation by two observations only. The results then obtained indicate that (the two) part-time working men had higher hourly earnings than other men (β=0.310, t=1.889). No other results are altered: therefore, the relevant observations were dropped from the data used in this chapter.

3 A Swedish university degree is specified in "points," where one point corresponds to one week of study and twenty points equal one completed semester of education. Thus, a degree with an educational length of three and a half years corresponds to 140 points. This is the stipulated time, which will not always correspond to the actual outcome.

4 Measures of normality and heteroskedasticity are presented in Table 6.2. These tests indicate that the residuals are homoskedastic in all regressions, and normally distributed in all but one case.

5 The marital status variable equals one for legally married individuals only, despite the fact that Richardson (1995) found that cohabiting men earned 50–60 percent of the "legally married" wage premium and that we know whether or not our respondents were cohabiting at the time of the 1992 survey. Cohabitation had no significant impact on the current salaries obtained by our sample, however.

6 Malkiel and Malkiel (1973) suggest that marriage will increase the turnover rates and absenteeism of women, due to divided responsibilities. The empirical evidence, however, is inconclusive (see e.g. Hill 1979; Goldin and Polachek 1987; Korenman and Neumark 1992a,b; Wood *et al.* 1993).

7 Korenman and Neumark (1992b) suggest that experience and tenure are endogenous variables in the wage equations of women: treating these variables as endogenous eliminated the overall return to time spent in the labor market, while, simultaneously, a negative wage effect of children became visible.

8 Regressions (not shown) using pre-university work history variables show that these events are of minor importance in the determination of earnings profiles for the current sample.

9 The average length of the respondents' total work experience equals 6.8 years. This is decomposed into experience obtained before entering (2.8 years) versus after leaving (4.0 years) the university. The respondents perceive and report that 90 percent of the labor market experience obtained after leaving the university has an educational relevant content. This information is based on the answers to the following question: "How much has your labour market experience (reported above) been related to your education in business regarding work tasks and the like?" All information concerning experience has been recalculated – by the respondents – to the amount that is equivalent to full-time work.

10 It can be argued that the weekly overtime depends on the salary obtained. Such a variable is therefore endogenous, and ought not to be included in a wage equation. The present analysis seeks, however, to explain an increasing female salary disadvantage. We therefore include this variable in our set of explanatory variables, in order to find out whether the return to working overtime differs between males and females in our sample.

11 Years of career interruptions = 1992 – [year of hire] – [years of (relevant and irrelevant) post-university experience] – [years of post-university unemployment] – [years of post-university education].

12 Such labor force withdrawals could obviously also be due to – for example – prolonged periods of illness or vacation.

13 According to Mincer and Ofek (1983) the wage rebound is due to the fact that eroded human capital can be cheaply and rapidly restored. Corcoran and Duncan (1979), on the other hand, argue that the rebound might just as well be caused by temporary mismatches and/or imperfect information on behalf of the employer at the return to the labor market.

14 The 1992 survey included questions not only about the amount, but also about the type – formal education versus trainee programs – of firm-provided education obtained. Regressions (not shown) indicate that time spent in trainee programs had a marginally significant impact on the wage growth obtained by men (β=0.072, t=1.906), but no other visible impact on earnings: consequently this information is excluded in the following analysis. We want, further, to stress that the firm-provided education variable used in the analysis refers to the total amount of firm-provided education obtained. This definition is based on Björklund and Regnér's (1993) conclusion regarding the general character of the

firm-provided education conducted in Sweden. Further, the variable is recalculated to equalize years of education, despite the fact that firm-provided education by definition never amounts to more than months.

15 Paid parental leave is legislated for in Sweden. It comprised, during the relevant time period, 360 days compensated at 90 percent of total full income (up to a ceiling of SEK 267,750/year in 1995 prices) and another 90 days compensated at SEK60/day. The compensation is paid by the National Social Security (see RFV 1993: 3: 5). Parents also have a legal right to to be absent 60 days/year and child (with sickness benefits) due to illness of the child (until the child reaches the age of 12) (RFV 1994: 17: 7) and to decrease their hours of work to 75 percent of full time (until the child reaches the age of 8).

16 Only 47 percent of the fathers of newborn children within the present educational category utilized any parental leave at all during 1989–90. Those who did spent on average between 50 and 60 days on parental leave/year (see RFV 1993: 3). The average number of days in "our" category thus resembles the average for the population at large.

17 Educational speed is calculated as the total amount of points obtained divided by the time (i.e., the number of weeks and months from the registration date to the last exam result registered) taken to obtain them. A higher value on this variable therefore means more points acquired in a given period. The graduation dummy equals one if the BA program in business was de facto completed, and zero if it was not.

18 More able individuals (those with more inherent ability, more education and better grades) are assumed to choose jobs that include a high degree of skill acquisition and post-school investments in human capital. This results in lower than average earnings during the apprenticeship period, but – once productivity increases – faster wage growth (cf. Mincer 1974).

19 It should be noted, however, that Corcoran *et al.* (1983: 499) found "little evidence that a prospective withdrawal from the labour force was associated with lower current wage growth." They therefore "call into question the likely disincentive effects of future withdrawals on current decisions about on-the-job training."

20 Although for current salaries the return was only marginally statistically significant (t=1.667).

21 If the different kinds of experience are included (together with their squares) in the wage equations simultaneously, the following results emerge: experience obtained before entering the university had no significant impact on the earnings profiles of either gender. Irrelevant experience obtained after leaving the university appears to have a negative impact on the wage growth (β =–0.102, t_m=–1.941; β_f=–0.100, t_f=–1.923), but not on the current salaries obtained by men and women alike. According to these (new) results, relevant experience has no significant impact on the wage growth, but a large and significant impact on the current salaries obtained by men (β=0.120, t=2.163). Women on the other hand appear to receive a negative return in terms of wage growth (β-0.102, t=–1.746) but no return in terms of current salaries. No other results are altered.

22 Wage growth equations (not shown) including education beyond the one obtained at the BA program in business indicate that such education had a significant effect on the the wage growth obtained by women (β=0.089, t=2.414) but not by men (β=0.026, t=0.603). No other results are altered.

23 The argument goes as follows: employees will have to pay part of the cost associated with general training through lower salaries. The training acquired increases productivity and, consequently, wages. This results in lower starting salaries and faster wage growth – i.e. a steeper earnings profile – for those who do, than for those who do not accept jobs with a high degree of skill acquisition and

firm-provided education. These steeper earnings profiles will eventually – when the "overtaking point" (Mincer 1974 and Willis 1986) is reached – intersect with the flatter earnings profiles of those who have not continued to invest in their human capital.

24 There is one exception: men who began a PhD or MBA program after graduating from the BA program in business had significantly lower current salaries than other men. Our data do not, regrettably, shed any light on the reason behind this result. We are inclined to believe that it is explained by the fact that these men had not yet finished their thesis, i.e., that they were still "in the program" at the time of the 1992 survey.

25 The absence of significant effects in the case of males could possibly be explained by a low variance in the relevant variables. Summary statistics show, however, that the variance is not lower among men than women. (These results are available from the author on request.)

26 This argument is supported by a survey among personnel managers conducted and reported by Agell and Lundborg (1995) where they concluded that "most firms consider job seekers in either of these states [i.e., long-term unemployment or labor market programs] as potentially less productive" (Agell and Lundborg 1995: 3).

27 Persson (1993) emphasizes that the difference in the hourly salary between part-time and full-time work is likely to be smaller in Sweden than in many other countries, since the unions have promoted equal terms, independent of hours of work.

28 Inclusion of the "1992 overtime" variable in the starting salary and wage growth equations of Table 6.2 alters no results presented there: neither coefficients nor t-values.

29 Our results will be slightly different if we calculate instead the female–male wage differential, i.e. $\ln W_f - \ln W_m = \Sigma\hat{\beta}_f(X_f - X_m) + \Sigma X_m(\hat{\beta}_f - \hat{\beta}_m)$. This is basically an indexation problem, and the two different results tend to provide an upper respectively a lower limit to the part of the observed wage gap that is explained versus left unexplained by the method of estimation and the coefficients used. We present results obtained in both ways in Table 6.3.

30 This issue as well as the issue of wage expectations (see the next section of the chapter) are discussed at length in a working paper (Fornwall 1996) in which the relevant statistics and tables are also given.

31 Several authors emphasize, as does Gustafsson, (Gustafsson and Lantz 1985) that although there has been a large change during the last decades (Ståhlberg 1991; Jonung and Persson 1994), the traditional division of labor within the family still exists in Sweden (Flood and Klevmarken 1990; Persson 1993; Jonung and Persson 1994).

32 We have already mentioned that only 7 percent of the legally permitted parental leave was utilized by men in 1989. While 43 percent of the women in the labor force (age 16–64) held part-time jobs in 1988, only 7 percent of the males did. There is a close connection between part-time work and small children; Sundström (1983, 1987) reports that part-time working women have more and younger children than full-time working women. Women were also absent more than men, due to their own illnesses (men=22.0 days/year; women=28.7 days/year) and the illnesses of others, i.e., their children (*Arbetsmarknaden i siffror*: 178). Björklund (1991: 288) analyzes the determinants of sick days in Sweden. He concludes, "[The] variable 'N of small children at home' is significant and relatively strong for women (+15.9 sick days/small child) while the effect of small children is small and insignificant for males."

33 Jonung (1983: 53) concludes that "[men and women in Sweden] within each sector work in different occupations, and can – within each occupation – be

found at different levels and in different assignments." Gustafsson (1983) reports that (among white-collar workers in the Swedish industry with a BA in business) 34.5 percent of the men, versus only 8.5 percent of the women, had executive positions.

34 According to the dual, or segmented, labor market theory, there is a primary as well as a secondary sector in the labor market. The primary sector is characterized by high-wage jobs and a substantial return on investments in human capital, the secondary sector is not.

REFERENCES

Agell, J. and Lundborg, P. (1995) "Theories on pay and unemployment: survey evidence from Swedish manufacturing firms", *Scandinavian Journal of Economics* 97, 2: 295–307.

Arbetsmarknaden i siffror 1970–1988 (1989) Statistiska Centralbyrån.

Becker, G.S. (1981) *A Treatise on the Family*, Cambridge MA: Harvard University Press.

—— (1985), "Human capital, effort, and the sexual division of labor," *Journal of Labor Economics* 3, 1: 33–58.

Berndt, R.E. (1991) *The Practice of Econometrics: Classic and Contemporary*, Reading MA: Addison-Wesley.

Blau, F.D. and Ferber, M.A. (1987) "Discrimination: empirical evidence from the United States," *American Economic Review* 77, 2: 316–20.

—— (1990) "Career plans and expectations of young women and men: the earnings gap and labor force participation," NBER Working Paper No. 3445.

Björklund, A. (1991) "Vem får sjukpenning? En empirisk analys av sjukfrånvarons bestämningsfaktorer" in *Arbetskraft, arbetsmarknad och produktivitet*, Expertrapport Nr 4 till Produktivitetsdelegationen, Stockholm: Allmäna förlaget.

Björklund, A. and Regnér, H. (1993) "Humankapital-teorin och utbildning på arbetsplatserna," in C. le Grand, R. Szulkin and M. Tåhlin (eds) *Sverige och arbetsplatserna – Organisation, personalutveckling, styrning*, Stockholm: SNS Förlag.

Blinder, A.S. (1973) "Wage discrimination: reduced form and structural estimates," *Journal of Human Resources* 8, 4: 436–55.

Corcoran, M. and Duncan, G.J. (1979) "Work history, labor force attachment, and earnings differences between races and sexes," *Journal of Human Resources* 14, 1: 3–20.

Corcoran, M., Duncan, G.J. and Ponza, M. (1983) "A longitudinal analysis of white women's wages," *Journal of Human Resources* 18, 4: 497–520.

Dickens, W.T. and Lang, K. (1985) "A test of dual labor market theory," *American Economic Review* 75, 4: 792–805.

—— (1988) "The reemergence of segmented labor market theory," *American Economic Review* 78, 2: 129–34.

Duncan, G.J. and Hoffman, S. (1979) "On-the-job training and earnings differences by race and sex," *Review of Economics and Statistics* 61, 4: 593–603.

Flood, L. and Klevmarken, A. (1990) "Tidsanvändningen i Sverige 1984," in *Kvinnors roll i ekonomin*, Bilaga 23 till Långtidsutredningen 1990, Stockholm: Allmänna förlaget.

Fornwall, M. (1996a) "Early labor market careers of young business economists in Sweden," Working Paper No. 1996:14, Department of Economics, Uppsala University.

—— (1996b) "Gender differences in pay among young professionals in Sweden," Working Paper 1996:15, Department of Economics, Uppsala University.

Goldin, C. and Polachek, S. (1987) "Residual differences by sex: perspectives on the gender gap in earnings," *American Economic Review* 77, 2:143–51.

Gronau, R. (1988) "Sex-related wage differentials and women's interrupted labor careers – the chicken or the egg?" *Journal of Labor Economics* 6, 3: 227–301.

Gustafsson, S. (1981a) "Male-female lifetime earnings differentials and labor force history," in G. Eliasson, B. Holmlund and F. Stafford (eds) *Studies in Labor Market Behavior: Sweden and the United States*, Stockholm: Industriens Utredningsinstitut.

—— (1981b) *Forskning om jämställdhet i arbetslivet*, Stockholm: Arbetslivscentrum.

—— (1983) "Kvinnors låga löner – kunskapskapital eller diskriminering?" in M. Lundahl and I. Persson-Tanimura (eds) *Kvinnan i ekonomin*, Stockholm: LiberTryck.

Gustafsson, S. and Lantz, P. (1985) *Arbete och löner – Ekonomiska teorier och fakta kring skillnader mellan kvinnor och män*, IUI and Arbetslivscentrum, Stockholm: Almqvist & Wiksell International.

Hill, M.S. (1979) "The wage effects of marital status and children," *Journal of Human Resources* 14, 4: 579–93.

Jonung, C. (1983) "Kvinnors och mäns yrken," in M. Lundahl and I. Persson-Tanimura (eds) *Kvinnan i ekonomin*, Stockholm: LiberTryck.

Jonung, C. and Persson, I. (1994) "Combining market work and family," Reprint Series No. 197, Department of Economics, Lund University.

Korenman, S. and Neumark, D. (1991) "Does marriage really make men more productive?" *Journal of Human Resources* 26, 2: 282–307.

—— (1992a) "Marriage, motherhood and wages," *Journal of Human Resources* 27, 2: 282–307.

—— (1992b) "Sources of bias in women's wage equations: results using sibling data," NBER Working Paper No. 4019.

Lazear, E.P. and Rosen, S. (1990) "Male–female wage differentials in job ladders," *Journal of Labor Economics* 8, 1, suppl.: 106–23.

le Grand, C. (1991) "Rörlighet och stabilitet på den svenska arbetsmarknaden," in *Arbetskraft, arbetsmarknad och produktivitet*, Expertrapport Nr 4 till Produktivitets-delegationen, Stockholm: Allmänna förlaget.

Löfström, Å. (1989) *Diskriminering på svensk arbetsmarknad*, Umeå: Umeå Economic Studies No. 196.

Lundberg, S.J. and Startz, R. (1983) "Private discrimination and social intervention in competitive labor markets," *American Economic Review* 73, 3: 340–7.

Maddala, G.S. (1983) *Limited Dependent and Qualitative Variables in Econometrics*, Cambridge: Cambridge University Press.

Malkiel B.G. and Malkiel, J.A. (1973) "Male–female pay differentials in professional employment," *American Economic Review* 63: 693–705.

Mincer, J. (1962) "Labor force participation of married women: a study of labor supply," in *Aspects of Labor Economics*, Princeton: NBER, pp. 63–97.

—— (1974) *Schooling, Experience and Earnings*, NBER, New York: Columbia University Press.

Mincer, J. and Ofek, H. (1982) "Interrupted work careers: depreciation and restoration of human capital," *Journal of Human Resources* 17, 1: 3–24.

Mincer, J. and Polachek, S.W. (1974) "Family investments in human capital: earnings of women," *Journal of Political Economy* 82: 76–108.

Neumark, D. (1993) "Sex discrimination and women's labor market interruption," NBER Working Paper No. 4260, Princeton: NBER.

Oaxaca, R.L. (1973) "Male–female wage differentials in urban labor markets," *International Economic Review* 14: 693–709.

Persson, I. (1993) *Svenska kvinnor möter Europa*, Bilaga 16 till Långtidsutredningen 1992, Stockholm: Allmänna förlaget.

Polachek, S.W. (1975) "Differences in expected post-school investment as a determinant of market wage differentials," *International Economic Review* 16, 2: 451–70.
RFV (1993:3) Riksförsäkringsverket informerar, Statistisk rapport.
—— (1994:15) Riksförsäkringsverket informerar, Statistisk rapport.
—— (1994:17) Riksförsäkringsverket informerar, Statistisk rapport.
Richardson, K. (1995) "The evolution of the marriage premium in the Swedish labor market 1968–1991," mimeo, Swedish Institute for Social Research, Stockholm University.
Rosen, S. (1986) "The theory of equalizing differences," in O. Aschenfelter and R. Layard (eds) *Handbook of Labor Economics*, vol. 1, Amsterdam: Elsevier.
Spence, M. (1974) *Market Signalling*, Cambridge MA: Harvard University Press.
Ståhlberg, A.C. (1991) "Skillnader i försäkringsförmåner eller icke-kontanta löneskillnader mellan kvinnor och män," in *Kvinnors roll i ekonomin*, Bilaga 23 till Långtidsutredningen 1990, Stockholm: Allmänna förlaget.
Sundström, M. (1983) "Kvinnor och deltidsarbete," in M. Lundahl and I. Persson-Tanimura (eds) *Kvinnan i ekonomin*, Stockholm: LiberTryck.
—— (1987) *Study in the Growth of Part-time Work in Sweden*, Forskningsrapport 56, Stockholm: Arbetslivscentrum.
Wadensjö, E. (1991) "Högre utbildning och inkomster," in *Arbetskraft, arbetsmarknad och produktivitet*, Expertrapport Nr 4 till Produktivitetsdelegationen, Stockholm: Allmänna förlaget.
Willis, R.J. (1986) "Wage determinants: a survey and reinterpretation of human capital earnings functions," in O. Ashenfelter and R. Layard (eds) *Handbook of Labor Economics*, vol. 1, Kidlington: Elsevier, pp. 525–602.
Wood, R.G., Corcoran, M.E. and Courant, P.N. (1993) "Pay differences among the highly paid: the male–female earnings gap in lawyer's salaries," *Journal of Labor Economics* 11, 3: 417–41.
Zetterberg, J. (1994) "Avkastning på utbildning i privat och offentlig sektor," Forskningsrapport Nr 125, Stockholm: Trade Union Institute for Economic Research.

Part III

GENDER AND PAY STRUCTURES

7

WAGE DIFFERENTIALS AND GENDER IN NORWAY

Pål Longva and Steinar Strøm

INTRODUCTION

In neoclassical economics it is assumed that wage rates depend on productivity-related characteristics. These can be measured by individual-specific human capital variables such as age, level and type of education, and working experience. In a neoclassical world there are no imperfections in the labor market. Productivity-related characteristics are priced out and wage differentials will occur only as a result of variation in skills across individuals. However, this result conflicts with the facts of life. Wage differentials beyond the return to observed human capital are present in economies with quite diverse institutions in the labor market. In particular, this is the case with respect to gender wage differentials. As pointed out by Blau and Kahn (1992), despite some reductions in the male–female pay gap since the 1950s, gender differentials persist in all industrialized countries.

Several explanations of the persistent measured wage differences have been given in the literature. Murphy and Topel (1987, 1990) claim that these differences may still not be at variance with the neoclassical model and that the wage differences among observationally similar workers are thus due to unobserved personal characteristics and unobserved job attributes which affect the utility of workers. In accordance with this view gender wage differentials may occur as the result of individual choice rather than as a consequence of discrimination or other imperfections in the labor market. For instance, in the Scandinavian countries many women work in the public sector where the pay tends to be lower than that for workers with similar skills in the private sector. One reason for this may be that it is easier to find part-time work and daycare facilities that can be combined with raising children than in the private sector. Moreover, since the risk of suddenly losing one's job tends to be less in the public sector, a married couple may decide to hedge against risk with the wife working in the public sector and the husband working in the private sector. The availability of part-time jobs varies across sectors with a higher frequency in the service sectors than in other parts of the economy. In relative terms there are far more women working in these sectors than in others. Interruptions in the job career for maternity leave could explain why employers might consider that women have a weaker and less predictable labor market attachment than men. Hence in a neoclassical environment the pay will be less. The neoclassical model thus explains measured wage differences as a consequence of deliberate choices in which a higher salary is substituted for other unobserved attributes of a job.

Recently neoclassical models have lost some ground as explanations of labor market behavior and hence of the measured wage differences. In the non-Walrasian school of thought, it has been argued that wage premiums may arise as a consequence of rent sharing (Katz and Summers 1989; Blanchflower *et al.* 1990) and of efficiency wages (Katz 1986; Krueger and Summers 1988). In the rent-sharing branch of this literature the emphasis has been on the role of trade unions. In unionized industries where firms are vulnerable to strikes and go-slow actions, for example, industries with a high capital–labor ratio, according to the union power theory one would expect wages to be higher than in other industries.

In recent empirical studies of wage differentials, the focus has been on explaining wage premia by industry, after checking for productivity-related individual characteristics. With some few exceptions, for example see Fields and Wolff (1995), the gender issue has not been accounted for. There are several reasons why industry wage premia may differ between men and women. First, as alluded to above, employers may believe that men have a higher degree of labor market attachment than women, and hence will be willing to invest more in their training and to pay a higher wage. Second, women tend to choose jobs in the service sector where they can find part-time jobs with relatively but certain low pay. These jobs tend to be less capital intensive and hence less attractive for rent-seeking unions. Moreover, in capital-intensive and natural resource extraction industries the firms may have strong incentives to introduce efficiency wages to avoid shirking.

In this chapter we estimate wage equations for men and women separately. We assume that wages depend on productivity-related characteristics. We allow for inter-industry wage differentials beyond the return to human capital. This framework enables us to answer questions such as: are women's inter-industry wage differentials as large and varied as men's? Is the ranking of industries by wage premia the same for women as for men? Is there any significant difference between the wage premia for men and women?

In order to correct for variation in hours, the dependent variable is the wage rate in a full-time job. Since individuals are not randomly assigned to full-time jobs, we have tried to account for labor supply selection effects by including labor supply variables among the regressors.

The microdataset we employ is unique for the following reasons:

- It includes all individuals in Norway who had a full-time job in 1991 – thus part-timers and workers with side jobs are excluded,

- Register files are combined to yield information about personal characteristics, different types of income, observation of industry affiliation and place of residence,
- The observation of place of residence means that we can include local unemployment rates among the covariates.
- The observation of earnings is based on declarations sent by the employers to the taxation authorities.
- These earnings declarations make it possible to add non-wage compensation – i.e., taxable benefits in kind – to wage income.

The observed mean female–male earnings ratio in our sample is 75.8 percent, which is the same size as that reported by others who have analyzed Norwegian labor market data. For example, Blau and Kahn (1992) find that the mean female–male earnings ratio for all full-time workers in Norway was 73 percent in 1982. In Barth and Mastekaasa (1993) the mean pay ratio in 1990 was found to be 77 percent in the private sector and 82 percent in the public sector. Their dataset was based on a small sample – around 0.2 percent of the large sample we are using – and the earnings observations were derived from the self-reporting of hourly wages among full-time as well as part-time workers. Individuals with multiple jobs were not excluded, either.

Based on the estimated wage equations the predicted female–male earnings ratio, evaluated at mean sample values, is found to be 77 percent. The difference between the log male wage and the log female wage is estimated to 0.266, evaluated at sample means. The decomposition of this gender-log-wage gap, using the conventional methodology, shows that as much as 70.7 percent can be attributed to discrimination. The second most important determinant of the gender-log-wage gap is the distribution of male and female workers across industries which contributes with 25.3 percent of the gap. Differences in human capital endowments and local labor market conditions stand for only 4.0 percent of the gap. Although not exactly identified, our results indicate that only a negligible part of the discrimination portion of the gap can be attributed to gender differences in inter-industry wage differentials. Given that these differentials are due to true industry-specific wage premia that on the whole are equivalent for men and women, it seems that a non-Walrasian, non-competitive labor market does not discriminate between gender to any significant extent. Here, our results differ from Fields and Wolff (1995), who found on data from the USA that the differences in wage premia contributed as much to the gender wage gap as the differences in the distribution of males and females across industries.

Although we find no significant gender differences in industry wage premia, our findings suggest that the magnitude of inter-industry wage differentials, after controlling for human capital and local labor market conditions, is much larger than previously found for Scandinavian labor markets: see, for example, Barth and Zweimuller (1992) and Edin and Zetterberg (1992). The main reasons why our results differ from the findings in these previous studies may be in the first place that we have added non-wage compensation to wage earnings. As reported in Krueger and Summers (1988), non-wage compensation reinforces rather than reduces inter-industry wage differences in the USA. The same appears to be the case in Norway. In a study of wage differentials in Finland, in which the sample was restricted to full-time workers and where non-wage compensation was added to wage income, Vainiomäki and Laaksonen (1995) get results that are not so different from ours. Second, our large sample approach enables us to include industries at a two-digit level that have been excluded in previous studies of the Norwegian labor market, for example, the oil and gas industries. Although we estimate the magnitude of the inter-industry wage differentials to be larger than previously obtained on Scandinavian data, the magnitude of the wage differences, after controlling for personal characteristics, is significantly smaller than the corresponding ones estimated by Krueger and Summers (1988) and Fields and Wolff (1995) on data from the USA.

The chapter is organized as follows. First we present the methodology used in analyzing earnings data. In the following two sections the data are described and the main results presented. Then we summarize and suggest some topics for future research.

METHODOLOGY

In order to examine the importance of industry affiliation and other factors in explaining the gender wage gap, we have estimated cross-section wage curves. The wage equation, one for each gender, is given by:

$$\log W_i = \Pi + \mathbf{X}_i\beta + \mathbf{L}_i\gamma + \mathbf{I}_i\alpha + \epsilon_i \tag{7.1}$$

where W_i denotes the observed hourly wage for individual i. Π is a constant term, **X** is a vector of human capital variables, **L** is a vector of variables characterizing the local labor market and **I** is a vector of industry dummies of dimension J, where J is the number of industry sectors – two-digit specification. α, γ and β are vectors of unknown coefficients. ϵ is a random variable assumed to be normally distributed with zero expectation and a constant and unknown variance.

The **X** vector contains human capital variables like age, age squared, education – number of years – education squared, and marital status. As shown in Blau and Kahn (1992), the female–male earnings ratios are quite different in the population of married and single workers. In this chapter we have included marital status among the covariates and we distinguish between married, divorced and never married. Occupation is not observed, and therefore not included among the covariates. However, occupation may correlate strongly with the industry dummies. We do not observe capital–labor intensity and union membership for all sectors and since we want to estimate inter-industry wage differentials based on a detailed two-digit specification of the industries, we have excluded these two variables from the set of covariates in this chapter. Elsewhere we have analyzed the impact on wages in some industries of capital/labor ratios and of union membership. As expected, both variables have a positive impact on wages, but the quantitative influence on wages is rather weak.

As emphasized by Blanchflower and Oswald (1994), local unemployment rates may have a negative impact on wage levels. The justification is that the wage formation in non-competitive labor markets may be affected by local labor market conditions. We have included unemployment rates at the place of residence (municipality). Moreover, northern Norway is very different from the south in the sense that southern Norway is far more densely populated, with a much greater variety in the industrial structure. Seen in a longer perspective, northern Norway has become depopulated, but in the short run north–south mobility in the labor force is rather low. In order to capture a possible important geographical segmentation of the labor market, we have included a regional dummy in the set of covariates.

As already mentioned, we are focusing only on full-time workers. The reason for this, in the first place, is that many part-time employees work outside ordinary working hours – weekends, late evenings, nights, seasons – and are compensated for this. To include these workers along with full-time workers may bias the results. Further, it is not evident that including part-time/full-time among the covariates will capture the entire effect of very different wage contracts. Second, some of the part-time work takes place in small firms with questionable accuracy in accounting, registration of hours and reporting to the authorities. These measurement errors may disturb our estimates. Like Vainiomäki and Laaksonen (1995) we will argue that our restriction of the sample will provide us with a more homogeneous sample of workers whose labor market attachment is strong.

The inter-industry wage differentials are defined as the wage premia relative to the reference industry, and are given by α_j where j=1, 2, . . , J. Let e_j denote the number of full-time employees in sector j, relative to the total number of full-time workers in the economy. The mean, employee-weighted, wage differential is $\alpha^* = J\ \Sigma(e_j\ \alpha_j)$. The relative industry wage premium, relative to the average worker, is then $\alpha_j - \alpha^*$. The wage premium for the reference industry is thus given by $-\alpha^*$.

The degree of wage dispersion is estimated by the employment-weighted and bias-adjusted standard deviation of the relative wage premia:

$$STD = \left(\sum_{j=1}^{J}[e_j(\hat{\alpha}_j - \sum_{s=1}^{J} e_s\hat{\alpha}_s) - (e_j\hat{\sigma}_j^2)]\right)^{1/2} \quad (7.2)$$

where ^ denotes estimates. Each differential is weighted by its employment share so that the wage differentials for large sectors count more in the calculation than the differentials for small sectors. As shown in Krueger and Summers (1988), the standard deviation for the estimated α is biased. Our measure takes this into account through the last term in the parentheses where $\hat{\sigma}_j^2$ denotes the estimate of the variance related to the estimate of α_j.

There are alternative ways of expressing and decomposing the gender wage gap: see, for example, Cain (1986) and Oaxaca (1973). The approach we have taken is an Oaxaca type of measure and decomposition. Let W_k denote the mean wage for gender k, k=f,m and let $y_k = \log W_k$. Clearly, from equation (7.1) we get:

$$y_m - y_f = \underbrace{(\pi_m - \pi_f) + X_f(\beta_m - \beta_f) + L_f(\gamma_m - \gamma_f) + I_f(\alpha_m - \alpha_f)}_{\text{discrimination}} + \underbrace{(X_m - X_f)\beta_m + (L_m - L_f)\gamma_m + (I_m - I_f)\alpha_m}_{\text{endowment}} \quad (7.3)$$

where the X, L and I vectors are evaluated at mean sample values.

Thus, the difference between the mean male and female log wage can be decomposed into differences in constant terms – first term, differences in rates of return to human capital endowments, local labor market conditions and sectoral composition, all evaluated at female endowments – second, third and fourth term respectively, gender differences in human capital endowments, local labor market conditions and sectoral composition of employment, all priced out at male rates of return – fifth, sixth and seventh term respectively. In the literature there is a tendency to tie wage discrimination by gender only to the second term – gender differences in the rates of return to human capital. Given that the labor market is non-competitive, one may also consider gender differences in inter-industry wage differentials and rates of return to local labor market conditions as part of the gender wage discrimination. However, it is not possible to identify the separate contributions of sets of dummy variables to the discrimination portion of the wage decomposition. In this study we therefore resort to decomposing the endowment portion.

THE DATA

The data are cross-sectional and obtained from a number of public registers that have been merged to create a comprehensive microdataset. The population consists of individuals in Norway between 16 and 70 years of age in 1991. As discussed above, we restrict our sample to full-time workers. In order to calculate an hourly wage in a full-time job from the annual earnings, we omit individuals who were registered for more than one job, and those who received public benefits. We ended up with 534,797 observations; 189,194 women and 345,603 men. This is a huge microdataset by any standard. Hourly wage has been calculated by dividing annual income by normal hours for full-time workers plus mean overtime for each gender. Individuals who earned more or less than four times the standard deviation from the mean of the hourly wage were omitted.

Table 7.A1 in the Appendix to this chapter gives summary statistics. The mean female wage rate relative to the mean male wage rate is equal to 0.758. Standard deviations are not shown in the table, but the coefficients of variation – defined as the ratio of the standard deviation to the mean – for female and male wages are 0.28 and 0.37, respectively. Thus, the degree of wage dispersion is higher among the males than among the females. From the data about employment by industry we observe that the female employment distribution is far more concentrated to a few sectors than is the male distribution. Industry 93, social and related community services, stands out as a typical female industry, whereas there is no really typical male industry. The mean of human capital variables and local labor market conditions are rather similar across gender. This is also the case for the dispersion of these variables, not shown in the table.

Figure 7.1 reveals the fact mentioned above that the mean wage as well as the degree of wage dispersion is higher for males than for females.

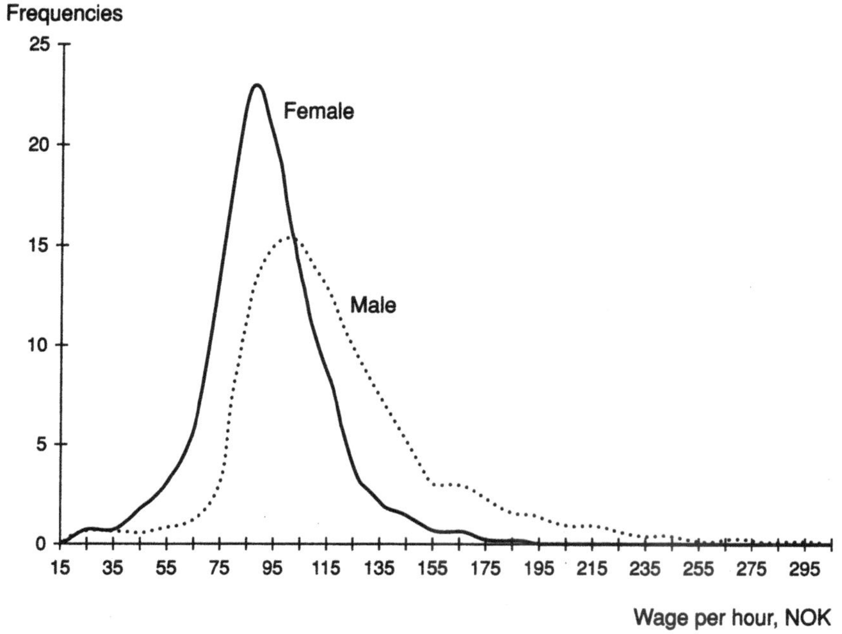

Figure 7.1 Distribution of hourly wage, Norway 1991

EMPIRICAL RESULTS

Wage regressions

Table 7.1 presents the estimates when all covariates – observable productivity characteristics, local labor market conditions, industry dummies – are included among the regressors. The estimates imply some important differences with respect to the effect of human capital and local labor market conditions on male and female wages. The wage level is a concave function of age for both sexes. For males the wage curve peaks at an age of 48 and for females at an age of 51. More marked, however, are the gender differences in the impact of marital status and education on wages. For females the hourly wage is estimated to be lower among married and divorced individuals than for never married individuals. For males we get the opposite result. The differences between the estimates for the two sexes are rather substantial and we should thus expect the female–male pay ratio to be much higher among single workers than among married workers. In fact, this is also confirmed by Blau and Kahn (1992) who report a pay ratio of 0.716 for married workers and 0.916 for single workers in Norway in 1982. For other industrialized nations they report similar differences in pay ratios. For reasons that are not clear to us, in most cases marital status has not been included among the covariates in previous studies of gender wage differentials using Scandinavian data. There might be several reasons for the wage differences associated with marital status like "hedging against risk" decisions among married workers, discriminatory practices in wage setting by employers, elements of selection that correlate with abilities, and differences in hours worked. In particular, if married men work longer hours – longer overtime – than the full-time average worker, and married women less than the average, this will show up in our sample as a higher wage rate than the normal wage rate among married men and a lower wage rate than the normal one among married women. These possible labor supply effects may be accounted for by including marital status among the covariates.

For feasible values of the education variable, the wage curve for both sexes is an increasing function of years of completed education. The elasticity of the wage level with respect to the education variable, evaluated at the mean sample value of education, is as much as two times higher for males than for females.

Geographical location has a different impact on male and female wages. For females the wage level is estimated to be 1.3 percent higher in southern Norway than in the north and for males it is estimated to be 4 percent higher – after controlling for human capital variables and industry affiliation.

The elasticity of the wage level with respect to the local unemployment rate is nearly the same across gender: for females it is estimated at –0.032 and for males at –0.038. These elasticities are significantly different from zero, as shown in Table 7.1, which is in accordance with the view of Blanchflower and Oswald (1994). However, the unemployment elasticities

Table 7.1 Log wage as a function of industry dummies, human capital variables and local labor market conditions, Norway 1991

Variable	*Females*		*Males*	
	Estimates	*t–values*	*Estimates*	*t-values*
Constant	3.351	217.8	2.961	266.1
Age	0.040	100.9	0.051	152.2
Age squared/100	–0.039	–84.5	–0.053	–140.7
Married	–0.100	–62.8	0.078	57.3
Divorced	–0.015	–6.2	0.053	25.3
Education	–0.002	–1.1	0.037	27.1
Education squared/100	0.187	21.4	0.042	7.5
Region	0.013	7.1	0.040	25.8
Local unemployment rate	–0.007	–13.7	–0.008	–19.9
Ind. code[a]				
11	–0.270	–21.5	–0.249	–34.0
12	–0.134	–3.5	–0.124	–11.9
13	0.133	4.4	0.047	4.1
21	0.123	2.9	0.267	14.4
22	0.345	62.5	0.583	161.4
23	0.137	4.3	0.089	8.9
29	0.012	0.4	0.131	14.6
31	0.023	5.4	0.082	27.7
32	–0.074	–10.2	–0.016	–2.1
33	–0.007	–0.9	–0.067	–17.5
34	0.158	36.4	0.172	57.0
35	0.145	27.5	0.157	49.9
36	0.062	5.1	0.095	17.0
37	0.165	19.1	0.139	38.8
38	0.078	18.5	0.101	45.2
39	0.050	4.1	–0.012	–1.3
41	0.015	2.1	0.009	2.7
42	0.010	0.2	–0.031	–2.1
50	0.004	0.7	0.062	27.5
61	0.097	31.7	0.131	59.3
62	–0.126	–45.8	–0.038	–14.0
63	–0.065	–14.5	–0.030	–5.3
71	0.101	28.1	0.109	47.9
72	0.049	15.2	0.013	4.5
81	0.138	44.7	0.165	47.2
82	0.207	40.0	0.315	54.2
83	0.131	40.8	0.225	84.5
92	0.037	3.6	0.023	4.1
93	–0.051	–24.2	–0.111	–46.4
94	–0.004	–0.8	–0.038	–7.0
95	–0.143	–23.9	–0.049	–13.2
96	0.128	1.5	–0.242	–1.5
R-squared	0.267		0.362	
Number of observations	189,194		345,603	

[a] Industry 91 is the reference industry.

we have found are considerably lower in numerical value than the elasticity hinted at as an empirical law in Blanchflower and Oswald (1994), namely −0.1. Our estimate is nearly identical to that of Edin and Zetterberg (1992) obtained with Swedish data.

Table 7.2 gives the R-square values from the different regressions. Human capital and local labor market variables explain slightly more of the wage variation than industry affiliation. This result differs from previous estimates on Scandinavian data: see, for example Barth and Zweimuller (1992) and Edin and Zetterberg (1992). The latter authors conclude: "While human capital variables and industry variables are of roughly equal importance in explaining wage variations in the United States, our estimates suggest that human capital variables are more than ten times as important as industry variables in Sweden." That our estimates are closer to the US result reported by Krueger and Summers (1988) may be due to a much wider industry coverage, exclusion of workers with part-time and/or multiple jobs, separate wage equations for males and females, and non-wage compensation added to wage earnings. Vainiomäki and Laaksonen (1995), who restrict the data as we have done, get a result in line with ours.

Inter-industry wage differentials

In Table 7.3 we present estimates of interindustry wage differentials for males and females. The estimates are derived from the estimates given in Table 7.1. Observe that almost all wage differentials are precisely determined. Table 7.3 shows that the wage premia range from 50.4 percent to −32.8 for males and from 33.5 percent to −28.1 percent for females. For both men and women, the top-ranked industry is oil and gas production and the bottom ranked is agriculture. As revealed by the reported estimate of Spearman's rank correlation[1] – 0.80 – the ranking of industries by wage premia is nearly the same for males and females.

As a summary statistic of the overall wage variability, we report, in Table 7.3, the employment-weighted and bias-adjusted standard deviation – STD (see equation 7.2 above). The use of employment weights, in particular for

Table 7.2 R-square analysis, Norway 1991

Variables	*Females*	*Males*
Human capital, local labor markets and industry dummies ("all")	0.267	0.362
Human capital and local labor markets	0.169	0.248
Industry dummies	0.108	0.164
"All" – industry dummies[a]	0.159	0.198
"All" – human capital and local labor markets[b]	0.098	0.114

[a] "Marginal impact of human capital variables and local labor markets"
[b] "Marginal impact of industry dummies"

males, is of importance. Adjusting for the Krueger–Summer bias is less important in our sample. The estimated weighted and adjusted standard deviations of inter-industry wage differentials indicate that there are substantial wage

Table 7.3 Estimated wage differentials relative to average for all industries and predicted female/male wage ratio by industry, after controlling for human capital variables and local labor market conditions, percent, Norway 1991

Variables		*Estimated wage differential (ranks in parentheses)*				*Predicted female/male wage ratio (%)*
		Females		*Males*		
Code	**Industry**					
11	Agriculture	–28.1	(33)	–32.8	(33)	83.1
12	Forestry	–14.5	(31)	–20.3	(31)	76.1
13	Fishing	12.3	(8)	–3.2	(18)	90.7
21	Coal mining	11.3	(11)	18.7	(3)	78.9
22	Crude petroleum and natural gas	33.5	(1)	50.4	(1)	64.7
23	Metal ore mining	12.6	(7)	1.0	(15)	88.4
29	Other mining	0.2	(22)	5.2	(10)	70.5
31	Food, beverages and tobacco	1.2	(20)	0.2	(16)	78.6
32	Textile, wearing apparel and leather	–8.5	(29)	–9.5	(23)	78.0
33	Wood and wood products	–1.8	(26)	–14.5	(29)	86.5
34	Paper, paper products and printing	14.8	(4)	9.2	(5)	81.5
35	Chemical	13.4	(5)	7.7	(8)	81.6
36	Stone, clay and glass	5.2	(16)	1.6	(14)	79.9
37	Basic metal	15.4	(3)	5.9	(9)	85.4
38	Machinery and equipment	6.8	(14)	2.1	(13)	80.8
39	Other manufacturing industries	3.9	(17)	–9.1	(22)	84.5
41	Electricity	4.7	(21)	–7.0	(21)	83.5
42	Water supply	–0.1	(23)	–11.0	(25)	–
50	Construction	–0.7	(24)	–1.6	(17)	78.8
61	Wholesale trade	8.6	(13)	5.1	(11)	80.4
62	Retail trade	–13.7	(30)	–11.8	(27)	76.7
63	Restaurants and hotels	–7.5	(28)	–10.9	(24)	80.8
71	Transport and storage	9.0	(12)	3.0	(12)	80.3
72	Communication	3.8	(18)	–6.6	(20)	86.4
81	Financial institutions	12.8	(6)	8.6	(6)	83.1
82	Insurance	19.7	(2)	23.5	(2)	74.2
83	Real estate and business services	12.0	(9)	14.6	(4)	75.8
91	Public administration and defense	1.1	(15)	7.9	(7)	82.8
92	Sanitary service	2.6	(19)	–5.6	(19)	85.1
93	Social and related community services	–6.1	(27)	–19.1	(30)	87.7
94	Recreational and cultural services	–1.5	(25)	–11.8	(26)	86.9
95	Personal and household services	–15.3	(32)	–12.9	(28)	82.5
96	International org. and embassies	11.7	(10)	–32.1	(32)	–
	All industries					77.2
Weighted and adjusted standard deviation (STD)		9.46		11.71		
Spearman's rank order correlation			0.80			

differentials in Norway. The magnitude of these differentials, as expressed by STD, is slightly larger among males than females. To some extent, this gender difference is due to the fact that female employment is far more concentrated to a few sectors than is male employment.

In the last column of Table 7.3 we also give the predicted female–male wage ratio by industry, after controlling for variation in human capital variables and local labor market conditions. The average female–male pay ratio is predicted to 0.772. The lowest female–male pay ratio occurs in the oil and gas industry, but it is worth noting that the gender pay ratios in the two financial sectors, insurance and real estate and business services, are also markedly below the average level. In the typical female industry, social and related community services, the pay ratio is much higher than the average level, 0.877 as compared to 0.772.

Decomposition of the pay gap

Table 7.4 reports the results from decomposing the log wage gap in the way shown by equation 7.3 above. As indicated, the predicted difference between the male log wage and the female log wage, evaluated at mean values, is 0.258. The table presents the relative contribution of different factors: the dominating factor turns out to be discrimination, which accounts for 70.7 percent of the gender wage gap. However, we must have in mind that discrimination also includes the unexplained portion of the wage gap captured by the difference in the constant terms. The gender difference in industry affiliation accounts for as much as 25.3 percent of the wage gap, indicating that females are to a larger degree than men employed in low wage industries.

The wage setting may differ between the private and the public sector. In order to capture any such differences we estimated separate regressions for the two sectors. As shown in Table 7.4 somewhat more of the wage gap – 2.6 percentage points, is explained by differences in human-capital endowments and local labor market conditions in the public sector compared to the private sector. The great number of individuals in our dataset also made it possible for us to estimate separate wage regressions for each industry. The results for the decompositions of industry-specific gender wage gaps are reported in Table 7.A2 in the Appendix.

CONCLUSIONS AND FUTURE RESEARCH

Despite some reductions in the male–female pay gap in the post-war period, gender differentials seem to persist in all industrialized countries. This is also the case in Scandinavian countries where the wage dispersion has been compressed as a consequence of a solidarity wage policy. Gender wage differentials may occur as the result of differences in the endowment of, and return to, human capital. Another source leading to a gender wage gap is gender

Table 7.4 Decomposition of the gender (log) wage gap, Norway 1991[a]

	Corrected for ind.		*Not corr. for ind.*		*Public sector*		*Private sector*	
Total gap	0.25756		0.25756		0.22288		0.25668	
Decomposition		%		%		%		%
Discrimination	0.18214	(70.72)	0.24734	(96.03)	0.18265	(81.95)	0.21705	(84.56)
End. human-capital	0.01037	(4.03)	0.01030	(4.00)	0.03977	(17.84)	0.04056	(15.80)
End. LLMC	–0.00015	–(0.06)	–0.00009	–(0.03)	0.00046	(0.21)	–0.00093	–(0.36)
Industry affiliation	0.06520	(25.31)						
Industry premium	0.00159	(0.62)						

[a] The following abbreviations are used: End. = Endowments; Ret. = Return; Ind. = Industry; LLMC = Local labor market conditions.

differences in inter-industry wage differentials and in the distribution of men and women between industries. Finally, imbalances in the labor market may have a different impact on female and male earnings. To test these hypotheses we have estimated wage curves on datasets covering all Norwegian individuals who had a full-time job in 1991. The empirical results indicate that the greatest part of the male–female pay gap can be explained by the differences in the rate of return to human capital. The second largest part is explained by the differences in the distribution of male and female workers between industries. The other factors, differences in inter-industry wage differentials, differences in human capital endowments and local labor market conditions, contribute together only a little more than 10 percent to the gender wage gap.

In future work we will try to embed wage curves in a matching framework, in which the behavior of firms and households, together with wage formation, are modeled. This modeling framework may provide us with a better tool for distinguishing between the effects of choices and of discrimination.

ACKNOWLEDGMENTS

This chapter is part of the documentation from the project "Firms and Job Seekers" at the SNF Centre for Research in Economics and Business Administration at the Department of Economics, University of Oslo. We gratefully acknowledge support from the Ministry of Local Government and Labor, and the Research Council of Norway. We would like to thank participants in the Arne Ryde Symposium, and Steinar Holden for comments.

NOTE

1 Spearman's rank correlation, ρ, is defined as $\rho=1-[6/(N^3-N)]\Sigma_j d_j^2$, where N is the number of industries, and d_j is the difference in rank for industry j between the two genders.

REFERENCES

Barth, E. and Mastekaasa, A. (1993) "Decomposing the male–female wage gap: within and between establishment differences," in E. Barth *Pay Differentials and Bargaining Institutions*, Økonomiske doktoravhandlinger (PhD thesis) 16, Department of Economics, University of Oslo.

Barth, E. and Zweimuller, J. (1992) "Labor market institutions and the industry wage distribution: evidence from Austria, Norway and the U.S.," *Empirica* 19, 2: 181–201.

Blanchflower, D. and Oswald, A. J. (1994) *The Wage Curve*, London: MIT Press.

Blanchflower, D. G., Oswald, A. J. and Garrett, M. (1990) "Insider power in wage determination," *Economica* 57: 143–70.

Blau, F. D., and Kahn, L. M. (1992) "The gender earnings gap: learning from international comparisons," *American Economic Review* 82, 2: 533–8.

Cain, G. G. (1986) "The economic analysis of labor market discrimination: a survey," in O. C. Ashenfelter and R. Layard (eds) *Handbook of Labor Economics*, New York: Elsevier.

Edin, P-A. and Zetterberg, J. (1992) "Interindustry wage differentials: evidence from Sweden and a comparison with the United States," *American Economic Review* 82, 5: 1341–9.
Fields, J. and Wolff, E. (1995) "Interindustry wage differentials and the gender wage gap," *Industrial and Labor Relations Review* 49, 1: 105–20.
Gibbons, R. and Katz, L. F. (1992) "Does unmeasured ability explain inter-industry wage differentials," *Review of Economic Studies* 59, 3: 515–35.
Katz, L. F. (1986) "Efficiency wage theories: a partial evaluation," in S. Fischer (ed.) *NBER, Macroeconomics Annual 1986*, Cambridge MA: MIT Press.
Katz, L. F. and Summers, L. H. (1989) "Industry rents: evidence and implication," *Brooking Papers on Economic Activity*: 209–75.
Krueger, A. B. and Summers, L. H. (1988) "Efficiency wages and the inter-industry wage structure," *Econometrica* 56, 2: 259–93.
Murphy, K. M. and Topel, R. H. (1987) "Unemployment, risk and earnings: testing for equalizing differences in the labor market," in K. Lang and J. Leonard (eds) *Unemployment and the Structure of Labor Markets*, Oxford: Basil Blackwell.
—— (1990) "Efficiency wages reconsidered: theory and evidence," in Y. Weiss and G. Fishelson (eds) *Advances in the Theory and Measurement of Unemployment*, London: Macmillan.
Oaxaca, R. (1973) "Male–female wage differentials in urban labor markets," *International Economic Review* 14, 3: 693–709.
Vainiomäki, J. and Laaksonen, S. (1995) "Inter-industry wage differentials in Finland: evidence from longitudinal census data for 1975–1985," *Labour Economics* 2, 2: 161–74.

APPENDIX

Table 7.A1 Summary statistics, means, Norway 1991

Variables			*Females*		*Males*	
Hourly wage (NOK)			87.34		115.23	
Age (years)			40.3		41.2	
Marital status (%)	Married		59.9		64.9	
	Divorced		10.8		7.8	
	Never married		29.3		27.3	
Education (years)			11.3		11.3	
Place of residence (%)	North		11.3		11.2	
	South		88.7		88.8	
Local unemployment rate (%)			4.6		4.7	
Employment by sector (percent of total in parentheses)						
Code	**Industry**					
11	Agriculture		422	(0.2)	1,558	(0.5)
12	Forestry		44	(0.0)	746	(0.2)
13	Fishing		72	(0.0)	600	(0.2)
21	Coal mining		35	(0.0)	234	(0.1)
22	Crude petroleum and natural gas		2,409	(1.3)	7,644	(2.2)
23	Metal ore mining		66	(0.0)	817	(0.2)
29	Other mining		71	(0.0)	1,009	(0.3)
31	Food, beverages and tobacco		4,591	(2.4)	13,350	(3.9)
32	Textile, wearing apparel and leather		1,326	(0.7)	1,363	(0.4)
33	Wood and wood products		1,009	(0.5)	6,937	(2.0)
34	Paper, paper products and printing		4,164	(2.2)	12,491	(3.6)
35	Chemical		2,695	(1.4)	11,144	(3.2)
36	Stone, clay and glass		457	(0.2)	2,769	(0.8)
37	Basic metal		921	(0.5)	7,927	(2.3)
38	Machinery and equipment		4,528	(2.4)	35,661	(10.3)
39	Other manufacturing industries		439	(0.2)	1,004	(0.3)
41	Electricity		1,308	(0.7)	9,109	(2.6)
42	Water supply		18	(0.0)	365	(0.1)
50	Construction		2,885	(1.5)	31,777	(9.2)
61	Wholesale trade		11,145	(5.9)	37,938	(11.0)
62	Retail trade		15,977	(8.2)	16,222	(4.7)
63	Restaurants and hotels		4,019	(2.1)	2,704	(0.8)
71	Transport and storage		6,867	(3.6)	31,700	(9.2)
72	Communication		9,322	(4.9)	13,535	(3.9)
81	Financial institutions		10,695	(5.7)	8,250	(2.4)
82	Insurance		2,754	(1.5)	2,525	(0.7)
83	Real estate and business services		9,428	(5.0)	17,947	(5.2)
91	Public administration and defense		19,299	(10.2)	29,966	(8.7)
92	Sanitary service		662	(0.3)	2,622	(0.8)
93	Social and related community services		67,123	(35.5)	25,851	(7.5)
94	Recreational and cultural services		2,416	(1.3)	2,885	(0.8)
95	Personal and household services		2,018	(1.1)	6,950	(2.0)
96	International org. and embassies		9	(0.0)	3	(0.0)
All industries			189,194	(100.0)	345,603	(100.0)

Table 7.A2 Decomposition of the gender (log) wage gap for each industry,[a] Norway 1991

Industry	*Total gap*	*Human cap. Endowment*	*Discrimination*	*LLMC*[b] *Endowment*
11	0.143	–0.003	0.151	–0.004
12	0.135	–0.072	0.207	0.000
13	0.067	–0.026	0.094	–0.001
21	0.266	0.010	0.259	–0.003
22	0.538	0.134	0.402	0.001
23	0.084	–0.010	0.083	0.010
29	0.273	–0.005	0.277	0.000
31	0.243	0.018	0.225	–0.001
32	0.236	0.020	0.216	0.000
33	0.093	–0.019	0.113	–0.001
34	0.200	0.010	0.195	–0.005
35	0.204	0.013	0.190	0.002
36	0.215	0.012	0.203	0.000
37	0.162	0.010	0.153	–0.001
38	0.232	0.041	0.192	–0.001
39	0.126	0.019	0.107	0.000
41	0.217	0.045	0.171	0.000
50	0.239	–0.003	0.242	–0.001
61	0.237	0.032	0.209	–0.005
62	0.267	0.010	0.257	0.000
63	0.232	0.060	0.170	0.001
71	0.200	0.018	0.186	–0.004
72	0.164	0.019	0.145	0.000
81	0.295	0.094	0.198	0.003
82	0.392	0.108	0.282	0.001
83	0.379	0.111	0.267	0.001
91	0.226	0.037	0.188	0.001
92	0.179	0.010	0.168	0.002
93	0.214	0.084	0.130	0.000
94	0.148	0.007	0.141	0.001
95	0.308	0.065	0.244	–0.002

[a] Industries 42 and 96 are not included due to lack of observations.
[b] LLMC=Local labor market conditions.

8

THE GENDER WAGE GAP IN FINNISH INDUSTRY 1980–94

Rita Asplund

INTRODUCTION

This study analyzes the development of the male–female wage gap for white-collar workers in Finnish industry over the years 1980–94, a time period covering both boom and deep recession. Of particular interest therefore is whether the relative labor market situation of female industrial workers has been notably affected by changes in economic activity and, especially, by the deep recession into which the Finnish economy plunged in the early 1990s.[1]

The sample data used come from individual level data collected by the Confederation of Finnish Industry and Employers (TT).[2] The database comprises a considerable amount of information about personal and job-related characteristics, as well as wages and various pay compensations such as fringe benefits, shift pays and bonuses. The data set covers each year during the period 1980–94, and has the properties of both panel and cross-section data. It thus opens a multitude of previously unexplored possibilities to examine in detail trends in the male–female wage gap in Finnish industry over the past fifteen years.

For several reasons, the analysis is restricted to white-collar industrial workers, with a further division according to occupational social status (technical, clerical and upper level white-collar workers) and industrial sector. One important reason for focusing on white-collar workers only is that the database for white-collar industrial workers contains, *inter alia*, information on formal schooling (degree and field), work experience and seniority, while the corresponding database for blue-collar industrial workers does not. The fifteen cross-section samples used in the study include between 6,400 and 9,600 individuals each.[3] The share of women has persistently been slightly less than 40 percent. The variation in sample size over the investigated time period reflects variations in the size of the underlying population resulting from structural changes in the economy and business cycle effects.

The study focuses on three aspects of the gender wage gap. The first section of the chapter gives an overall view of trends in male and female white-collar wages in Finnish industry by comparing the overall dispersion of male and female wages as well as the wage levels of males and females for selected percentiles. Underlying the observed trends in male–female wage differences is, *inter alia*, the pattern of wage mobility among male and female workers: that is, the individuals' mobility within the wage distribution. The second section of the chapter shows that not only is the starting position, i.e. the origin wage decile, on average much lower for female than for male white-collar workers. In addition there are notable gender-specific differences in the pattern of wage mobility. Moreover, the deep recession in the early 1990s turned out to have exerted a clearly negative influence on the relative wage position of female white-collar workers as well as on their opportunities for moving up the wage hierarchy.

The sections that follow analyze trends in the male–female wage gap by estimating broadly defined human capital wage equations for each relevant year. The gender effect is accounted for in two traditional ways. First, the wage equation is supplemented with a gender dummy variable with a value of 1 if the individual is a female. This gives the proportion of the observed wage differentials between male and female white-collar workers that cannot be explained by the personal and job-related characteristics accounted for in the estimations. Second, separate wage equations are estimated for male and female white-collar workers in order to investigate whether they are rewarded differently for the same characteristics and, especially, for the same amount of acquired human capital. These estimation results are then used to calculate the extent of wage discrimination in Finnish industry over the years 1980–94. Concluding remarks are given in a final section.

TRENDS IN WAGE LEVELS AND WAGE DISPERSION

In 1980, the nominal total hourly wage amounted on average to FIM31.70 for male white-collar workers and FIM19.60 for female white-collar workers, indicating that the average female wage level was only some 62 percent of the average male wage level among white-collar workers in Finnish industry. This relatively large gender wage gap is no doubt partly explained by the wage concept used, total hourly wages, which apart from the normal wage also includes different types of pay compensation such as fringe benefits. It is by now a stylized fact that pay compensations are more heavily concentrated to male workers.

By 1994, the nominal total hourly wage level of male white-collar workers had increased to FIM82.90 which gives an average growth rate of 7.7 percent a year. Among female white-collar workers the total hourly wage level by 1994 had risen to FIM57.00 giving an average growth rate of 8.6 percent per annum. Due to the more rapid growth of female wages, the female–male wage differential narrowed slightly over the investigated time period as well; in 1994 it amounted to some 69 percent.

The dispersion of total hourly wages among female and male white-collar workers in Finnish industry over the years 1980–94 is displayed in Figures 8.1 and 8.2 using three different measures of wage dispersion. Overall dispersion is measured by the standard deviation of log total hourly wages. Changes in the two tails of the wage distribution are captured by the LOG(P90/P10) distribution, where P90 and P10 refer to the wage level of the ninetieth and tenth percentiles, respectively. The LOG(P75/P25) measure displays whether eventual changes in the tails have been reflected throughout the wage distribution.

The Figures reveal a clearly higher overall dispersion of male white-collar industry wages than of female ones. The gender gap in overall wage dispersion narrowed slightly toward the end of the 1980s, but remained roughly unchanged in the deep recession years of the early 1990s. In 1994, though, the development seems to have shifted back to the general course that prevailed up to 1990. Similar overall trends are discernible in both the LOG(P90/P10) and the LOG(P75/P25) dispersion measures.

Figure 8.2 further indicates that the LOG(P75/P25) wage distribution is highly similar among Finnish and Swedish female white-collar workers, and has also developed quite similarly. Comparison of males, on the other hand, points to a much more compressed wage structure among male white-collar workers in Sweden. Hence, a strong similarity in labor market institutions across countries does not rule out the possibility of notable differences in wage dispersion.

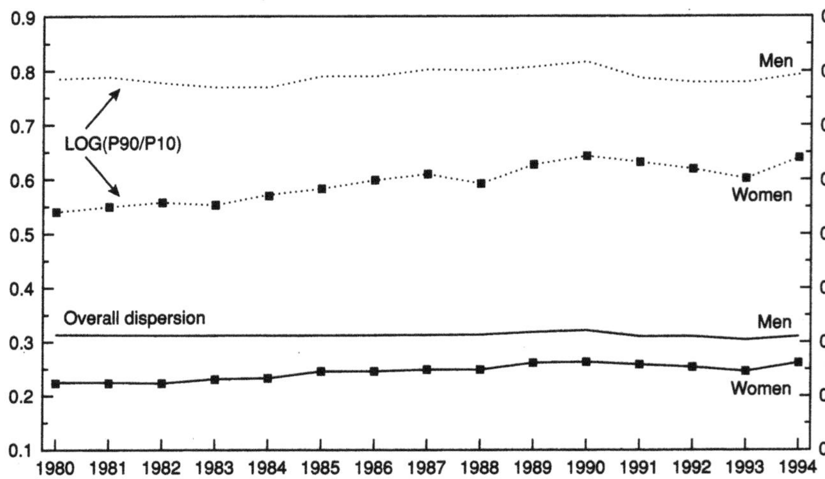

Figure 8.1 Trends in overall wage dispersion measured as the standard deviation of log total hourly wages and in the LOG(P90/P10) wage distribution

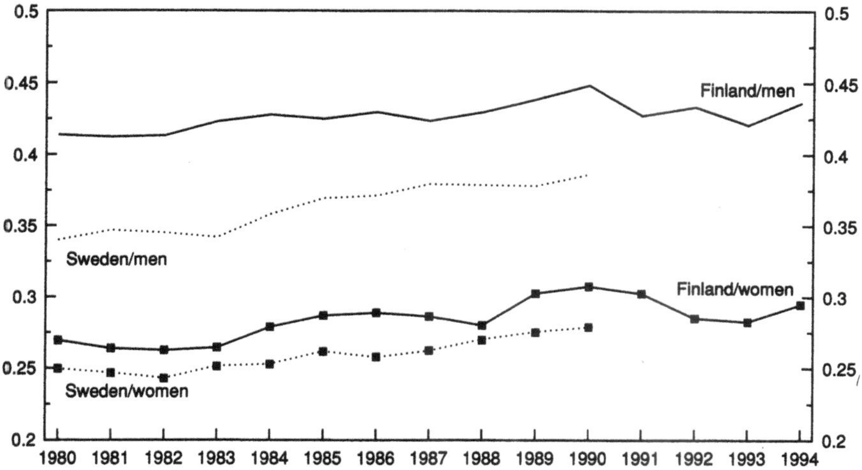

Figure 8.2 Trends in the LOG(P75/P25) wage distribution compared to male and female white-collar workers in the Swedish private sector
Source: The figures for Sweden are from Edin and Holmlund (1992)

WAGE MOBILITY

The distribution of male and female white-collar workers within the wage hierarchy of Finnish industry is very uneven. The overwhelming dominance of females in the lower tail of the wage distribution and of males in the upper tail is astounding. In 1980, over 95 percent of the white-collar workers situated in the lowest wage decile were females, whereas some 98 percent of the white-collar workers situated in the highest wage decile were males. Of all white-collar workers located in the lower half of the wage distribution, some 65 percent were women. Over 90 percent of those located in the upper half of the wage distribution were men.

The situation changed slightly in the boom years of the late 1980s. There was a clear, albeit modest, shift of females upwards in the wage hierarchy. The share of females in the lower half of the wage distribution dropped to some 61 percent, while their share in the upper half of the wage distribution rose to some 14 percent. The deep recession in the early 1990s, however, put an end to and even reversed this trend. In 1994, though, the development seems to have moved back to pre-recession tracks, with slowly increasing shares of females in the higher wage deciles.

In view of the strong segmentation of the white-collar wage distribution, it is of interest also to investigate and compare the stability and mobility within the wage hierarchy of male and female white-collar industrial workers. Is it possibly so that females not only enter relatively low wage positions but, moreover, also tend to be locked into these low wage deciles for several years? Or do they have the possibility to move rapidly upwards in the wage hierarchy already within a few years?

In brief, a comparison of the stability and mobility patterns of male and female white-collar workers indicates the following. The probability among white-collar workers located in the lowest wage deciles of still belonging to the same wage decile, say, four years later is notably higher for women than for men. Moreover, this tendency strengthened markedly during the deep recession in the early 1990s.

Female white-collar workers also seem to have a clearly lower probability of retaining their relative wage position, especially when situated in the highest wage deciles. Put differently, female white-collar workers tend to have a higher probability of moving downward in the wage distribution, i.e., of lagging behind in promotions and wage growth, than their male counterparts. This tendency is discernible at practically all decile levels. Over the past fifteen years, female white-collar workers have, moreover, seen a steady weakening in their relative wage position, while the trend for their male colleagues points to a notable decrease in the probability of shifting down into lower wage deciles.

These differences between genders in the patterns of downward mobility have their counterparts in the patterns of upward mobility within the wage hierarchy. In particular, the probability of moving up from the lowest wage deciles within four years is much higher among male white-collar workers. This trend has strengthened considerably when comparing the early 1980s to the early 1990s, and especially with respect to the lowest wage decile. In addition, the increased wage stability of females in the early 1990s seems to have occurred primarily at the expense of upward mobility.

These gender-specific differences in mobility patterns within the white-collar wage distribution of Finnish industry mediate the combined effect of two underlying forces: first, the degree of mobility of females within the female wage distribution as compared to that of males within the male wage distribution; second, shifts of the female wage distribution relative to the male wage distribution. Comparison of the male and female wage distributions reveals that the female wage distribution conceals a notably higher degree of wage mobility. This outcome is no doubt partly due to the more compressed wage structure of female white-collar workers (see Figure 8.1) and the consequently higher probability of shifting between wage deciles.

In the early 1990s, the female wage distribution remained roughly unchanged relative to the male wage distribution: the average wage level of female white-collar workers was located approximately at the twelfth percentile in the male white-collar wage distribution. In other words, nearly 90 percent of the male white-collar workers in Finnish industry earned more than the average female white-collar worker. In 1980, this figure was some 95 percent of the male white-collar workers.[4] Shifts in the female wage distribution relative to the male wage distribution thus seem to have played a minor role. Instead the dominant explanation is found in major differences in the degree of mobility within the female and the male wage distribution, respectively. This aspect definitely deserves further research.

As a concluding remark it should be emphasized that the above analysis of wage mobility is done in a very traditional way in the sense that the focus is merely on the transitions of those individuals for whom a positive wage is observed in both the starting and the destination year. This approach can be criticized for overlooking the potential presence of two selectivity processes influencing the observed mobility patterns. First, it ignores the potential sample selection bias associated with panel attrition, that is, with the fact that some individuals are no longer observed (do not have a positive wage) in the destination year. Second, individuals start in different wage deciles, i.e., differ in their origin decile, depending on their background characteristics. Both types of selectivity are covered in two forthcoming studies attempting to explain observed mobility patterns: one on wage mobility in Finnish industry in 1980–94 (Asplund and Bingley 1996) and one comparing wage mobility in Denmark and Finland (Asplund, Bingley *et al.* 1996). It is noteworthy that both selectivity processes are found to exert a non-negligible influence on individual wage mobility, more so for men than for women.

THE MALE–FEMALE WAGE GAP

Direct comparison of male and female average wage levels can always be criticized for neglecting personal and job-related differences between men and women, differences that are more or less strongly reflected also in wages and thus in the gender wage gap. A frequently used way to circumvent this criticism is to standardize for these types of differences by estimating wage equations comprising a broad set of wage-relevant variables.

This is also the approach used in the present study. More precisely, broadly defined wage equations of the Mincer type are estimated for all sample white-collar workers as well as for crucial white-collar subcategories (by occupational status and industrial sector). In the whole sample equations, log total hourly wages are regressed on a vector of explanatory variables including formal education (degree and field), total years of work experience, seniority (defined as years in the current employment relationship), type of working tasks (administration, production, etc.), region, plant size, occupational status (clerical, technical, upper level), and industrial sector (thirteen in all). Variables were also added reflecting the female dominance at each plant[5] and the mobility of individuals.[6]

The gender aspect is accounted for in two different ways; first, by adding a gender dummy to the full-sample wage equation; second, by estimating separate wage equations for male and female white-collar workers.[6]

The same analytical framework is applied to the various subcategories investigated. A distinction is hereby made between three occupational, social status categories: upper level, technical and clerical white-collar workers. From the gender point of view, these three categories are interesting mainly because they can be classified as typical male- or female-dominated worker categories.

In 1980, the share of women among upper level and technical white-collar workers was less than 14 percent. Despite a slight increase in the female share (to around 17–18 percent) over the past fifteen years, they are still to be classified as typical male occupational status categories. In contrast, over 77 percent of the white-collar workers in clerical jobs were women in 1980. By 1994 the female share had increased to over 80 percent.

Of the eight industrial sectors investigated, three can be classified as female dominated, at least when it comes to the white-collar personnel. These are clothing industries (over 70 percent), textile industries (around 60 percent), and printing and publishing (around 60 percent). In the other five industrial sectors, the share of females is less than 50 percent (chemical industries over 40 percent; manufacture of paper and wood products less than 40 percent; manufacture of metal products and construction less than 30 percent).

The estimated gender wage gaps for the whole sample and for the various subcategories for the years 1980–94 are displayed in Figures 8.3, 8.4 and 8.5, which for illustrative reasons had to be drawn using different scales. The results obtained from using the gender dummy variable approach indicate that the overall male–female wage gap declined from some 26 percent in 1980 to around 20 percent in 1991. After this bottom year of the recession the overall gender wage gap among white-collar workers seems, however, to have increased slightly, amounting to some 21 percent in 1994.[8] These male–female wage gaps standardized for differences in personal and job-related characteristics across genders also show that the gender wage gap adjusted for differences in background characteristics is some 10 percentage points smaller than the male–female wage differential calculated from average wage levels (some 38 percent in 1980, and around 31 percent in 1994).

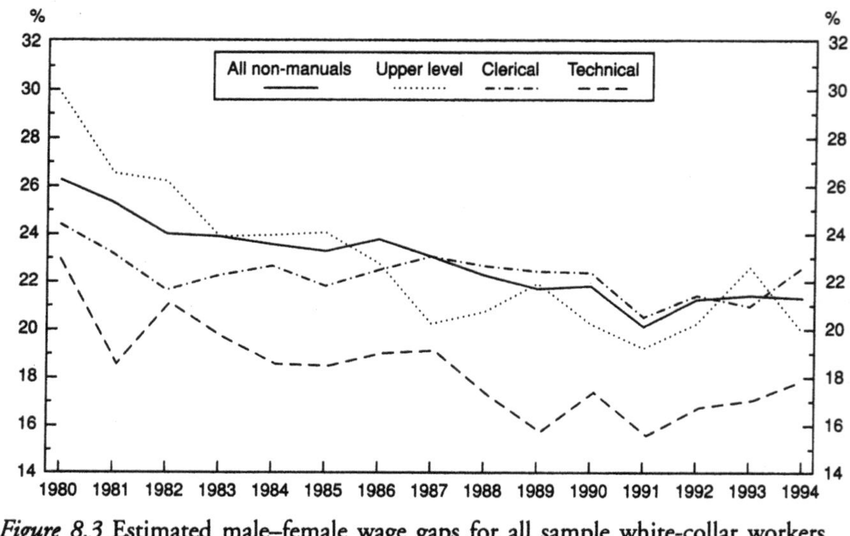

Figure 8.3 Estimated male–female wage gaps for all sample white-collar workers and by occupational status, 1980–94

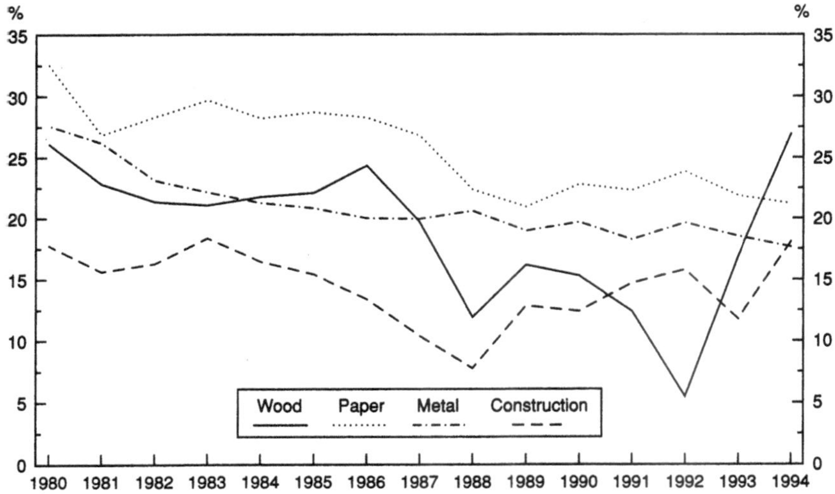

Figure 8.4 Estimated male–female wage gaps for industrial sectors with a relatively low share of female white-collar workers, 1980–94

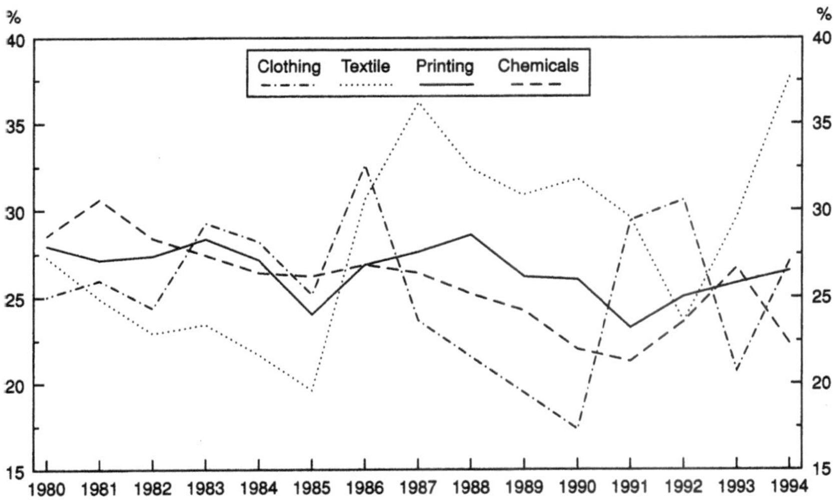

Figure 8.5 Estimated male–female wage gaps for industrial sectors with a relatively high share of female white-collar workers, 1980–94

The same overall trend is reflected in the gender wage gaps estimated for the three occupational status categories. The largest drop in the male–female wage gap is observed among upper level white-collar workers: from 30 percent in 1980 to 19 percent in 1991, followed by minor (insignificant) variations over the years 1991–4. A strong decline in the gender wage gap has also occurred among technical white-collar workers, although the starting point was notably lower (some 23 percent in 1980) than among upper level white-collar workers. By 1991, the gender wage gap among technical white-collar workers had declined to below 16 percent, but rose to nearly 18 percent in 1994. Again, however, the changes after 1991 turn out to be statistically insignificant. The female-dominated category of clerical white-collar workers displays a slowly but very erratically declining male–female wage gap. In 1980, the gender wage gap among clerical white-collar workers amounted to slightly more than 24 percent, and at the end of the investigated time period to some 22.5 percent, a difference that is statistically insignificant according to a simple t-test. In effect, since the mid-1980s, the gender wage gap has almost persistently been highest in this female-dominated occupational status category.

These same patterns are largely repeated in the eight industrial sectors investigated in the sense that the gender wage gap is on average smaller and displays a distinctly declining trend among white-collar workers in the more male-dominated branches (Figure 8.4). The male–female wage gap in the sector manufacture of paper products dropped from some 32 percent in 1980 to some 21 percent in 1994. White-collar workers in the sector manufacture of metal products experienced over the same time period a decline in the gap from around 27 percent to some 18 percent. Also in "manufacture of wood products" the gender wage gap narrowed substantially, especially in the latter half of the investigated time period. By 1994, however, the gender wage gap in this particular sector had returned to the 1980 level, or almost 27 percent. The male–female wage gap has persistently been relatively small in construction (less than 20 percent), and seems to have imitated some kind of business cycle behavior.

The estimation results point to notably larger gender wage gaps in the more female-dominated industrial sectors (Figure 8.5). An almost identical trend is observable among white-collar workers in the printing and publishing and the chemical industries, with a somewhat jumpy drop in the gender wage gap up to 1991, followed by a clear "recovery" of male wages in the past few years. In both sectors, the male–female wage gap amounted to some 26 percent in 1993 compared to some 28 percent in 1980.[9] No clear trends are discernible in the gender wage gap estimated for the strongly female-dominated clothing and textile industries, but this is partly due to small sample sizes in these two sectors.

MALE–FEMALE DIFFERENCES IN HUMAN CAPITAL RETURNS

The previous section has shown that part of the wage differentials observed between male and female white-collar workers in Finnish industry is explained by differences in measurable personal and job-related characteristics. At the same time, however, a considerable part of the gender wag gap remains unexplained as indicated by the parameter estimates of the gender dummy variable. Generally this unexplained share of the observed gender wage gap, at least in part, is argued to be due to discrimination of women in the labor market.

A frequently raised question therefore is why females are generally less rewarded for observationally equivalent qualifications and working tasks. So far the international literature can offer no widely accepted explanation(s) for this phenomenon. Moreover, most of the effort has been directed toward providing convincing empirical evidence on the factually weaker labor market and, especially, wage situation of women. This is also the main purpose of the subsequent analysis.

In particular, this section explores possible differences in the reward to human capital (formal education, work experience, seniority) between male and female white-collar workers in Finnish industry over the years 1980–94.[10] Such differences are also of interest in view of, on the one hand, the rapidly growing share of female students, the relatively high educational level of females and their high labor force participation and, on the other hand, the increasing emphasis that international debate and research put on education, training and lifelong learning at the individual, firm and economy levels.

The development of the estimated average return to an additional year of schooling for all sample white-collar workers and separately for males and females is displayed in Figure 8.6. The overall trend in the average wage effect of an additional year of school was quite similar for male and female white-collar workers in the 1980s with small (insignificant) annual changes in the average return to school.

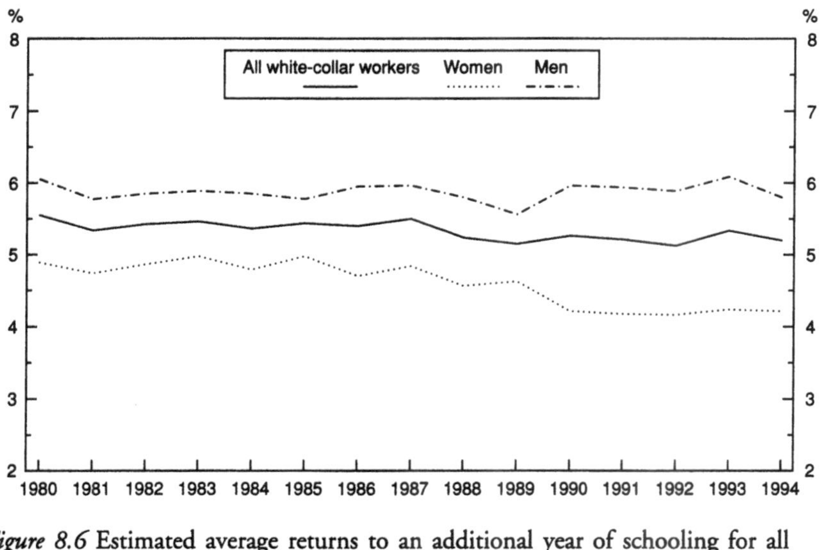

Figure 8.6 Estimated average returns to an additional year of schooling for all sample white-collar workers and separately for males and females

In contrast, in the early 1990s, the average return to an additional year of schooling developed very differently among male and female white-collar workers: the average return of females dropped permanently to around 4 percent per annum, whereas the average return of males rose, also permanently as it seems, to around 6 percent per annum, thus widening the gender gap in average returns to additional schooling to nearly 2 percentage points.[11] Probably even larger effects of the deep recession in the early 1990s on the returns to schooling would have been obtained had it been possible to account for the high unemployment rates in these years (see Westergård–Nielsen 1996).

These gender differences in the estimated returns to additional years of schooling, however, conceal notable differences between male and female white-collar workers in the average returns to educational degrees.[12] These differences are shown in Figure 8.7, which contains a maximum of information, but still clearly reveals the following. First, with few exceptions the average return to acquiring an additional degree after having completed compulsory schooling (=9 years) is significantly lower for female than for male white-collar workers at all educational levels.[13]

Second, the estimated returns to educational degrees have declined significantly among female white-collar workers over the past fifteen years. In contrast, among male white-collar workers the average returns to educational degrees declined only slightly or remained roughly unchanged in the 1980s, and have shown an upward trend since the beginning of the present decade. A most conspicuous finding is that by 1993 this development had resulted in a situation where the average return for females to a particular educational degree had dropped to the same level as the average return for males to the closest lower educational degree. More precisely, in 1993 the average return for females to a university degree was very close to the average return for males to a short non-university degree. Likewise, the average return for female white-collar workers to a short non-university degree had declined by 1993 to that for male white-collar workers to a high school (upper secondary) degree. The return for females to a high school (upper secondary) degree, in turn, was of approximately the same size as the return for males to a vocational school (lower secondary) degree. A break in this trend seems to have occurred, however, in 1994. In particular, the return to education appears to have increased slightly at all levels among female white-collar workers, whereas their male counterparts have experienced a decline in the average returns to educational degrees. A t-test indicates, though, that these changes between 1993 and 1994 are statistically insignificant for a majority of the education degree levels.

A third noteworthy result is the discovery that there were no wage effects in the early 1980s for people acquiring a vocational school (lower secondary) degree after having completed primary schooling. In the mid-1980s the situation worsened further. For female white-collar workers the acquisition of a

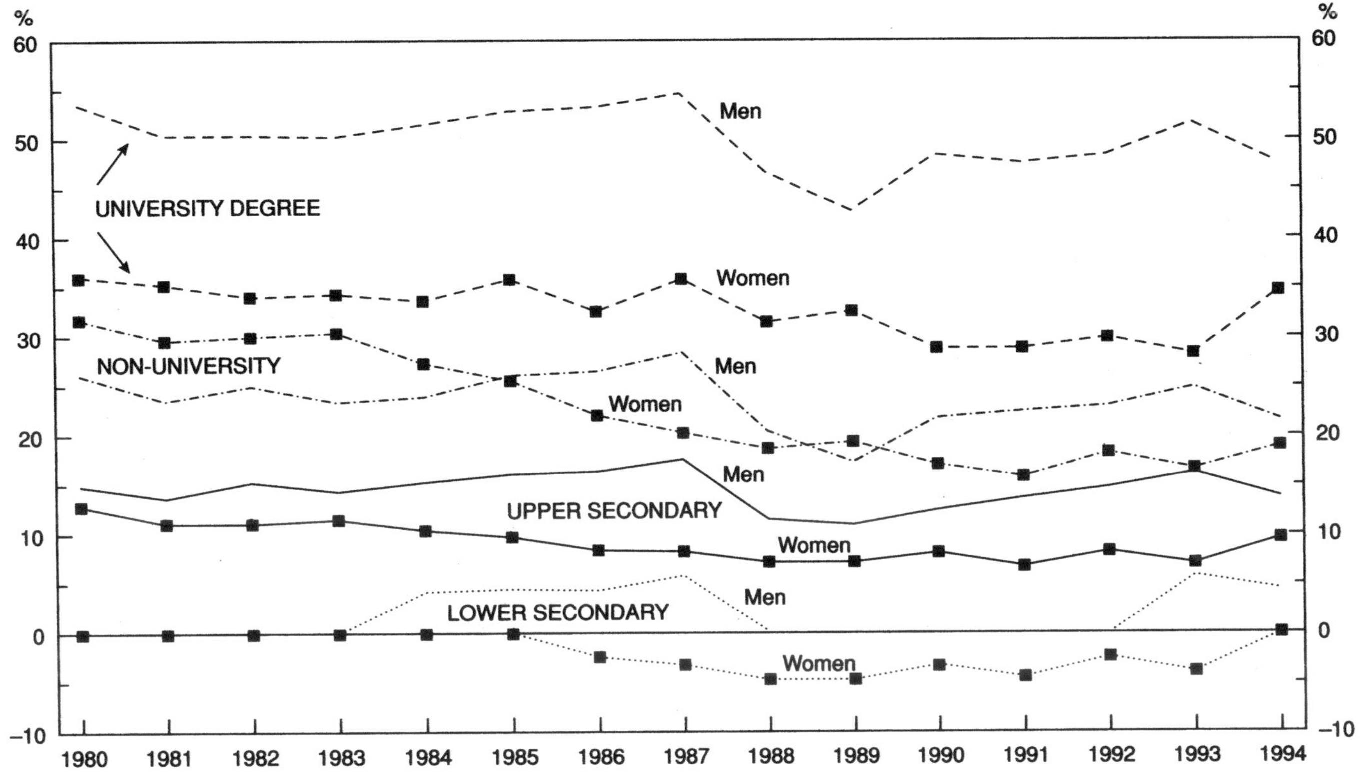

Figure 8.7 Estimated average returns to educational degrees compared to a basic education (= 9 years) only, by gender

vocational school (lower secondary) degree turned into a demerit, and stayed so up to 1993. In other words, females in white-collar positions seemed generally to be better off, at least monetarily, if they were satisfied with a basic education instead of investing in a few additional years of vocational education. This, of course, does not rule out the possibility that a lower vocational degree is still preferable because it could lead to a nicer working environment and/or more meaningful working tasks. The situation is slightly better for male white-collar workers: the wage differential between a basic education and a vocational school (lower secondary) degree has been minor or negligible, but still persistently non-negative. The weak rewarding of short vocational educations in the Finnish labor market is a puzzle.

Huge gender differences are also found in the wage effects of total work experience and of seniority (measured as the length of the current employment relationship). Moreover, these gender gaps have increased further in the deep recession in the early 1990s, as can be seen from Figures 8.8 and 8.9. The experience–wage profiles of male and female white-collar industrial workers were very similar in shape in 1980, albeit with a substantially flatter curvature for the female experience–wage profile. For both genders, the maximum point of the experience–wage profile was reached after 31 years in the labor market.

By 1994, the situation had changed dramatically, not least for female white-collar workers. Compared to 1980, the accumulation of work experience was reflected slightly more strongly in male white-collar wages, resulting in a minor shift upwards of the top point of the experience–wage profile.

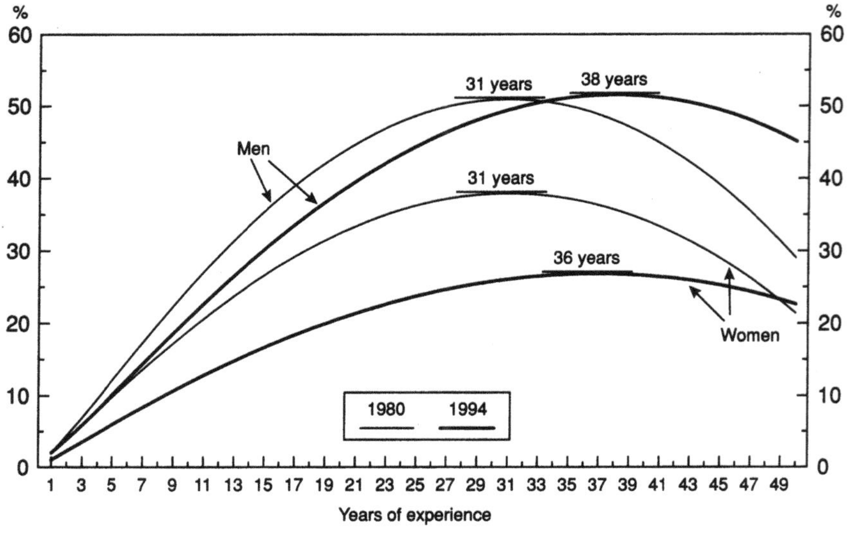

Figure 8.8 Estimated experience–wage profiles for 1980 and 1994, by gender

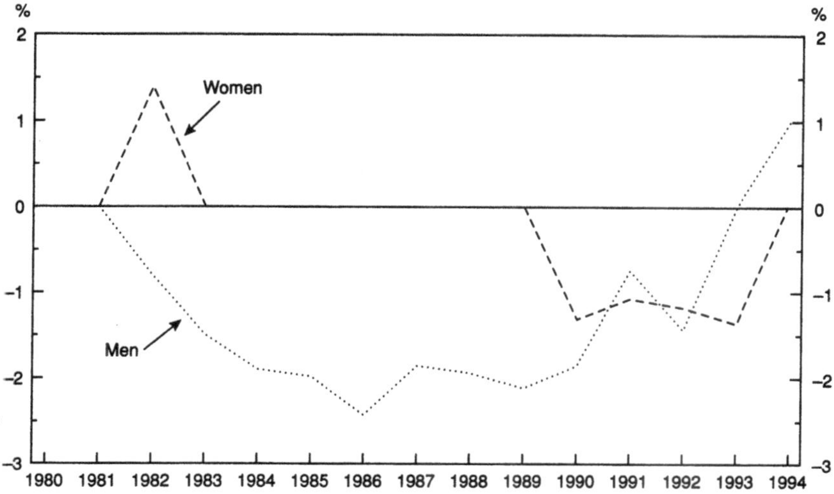

Figure 8.9 Estimated average wage premium (%) of ten years of seniority compared to newly hired (seniority less than one year)

But due to the slower growth rate, it took seven more years in the labor market to reach it as compared to the situation fifteen years earlier. Over the same time period the experience induced growth in female white-collar wages declined substantially, thus further widening the gender gap in the wage effects of work experience.

Broadly speaking, the wage effects of seniority tend to be very small, but nevertheless clearly more favorable for female workers. This finding also supports results obtained in previous studies of wage determination in the Finnish labor market (e.g. Asplund 1993). Again, however, the situation varied markedly over the fifteen-year period investigated. For most of the 1980s the length of the current employment relationship is estimated to have had no significant effect on female white-collar industry wages. Among male white-collar workers, the relative wage position of those having a long employment relationship turned negative in the first half of the 1980s. In other words, when comparing two male white-collar workers differing only in the length of the current employment relationship, the newly hired male was paid significantly more. If seniority is given a traditional human capital interpretation this means that the acquired firm-specific training had become a demerit for male white-collar workers in Finnish industry.

Again a clear break in overall trends can be observed at the beginning of the 1990s, and by 1993 the situation with respect to seniority induced wage effects had been reversed for male and female white-collar workers. Specifically, the impact of seniority on female white-collar wages had turned negative, whereas the negative impact of seniority on male white-collar wages had become insignificant. In 1994 a weak positive wage effect of seniority was observed for the first time among male white-collar workers. Simultaneously the situation for female white-collar workers seems to have turned back to the "traditional" one with no significant effects on wages of the length of the current employment relationship.

WAGE DISCRIMINATION

Following Oaxaca (1973) and Chiplin (1979), a proxy measure of the extent of wage discrimination in the Finnish labor market for white-collar industrial workers over the years 1980–94 can be calculated using the regression results obtained from estimating wage equations separately for male and female white-collar workers.[14] These estimation results have been discussed only in relation to the human capital variables accounted for in the estimated wage models.

In brief, the Oaxaca index for discrimination splits the observed difference in average (log) hourly wages between male and female white-collar workers into two parts: one part that is interpreted as the wage difference originating in differing – observable – background characteristics; and a second part that can be interpreted as the discriminating component of the observed wage differential, or actually the male–female wage differential caused by different remuneration of the broad set of background characteristics accounted for in the estimated gender-specific wage equations.

Specifically, female white-collar wages are compared to male white-collar wages based on the explanatory variables included in the estimated wage models and the wage structure of male white-collar workers (as given by the estimated coefficients of the various explanatory variables). It is also noteworthy that compared with the wage gap measure – the coefficient of the female dummy variable – obtained from the pooled regressions as reported above, this Oaxaca measure of the male–female wage gap has the advantage of not being dependent on the gender composition of the labor force.

The development of the two components, i.e., the background characteristic component *(1 + d)* and the remuneration component *(1 + c)*, for the years 1980–94 for white-collar workers in Finnish industry is illustrated in Table 8.1. The product of the two components gives (with slight discrepancies for rounding off) the average male–female wage ratio observed among white-collar workers in Finnish industry.

The gross male–female wage ratio was extremely high in the beginning of the investigated time period – 1.62 in 1980. By 1994 it had dropped to some 1.45, indicating that male white-collar workers earned on average some 45 percent more than their female colleagues. As is evident from Table 8.1, these fairly large gross differences in male and female white-collar total hourly wages are caused by highly differing background characteristics resulting from

Table 8.1 Components of the male–female gross wage differential among white-collar industrial workers, 1980–94

		Within occupation and working task categories		*Between occupation and working task categories*	
Year	*Observed male–female hourly wage ratio among white-collar workers*	*Component from different wage-relevant background characteristics (1+d)*	*Remuneration component originating in different coefficients (1+c)*	*Component from different wage-relevant background characteristics (1+d)*	*Remuneration component originating in different coefficients (1+c)*
1980	1.617	1.232	1.279	1.150	1.372
1981	1.565	1.195	1.278	1.130	1.352
1982	1.538	1.187	1.262	1.122	1.335
1983	1.538	1.187	1.266	1.115	1.347
1984	1.530	1.186	1.262	1.114	1.343
1985	1.538	1.201	1.255	1.113	1.354
1986	1.530	1.179	1.273	1.106	1.356
1987	1.509	1.165	1.271	1.096	1.352
1988	1.494	1.153	1.271	1.088	1.348
1989	1.488	1.158	1.263	1.087	1.345
1990	1.484	1.155	1.263	1.085	1.345
1991	1.472	1.166	1.245	1.090	1.331
1992	1.476	1.171	1.258	1.097	1.337
1993	1.476	1.154	1.258	1.073	1.353
1994	1.453	1.137	1.260	1.057	1.357

Notes: Due to rounding errors the product of the two components yields only approximately the observed male–female wage ratio. The difference between the calculations for "within" and "between" occupation and working task categories lies in the specification of the estimated gender-specific wage models. In particular, the "within" calculations refer to estimations also controlling for gender differences in occupational and working task structures, while the "between" calculations are based on estimations overlooking such differences across genders.

a distinct labor market segmentation, especially when it comes to the industrial sector, occupational status and working tasks. The wage gap is attributable to an even larger extent, however, to unequal remuneration of these characteristics in the Finnish industrial labor market.

The wage gap due to differing background characteristics across male and female white-collar workers amounted to some 23 percent in 1980, but since then has shown a declining trend with temporary increases in the mid-1980s and during the recession years in the early 1990s. By 1994 the wage gap caused by gender-specific differences in background characteristics had declined to less than 14 percent, out of a gross wage gap of some 45 percent. In contrast, the wage gap due to discrimination, i.e., to different coefficients in the estimated wage models, has remained almost unchanged over the past fifteen years: the amount of discrimination has remained constant in the interval 26 to 28 percent, except in the deep recession year of 1991 when it was slightly lower, or 24.5 percent.

The stability over time in the discrimination component is remarkable. One might argue, however, that this outcome is at least partly due to accounting for occupational segregation effects in the estimation of gender-specific wage equations, i.e., to the inclusion of dummy indicator variables for occupational status and working tasks. By recognizing that male and female white-collar workers differ notably in their distribution across both occupational and working task categories, the analysis is restricted to uncovering the potential presence of wage discrimination within occupational and working task categories.

If, on the other hand, no account is made of gender-specific differences in the distribution across these two job-related characteristics, the changes in the discrimination component over the past fifteen years could be expected to be more pronounced. The results reported in the last two columns of Table 8.1 do not seem to support this hypothesis of a decline over time in the extent of occupational segregation and thereby also in the amount of wage discrimination, however. As is to be expected, the amount of discrimination is notably higher when not accounting for occupational segregation, but the variation over time in the discrimination component is still surprisingly small.

When comparing these results with corresponding calculations for the whole Finnish labor market for the year 1987, the overall gross wage gap as well as the background characteristics and discrimination components are remarkably high. According to calculations reported in Asplund, Barth *et al.* (1996), the gross male–female wage ratio in the Finnish labor market was 1.20 in 1987. The background characteristics of the male and female labor force were found to be remarkably equal: the wage gap due to the characteristics component amounted to only 1.6 percent. The discrimination component, on the other hand, was calculated to be close to 20 percent, or clearly higher than in the other Nordic countries.

No doubt there are several reasonable explanations for these differences in results for the Finnish labor market as a whole and for white-collar industrial workers. Apart from the different data sets used and worker categories analyzed, the set of explanatory variables accounted for in the estimated wage models also differs in several important respects. Moreover, the explanatory power of the white-collar wage equations is about double the explanatory power of the whole labor market wage equations. The use of total hourly wages is also of importance (i.e., inclusive of fringe benefits and other bonuses) in the white-collar worker analysis instead of using only normal hourly wages as in the analysis for the whole Finnish labor market.

The overall impression thus is that the amount of wage discrimination among white-collar industrial workers has remained roughly unchanged over the past fifteen years. However, a word of caution is justified in this context. Since the remuneration component is actually a residual, it may reflect not only discriminatory forces but also unobserved productivity differences across genders. This is because the estimated wage models do not account for all factors – observable as well as unobservable – that potentially influence the productivity of men and women. Although the explanatory power of the estimated wage functions is comparatively high (in the interval 0.634 to 0.553 for men and 0.595 to 0.550 for women), a considerable part of the observed gross wage differential between male and female white-collar workers in Finnish industry remains unexplained. Moreover, the explanatory power of the estimated wage functions for male white-collar workers has declined steadily over the investigated time period, indicating the growing importance of wage-related variables overlooked in the present model specifications. But equally important to note is that these unmeasured variables may reflect not only productivity but also discriminatory differences between men and women.

CONCLUDING REMARKS

The purpose of this study was to uncover trends in wage levels, wage dispersion, wage mobility patterns and rates of return to human capital endowments among male and female white-collar workers in Finnish industry for the years 1980–94. Attempts have also been made to measure the extent of wage discrimination in this particular sector of the Finnish economy. The analysis has utilized fifteen broad representative cross-section data sets sampled from the individual level database of the Confederation of Finnish Industry and Employers. The wage concept used throughout the analysis refers to total hourly wages: i.e., to the sum of normal wages and various pay compensations such as fringe benefits.

In 1994 female white-collar workers earned some 69 percent of the average male white-collar wage, compared to 62 percent in 1980. Apart from earning much less than their male colleagues, the female white-collar workers are also characterized by a much more compressed wage structure. The gender gap in wage dispersion did however narrow slightly towards the end of the 1980s, but then remained roughly unchanged in the early 1990s.

The analysis has also revealed a remarkably strong concentration of females in the lower half of the white-collar wage distribution, especially in the lowest wage decile. Moreover, the minor shifts toward a more even distribution of males and females across wage deciles that could be observed in the 1980s seem to have stopped in connection with the recession in the early 1990s. The female white-collar workers situated in the lowest wage deciles also have a relatively high probability of being locked for several years into the lower tail of the wage distribution. Female white-collar workers also tend to have a higher probability of shifting down into lower wage deciles. Moreover, these tendencies seem to have intensified during the recession years in the early 1990s.

The gender wage gap estimated by means of a female dummy variable implies that the male–female difference in white-collar wages in Finnish industry declined from some 26 percent in 1980 to around 20 percent in 1991. By 1994 the gender wage gap had increased to around 21 percent. The same overall trend, with the bottom year of the recession (1991) marking a trend break, is reflected in the gender wage gaps estimated for three occupational status categories and eight industrial sectors.

The overall trend in the estimated average wage effect of an additional year of schooling was fairly similar for male and female white-collar workers in the 1980s, retaining the male–female gap in the return to additional years of schooling at around one percentage point. In the early 1990s, the estimated average return for females dropped to close to 4 percent per annum, whereas the average return for males rose to around 6 percent per annum.

Notable differences between male and female white-collar workers exist also in the returns to educational degrees. Moreover, the estimated returns of female white-collar workers have declined steadily at all educational levels over the past fifteen years. Among male white-collar workers, in contrast, the returns to different educational degrees changed only slightly in the 1980s, and since the turn of the decade have shown a clear upward trend. By 1993 this development had resulted in a situation where the average return for females to a particular educational degree was of approximately the same magnitude as the average return for men to the closest lower educational degree. A minor narrowing of the gender gap in educational returns seems, though, to have occurred in 1994.

Huge gender differences are also found in the wage effects of total work experience and of seniority, measured as the length of the current employment relationship. These gender gaps have widened further in the deep recession in the early 1990s as well.

Thus these findings concerning the wages and reward of human capital endowments of male and female white-collar workers indicate that the deep recession into which Finland plunged at the beginning of the 1990s impaired the relative labor market position of female white-collar workers in Finnish industry. But simultaneously, results for 1994 indicate that the recovery of the Finnish economy is slowly changing the labor market patterns of males and females back to the general course of narrowing gender gaps that prevailed prior to the recession.

Finally, calculations of the extent of gender wage discrimination among white-collar workers in Finnish industry using the Oaxaca index point to negligible changes over the past fifteen years. In other words, the decline in the gross male–female wage ratio is entirely attributable to a narrowing of the wage gap arising from differing background characteristics of the male and female white-collar personnel in Finnish industry.

ACKNOWLEDGMENT

I want to thank my commentator at the Arne Ryde symposium, Per-Anders Edin, for his many constructive suggestions. Any remaining errors and omissions are, of course, mine.

NOTES

1 Between 1991 and 1993, over 400,000 jobs (over 130,000 industry jobs) were lost, resulting in unemployment rates of 20 per cent and more.

2 The TT database is representative of the manufacturing sector only, of which it covers some 75 per cent. The database includes just a minor part of firms engaged in construction and private services.

3 The samples are restricted to white-collar workers with full-time employment. The exclusion of part-time workers, however, is not likely to bias to any notable extent the male–female results to be presented because of the small share of part-time workers in private sector employment (Asplund, Barth *et al.* 1996) and, especially, in private sector manufacturing (around 1 per cent in total, 2.1 per cent for women and 0.5 per cent for men according to the 1987 Labour Force Survey).

4 Most of the improvement in the female white-collar wage distribution relative to the male white-collar wage distribution occurred between 1980 and 1982 (from the fifth to the eighth percentile) and between 1986 and 1990 (from the ninth to the twelfth percentile).

5 Dummy variable taking the value of 1 if over 50 per cent of the white-collar personnel are females.

6 Dummy variables were used for "entrants" (newcomers in the firms covered by the TT database) and "leavers" (individuals no longer employed in a TT member firm in the next year).

7 Variable definitions and estimation results as well as other results left out from the text are available from the author upon request.

8 These changes over time are statistically significant at the 1 percent level according to a simple t-test. Unless otherwise indicated, this holds also for all other changes over time discussed in the text.

9 The drop in the gender wage gap in chemical industries after 1993 is statistically insignificant.

10 Existing empirical evidence for Finland points to clearly lower returns to human capital of females employed in the private sector as compared both to those of their male counterparts and to those of their female colleagues in the public sector (Asplund 1993).

11 Unless otherwise indicated, the gender differences in the estimated wage effects of the various explanatory variables included in the estimated wage equations are statistically significant according to a simple t-test.

12 The four educational degrees distinguished are: lower secondary education (= less than three years in a vocational education institution, giving a total of 10–11 years of schooling); upper secondary education (= about three years in a vocational education institution or matriculation, giving a total of 12 years of schooling); short non-university degrees (giving a total of about 13–14 years of schooling); university degrees (BA and MA levels and higher, giving a total of at least 15 years of education).

13 The only exceptions are short non-university degrees in the first half of the 1980s and in the late 1980s, and lower secondary degrees in the early 1980s.

14 For details and discussion of this particular measure of the amount of wage discrimination, see e.g. Asplund, Barth *et al.* (1996).

REFERENCES

Asplund, R. (1993) *Essays on Human Capital and Earnings in Finland*, Helsinki: ETLA The Research Institute of the Finnish Economy, Series A18.

—— (1994) *Wage Differentials, Wage Mobility and Skills in Finnish Industry*, Helsinki: ETLA The Research Institute of the Finnish Economy, Discussion Papers No. 525.

Asplund, R., Barth, E., Smith, N. and Wadensjö, E. (1996) "The male–female wage gap in the Nordic countries," in E. Wadensjö (ed.) *The Nordic Labour Markets in the 1990s*, Part I, Amsterdam: North-Holland.

Asplund, R. and Bingley, P. (1996) *Wage Mobility in Finnish Manufacturing 1980–1994*, Helsinki: ETLA The Research Institute of the Finnish Economy.

Asplund, R., Bingley P. and Westergård-Nielsen, N. (1996) "Wage mobility in Denmark and Finland. A comparative study for the years 1980–1994," in *International Comparisons of Wages*, Paris: DARES & INSEE, seminar report.

Chiplin, B. (1979) "An evaluation of sex discrimination: some problems and a suggested reorientation," in C.B. Lloyd, E.S. Andrews and C.L. Gilroy (eds), *Women in the Labour Market*, New York: Columbia University Press.

Edin, P-A. and Holmlund, B. (1992) *The Swedish Wage Structure: The Rise and Fall of Solidarity Policy?*, Uppsala: Uppsala University, Department of Economics, Working Paper 1992: 13.

Oaxaca, R. (1973) "Male–female wage differentials in urban labour markets," *International Economic Review* 14: 693–709.

Polachek, S.W. and Siebert, W.S. (1993) *The Economics of Earnings*, Cambridge: Cambridge University Press.

Westergård-Nielsen, N. (1996) "Wage differentials in the Nordic countries," in E. Wadensjö (ed.) *The Nordic Labour Markets in the 1990s*, Part I, Amsterdam: North-Holland.

9

FRINGE BENEFITS AND GENDER GAPS: THE FINNISH CASE

Lena Granqvist

INTRODUCTION

Economists generally measure an employee's compensation by money wages. But money wages alone may be an inadequate measure of labor compensation in, for example, studies of gender wage differentials as they omit fringe benefits. Ignoring fringe benefits in the analyses may lead to misjudgments regarding the extent of discrimination. Why are fringe benefits omitted from the earnings equation? They are often left out due to lack of data, or because it is thought that they make up only a small part of total compensation, in which case the analytical results would be unchanged. There are numerous studies of male–female earnings differentials, but only a handful have analyzed the role of fringe benefits in these differences: see, for example, Leibowitz (1983); Ståhlberg (1990); Knudsen (1991); and Currie (1993). My earlier research results (Granqvist 1994) suggest that the sex of the employee is a variable that contributes to explaining the incidence of fringe benefits.

Labor compensation, or total wage, can be divided into money wage and non-wage benefits; the latter can further be divided into earnings-related insurance rights and conventional fringe benefits. Non-pecuniary wage benefits such as working conditions can also be included in the total wage measure. In the literature the definition of fringe benefits is varied, which makes international comparisons difficult, but a clear dividing line can be drawn between the USA and Europe. In the USA the most important fringe benefits are the insurance rights, which constitute a considerable part of the total wage compared to the fringe shares in Europe. This reflects the different roles of the public sector. However, there is also a trend toward more employer responsibility in Europe (see, for example, Rein and Wadensjö 1997).

There are many theories and empirical findings concerning the incidence of fringe benefits in labor compensation. In brief, according to these findings there are differences in fringe benefits between sectors, industries, and occupational and educational groups, differences that are attributed to labor market status, and to money wage levels. Female workers differ from male workers in most of these aspects. The question therefore is whether there remains a "true" gender gap associated with fringe benefits after considering the aspects above.

For example, different methods of payments may reflect differential treatment of men and women by firms. Chauvin and Ash (1994) analyze how the pay gap varies by type of pay: total pay, base pay, and contingent pay. They find that within narrowly defined jobs, most of the unexplained difference in total pay between men and women in the sample was due to gender differences in the portion of pay that was contingent on job performance, which among other things may reflect differential treatment of men and women by the employer. This might also apply to fringe benefits: a firm may use the benefits as a "hidden tool for discrimination." Accordingly, an employer with a "taste for discrimination" has the possibility of showing his favoritism of certain employees, for example males, by using fringe benefits as extra rewards that may not show up in regular wage statistics.

Because fringe benefits are thought to be related to the education and occupational status of the employee, Townsend (1979), for example, has proposed that fringe benefits play a part in maintaining inequality between blue-collar and white-collar workers. This may suggest that fringe benefits are more unequally distributed than money incomes. A related possible factor affecting the level of fringe benefits is the relative job positions of the employees. Employees in leading positions are expected to be more likely to have fringe benefits (Knudsen 1991). Given that male employees are generally more often in leading positions than female employees, an inclusion of fringe benefits in the wage measure would lead to a broadening of the gender wage gap.

An issue that is rarely investigated is how the inclusion of fringe benefits in the earnings equation affects the gender differences in the returns to education. The few available studies show that including fringe benefits in the earnings equation affects the returns to human capital variables only to a small extent (Smeeding 1983). Using Finnish microdata from 1987, Asplund (1993) shows that the estimation results obtained when including fringe benefits do not significantly differ from the estimation results without fringe benefits. However, Fornwall's (1994) results from regressions on Swedish data indicate that "education and educational achievements have a different impact on the fringe benefits than on the salary received."

The aim of this chapter is to analyze the gender wage gap and the changes in men's and women's returns to human capital due to the inclusion of fringe benefits in the earnings equation. The effects of fringe benefits on male–female wage differentials are studied by decompositions of the gender wage gap. Finnish microdata from 1989 will be utilized.[1] The chapter is organized as follows. In the next section the data are discussed. In the following two sections the model is presented and the regression results discussed. Then decompositions of the wage gap are reported. The chapter ends with a summary.

THE DATA

The data set used in this chapter stems from an annual income distribution survey for 1989 compiled by the Central Statistical Office of Finland. The data on fringe benefits are quite detailed; the surveys include a variety of questions about different fringe benefits.[2] In Finland there are tax roll data on the most common fringe benefits, but the taxation values of the fringe benefits are below market values. However, this data set also includes fringe benefits that are tax exempt, and the values are based on the valuations made by the one who receives them.[3] The total value of fringe benefits per individual is calculated from and based upon answers from the survey about certain fringe benefits such as car, meal, housing, insurance, and interest benefits, and a couple of recreation benefits like theater tickets. The estimates are based on questions like: How much did you yourself pay for the benefit? – What is the value of the benefit?

After deleting individuals with missing or zero values on the labor force participation variables, those outside the 16–65 age interval, and those with no money wage, the remaining data set consists of 3,993 to 6,118 individuals depending on the labor force participation criterion used. I use two different subsamples: a sample consisting of employees working at least one month full-time or part-time in their main occupation during the year, and a sample of full-time, full-year employees. The two subsamples reflect employees with different degrees of labor market attachment. Another reason for not excluding the non-full-year employees is the possibility of including women who are out of the labor market for a part of the year due to childbearing and child rearing. The share of full-year workers is 67 percent in this sample. Moreover, according to Kim and Polachek (1994), using two samples and comparing the results may enable us to draw conclusions about the effect of selectivity. The gender distribution of the full-time, full-year employees is 54 percent for males and 46 percent for females. Accordingly, despite the restriction to full-time work, women are well represented, which reflects the fact that part-time work is unusual among Finnish women. For the larger sample, the gender distribution is 49 percent females and 51 percent males. The proportion of employees who worked part-time at least one month during the year is 6.9 percent. The share of females who worked part-time at least one month is 10.4 percent. Six percent of the female employees worked part-time for the whole year.

There is no information about the number of hours worked, so I control for the extent of participation on the labor market during the studied year, measured as months of employment, by dividing the annual labor income by months of employment receiving a monthly wage. More information about the samples used can be found in Table 9.A1 in the Appendix.

Annual, before-tax money wage from the main occupation is the basis of the dependent variables which are employed in the regressions. This type of compensation includes overtime and vacation pay, but I cannot separate them, even though information about the employee working overtime is available. Therefore I include three dummy variables indicating the extent of overtime work during the year in every regression.

A variable measuring total earnings was constructed by adding the total value of fringe benefits to the money wage. The share of full-time, full-year employees with positive total fringe values amounted to 30.3 percent of the sample. The mean of fringe benefits as a share of the money wage was about 5 percent and the maximum 60 percent. About 3 percent of the employees with fringe benefits had shares greater than 20 percent.

An inspection of the sample means of the female and male annual money wages shows that women earned on the average 75 percent of the male earnings. The corresponding figure for the sample means of the female and male total value of fringe benefits is about 50 percent. This indicates that including the fringe benefits in the wage measure may broaden the gender wage gap.

THE MODEL

The total wage includes two parts: money wage, W (monthly or annual), and the total annual value of fringe benefits, F. The total wage is $Y = W+F$. Fringe benefits can be thought of as a certain proportion, k of the money wage, i.e., $F = kW$, and $Y = W+kW = (1+k)W$.

The hypothesis to be tested is whether this proportion k is constant for both females and males. If so, there are no changes in the coefficients of the wage level equation from using an extended wage measure that can be attributed to gender effects. To put it differently, does leaving out fringe benefits from the wage equation lead to bias in the estimated returns to human capital in a gender respect?

To be able to use the model in a Mincer equation context, the logarithm $\ln Y = \ln(1+k)+\ln W$, that is, $y = f+w$, is taken as an alternative expression for the total wage. The term $\ln(1+k) = f$ is the log of the fringe value expressed in the proportional way presented above. Accordingly, the problem with the large proportion of zero fringe earners in the sample is also solved; utilizing f as the dependent variable in a wage equation enables the inclusion of zero values on fringe benefits: for example when $k = 0$, $\ln 1 = 0$.

I assume that w, f, and y are determined by:

$$
\begin{aligned}
w &= X\beta_w + \epsilon_w, \\
f &= X\beta_f + \epsilon_f, \qquad (9.1) \\
y &= X(\beta_w + \beta_f) + (\epsilon_w + \epsilon_f)
\end{aligned}
$$

where X is a vector of independent variables. These equations imply that:

$\beta_y = \beta_w + \beta_f$ and that $\beta_f = \beta_y - \beta_w$.

The error terms are assumed to be normally distributed with non-zero, off-diagonal terms in the variance–covariance matrix. Thus, money wages and fringe benefits are assumed to be related through the disturbance terms for each observation.

Why would fringe benefits and money wages be related to each other in that way? It is not unlikely that some unmeasurable characteristics of a given employee have similar effects on the disturbances of the money wage equation and the fringe share/total wage equation.

Hence, one has to use a GLS estimator to estimate the seemingly unrelated regressions model (SUR): that is, jointly to estimate either w and y or w and f. Estimating two of the equations together gives the coefficients of the third equation. Using this framework makes joint cross-equation tests possible.[4]

The equations are extended Mincer equations containing traditional human capital variables plus job-related characteristics, which are predicted to influence the wage level. There are four dummy variables indicating the number of children under 18 years of age living at home, one dummy indicating at least one month of part-time work during the year, and three dummies indicating the extent of overtime hours during the year. In addition, there are fifteen industry indicators, and a sector dummy for the private sector. A dummy for living in the southern parts of Finland is included: these parts are the most urbanized.

Instead of a continuous schooling variable, I use dummy variables to indicate the highest education level completed by each individual. In order to provide easy translations from the regression results to the text, the dummy coefficient is here interpreted as a rough approximation of the average percentage change in the wage from having completed the educational level compared to the chosen base level of education, though this approximation is very rough for coefficients larger than 0.10.[5]

I had no direct information on work experience. Therefore the variable is constructed as the difference between age and years of schooling minus seven – the latter variable is constructed by translating the educational degrees to years of schooling. However, the potential experience variable may be a poor proxy for the actual experience, especially for women, overestimating the length of the work experience. All the same, the effect of omitting actual labor market experience could be minimized by the inclusion of the number of children living at home, which has been shown to be a good proxy for labor force participation interruptions (Blau and Beller 1988).

The dependent variables are the logarithm of the monthly or yearly wage, depending on the subsample studied. The fringe benefits are alternatively excluded and included in the respective dependent variables. To test for correlation between the disturbances in the money wage equation and the fringe share equation, I use the Lagrange multiplier statistic suggested by Breusch and Pagan (1980).[6] The Breusch–Pagan test of independence was rejected for both samples. However, performing tests using the separate female and male groups led to a rejection of the independence hypothesis for the two male samples, but not for any of the female samples. This indicates that there exist gender-specific (male) unmeasured factors that relate money wages to fringe benefits. This may be an effect of unobserved ability bias that can be different for men and women due to different preferences for fringe benefits (Lazear 1995: 60–61).

EFFECTS OF INCLUDING FRINGE BENEFITS

The results from the regressions using the money wage and the total wage as the dependent variables are shown in Tables 9.1 and 9.2. Because the total wage equation is constructed as a sum of the money wage and fringe share equation as described above, it is possible to derive the fringe share coefficient vector as the difference between the coefficients of the total wage and the money wage equations. For example, in Table 9.1 the coefficient of the female dummy in the fringe share equation is: (–0.179–(–0.173)) = –0.006. The Fs in the total wage columns in Table 9.1 denote that the coefficient of the fringe share equation is significant at the 10 percent level.

The woman dummy coefficients in the wage level regressions without fringe benefits (Tables 9.1 and 9.2) show gender gaps of 17–26 percent. The large difference between the first and the second sample is certainly due to the fact that the employee group is much more heterogeneous in the first sample: men who may be unemployed for a couple of months during the studied year are compared, for example, to female high-income earners who are out of the labor market for some months due to maternity leave. The part-time workers and those with summer jobs also contribute to the heterogeneity of the sample. Asplund (1993) gets coefficients of about 19 percent in similar regressions on Finnish microdata for 1987. Comparison of the woman dummy coefficients in both Table 9.1 and Table 9.2 shows that including fringe benefits seems to broaden the gender gap, ceteris paribus. The returns to different educational levels seem to increase somewhat except for the lowest educational level.

The hypothesis of equal coefficient vectors across equations is tested using an F-statistic analogous to that for the single equation case (Judge *et al.* 1985: 475). The hypothesis of equal coefficient vectors (except for the constants) is rejected for every employee group for both samples at the 5 percent level. The tests of the coefficient groups show that fringe benefits affect the returns to education for males but not for females. On the other hand, fringe benefits do not seem to affect the returns to experience to any greater extent. The relative inter-industry differences are affected by fringe benefits, more so for females than for males.

I also tested equality between separate coefficients across the equations in order to find out which variables generate the differences discussed above.

Italicized coefficients in the total wage columns in Tables 9.1 and 9.2 indicate statistically significant differences between the money wage and the total wage coefficients. The woman dummy coefficient increases in absolute value in both samples. It is obvious that there are gender differences in the returns to education in both samples. For males, every educational level except the lowest one shows a significant increase in the average return beyond the basic level when fringe benefits are included. This is not so for females except in one case: women with an undergraduate university education working full-time, full-year have a significantly higher return to their education when fringe benefits are included. But this is another side of what I call the "positive fringe effect" for females in the female-dominated bank sector (see Granqvist 1996). This educational level is most typical for women working in the banking and insurance industry, where fringe benefits usually take the form of subsidized loans, which are valuable benefits compared to many others.

Nevertheless, the quantitative differences are quite small. In order to get an impression of the values, I calculated the percentage changes between the coefficients using the adequate percentage interpretation of dummy variable coefficients exceeding 0.1: that is, exp(coefficient)–1. The gender wage gap increases by 3.7 percent in the first sample and by 2.6 percent in the second sample. The calculations also show that for males in the first sample the average returns to the four highest educational levels increase within a range of 4.4–6.9 percent (on average 5.4 percent) due to fringe benefits. For males in the second sample the range is 4.0–6.5 percent (on average 5.6 percent). The only significant change for women is in the second sample and amounts to about 2.4 percent.

In contrast, the coefficients on the experience variables do not show any significant changes due to fringe benefits. Somewhat surprisingly, women working full-time with at least four children seem to be compensated by fringe benefits – the "punishment" of several children gets smaller. Another thing to notice from a gender point of view is that the number of children under 18 years old who live at home in most cases has a strong negative effect for female employees: on the other hand, only for male employees with at least four children does fatherhood have a negative impact on earnings (see Table 9.1). Although part-time work has a significantly negative impact on the female wage level, an inclusion of fringe benefits does not change the coefficients in a significant way.

There seem to be a couple of industries which have high levels of fringe benefits compared to the metal industry for both males and females: the wholesale and retail industry, the finance and insurance industry, the professional and scientific services industry, and other services. For the first sample, the negative wage differential for males in the professional and scientific services industry and in other services compared to males in the metal industry decreases due to fringe benefits. This is also the case for the males in the professional services industry in the second sample. In this sample both females and males working in the finance and insurance industry increase their positive wage differentials compared to the reference industry. The increase is about 32 percent for both. In order to control for segregation effects, I replaced the industry dummies with a variable for the female share in every industry. However, this variable was insignificant in both samples and accordingly did not affect the female dummy variable.

The sector dummies in Table 9.1 unexpectedly show negative signs: there are penalties from working in the private rather than the public sector. But this may be due to the fact that this sample includes employees with short periods of employment and temporary jobs. Labor contracts regulated by the public sector trade unions may in some cases be more favorable for this group of employees than the conditions of the private sector. But the negative sign could also be due to an omitted interaction effect between sector and occupational groups. Asplund (1993) shows that differences in human capital returns tend to be larger between occupational categories than between sectors. However, the negative sign does not show up in the fringe benefit share equation: for example, males in the private sector have a significantly larger fringe benefit share than males in the public sector (–0.226–(–0.237))=0.011. For the second sample the signs are the expected ones. Fringe benefits significantly increase the wage differentials between those in the private sector and women working in the public sector. Fringe benefits also seem to increase the wage inequalities between employees living in the urbanized southern parts of Finland and those living outside this area.

Hence, the conclusion is that including fringe benefits in the traditional extended earnings equation significantly increases the gender wage gap in both samples. Moreover, for males the returns to the four highest educational levels beyond the reference level increase. The hypothesis of fringe benefits being a constant proportion of the money wage is thus rejected for men. Excluding fringe benefits from the wage measure underestimates the returns to education for males but not for females. This means that gender differences in the returns to human capital estimated from the money wage equations do not reveal the true gender differences. However the bias of not using an extended wage measure is quite small.

DECOMPOSITIONS OF THE WAGE GAP

In order to analyze the wage gap between men and women when fringe benefits are excluded and included respectively, I use the conventional Oaxaca–Blinder decomposition method (Oaxaca 1973; Blinder 1973). Utilizing the results from the separate regressions for the female and male employee groups, the wage gap can be decomposed into differences in the averages of the independent variables, i.e., endowments of human capital and other characteristics, and into differences in average returns to human capital

Table 9.1 SUR regressions for 1989 using different wage measures. Employees aged 16 to 65 working at least one month in their main occupation[a]

	All		*Female*		*Male*	
	Money wage	*Total wage*	*Money wage*	*Total wage*	*Money wage*	*Total wage*
Intercept	8.687**	8.687**	8.535**	8.543**	8.658**	8.644**F
	(0.086)	(0.087)	(0.151)	(0.151)	(0.123)	(0.123)
Woman dummy	–0.173**	*–0.179***F				
	(0.032)	(0.032)				
Educational level dummies:						
Basic ed.	0	0	0	0	0	0
Lower voc. ed.	0.088*	0.087*	0.076	0.074	0.101+	0.101+
	(0.037)	(0.037)	(0.048)	(0.048)	(0.056)	(0.056)
Upper voc. ed.	0.240**	*0.249***F	0.224**	0.224**	0.249**	*0.264***F
	(0.042)	(0.042)	(0.052)	(0.052)	(0.065)	(0.066)
Short non-univ. ed.	0.525**	*0.538***F	0.465**	0.468**	0.588**	*0.611***F
	(0.067)	(0.067)	(0.083)	(0.083)	(0.104)	(0.105)
Undergrad. ed.	0.577**	*0.590***F	0.583**	0.589**	0.569**	*0.591***F
	(0.097)	(0.097)	(0.106)	(0.107)	(0.181)	(0.182)
Graduate ed.	0.717**	*0.727***F	0.805**	0.801**	0.647**	*0.668***F
	(0.068)	(0.068)	(0.091)	(0.091)	(0.101)	(0.102)
Work exper.	0.039**	0.039**	0.032**	0.032**F	0.047**	0.047**F
	(0.004)	(0.004)	(0.005)	(0.005)	(0.007)	(0.007)
$(Exp^2)/1{,}000$	–0.831**	–0.836**	–0.665**	–0.660**	–1.025**	–1.037**F
	(0.108)	(0.108)	(0.137)	(0.137)	(0.166)	(0.167)
Child dummies						
1 child	–0.053	–0.055	–0.067	–0.072 F	–0.035	–0.037
	(0.036)	(0.036)	(0.046)	(0.046)	(0.056)	(0.056)
2 children	–0.098*	–0.099*	–0.170**	–0.172**	–0.024	–0.024
	(0.040)	(0.040)	(0.051)	(0.051)	(0.060)	(0.060)
3 children	–0.189**	–0.193**	–0.325**	–0.330**	–0.067	–0.071
	(0.061)	(0.061)	(0.078)	(0.078)	(0.092)	(0.091)
At least 4 children	–0.273**	–0.274**	–0.078	–0.079	–0.412**	–0.417**
	(0.106)	(0.107)	(0.139)	(0.139)	(0.159)	(0.160)
Part–time dummy	–0.354**	0.353**	–0.423**	–0.421**	–0.158	–0.158
	(0.056)	(0.057)	(0.058)	(0.058)	(0.118)	(0.118)
Overtime dummies						
Overtime1 (< 50 h/y)	0.160**	*0.157***F	0.130**	0.129**	0.176**	*0.171***F
	(0.038)	(0.038)	(0.048)	(0.048)	(0.059)	(0.059)
Overtime2 (50–99 h/y)	0.232**	0.231**	0.243**	0.240**	0.219**	0.221**
	(0.058)	(0.058)	(0.081)	(0.081)	(0.083)	(0.083)
Overtime3 (> 100 h/y)	0.261**	0.259**	0.203*	0.201*	0.288**	0.286**
	(0.057)	(0.057)	(0.086)	(0.087)	(0.079)	(0.079)
Industry dummies						
Food, drink, tobacco	–0.033	–0.029	–0.013	–0.007	–0.034	–0.031
	(0.098)	(0.098)	(0.159)	(0.160)	(0.143)	(0.143)
Mining, petroleum, chemical	0.004	0.019 F	–0.060	–0.056	0.036	0.055 F
	(0.120)	(0.120)	(0.206)	(0.207)	(0.157)	(0.158)
Metal, mechanical, shipbuilding	0	0	0	0	0	0
Textiles	–0.176	–0.171	–0.194	–0.187	0.092	0.088
	(0.118)	(0.119)	(0.159)	(0.159)	(0.288)	(0.289)

Table 9.1 Continued

	All		*Female*		*Male*	
	Money wage	*Total wage*	*Money wage*	*Total wage*	*Money wage*	*Total wage*
Timber, furniture	–0.183+	0.182+	–0.030	–0.027	–0.220+	–0.219+
	(0.106)	(0.106)	(0.228)	(0.229)	(0.129)	(0.130)
Paper, printing, publishing	0.112	0.110	0.154	0.158	0.103	0.099
	(0.089)	(0.089)	(0.163)	(0.163)	(0.115)	(0.115)
Other manufacturing	–0.032	–0.034	–0.029	–0.032	–0.028	–0.030
	(0.107)	(0.107)	(0.199)	(0.200)	(0.135)	(0.135)
Construction	–0.046	–0.044	–0.149	–0.141	–0.044	–0.040
	(0.074)	(0.074)	(0.186)	(0.186)	(0.088)	(0.089)
Gas, electricity, water	0.068	0.065	0.148	0.143	0.041	0.040
	(0.134)	(0.134)	(0.293)	(0.294)	(0.163)	(0.163)
Transport, communication	–0.046	–0.047	–0.051	–0.048	–0.041	–0.043
	(0.078)	(0.079)	(0.152)	(0.152)	(0.099)	(0.099)
Wholesale, retail	–0.131+	–0.115 F	–0.116	–0.110	–0.126	–0.099 F
	(0.071)	(0.072)	(0.136)	(0.136)	(0.096)	(0.096)
Finance, insurance, real estate	0.020	0.068 F	0.065	0.121 F	0.008	0.041 F
	(0.089)	(0.089)	(0.144)	(0.144)	(0.149)	(0.149)
Professional and scientific services, education	–0.176*	*–0.162** F	–0.126	–0.110 F	–0.216+	*–0.203*+F
	(0.079)	(0.079)	(0.141)	(0.141)	(0.113)	(0.113)
Other services	–0.252**	*–0.244***F	–0.194	–0.185	–0.287**	*–0.278*** F
	(0.071)	(0.071)	(0.133)	(0.136)	(0.102)	(0.102)
Agriculture, forestry, fishing	–1.569**	–1.564**F	–1.354**	*–1.340***F	–1.665**	–1.662**
	(0.082)	(0.082)	(0.155)	(0.155)	(0.105)	(0.106)
Private sector dummy	–0.175**	*–0.169***F	–0.135**	–0.133**	–0.237**	*–0.226***F
	(0.041)	(0.041)	(0.048)	(0.048)	(0.069)	(0.070)
South dummy	0.101**	*0.106***F	0.098**	*0.102***F	0.104*	*0.110**F
	(0.029)	(0.029)	(0.036)	(0.036)	(0.045)	(0.046)
# of observations	6,118	6,118	2,978	2,978	3,140	3,140
"R^2"	"0.1825"	"0.1837"	"0.1721"	"0.1726"	"0.1893"	"0.1910"

[a] Dependent variable ln (monthly wage). Coefficients for the fringe share equation ln(1+k) calculated as the difference ($\hat{\beta}_{(total\ wage)} - \hat{\beta}_{(money\ wage)}$). Standard errors in parentheses.
[b] + significant at 10% level; * significant at 5% level; ** significant at 1% level.
[c] Italicized coefficients in the total wage equations significantly differ from the corresponding coefficients in the money wage equation according to the computed F-tests. The hypothesis of equal coefficients is rejected at the 5% level and below. Coefficients followed by an F indicate a significant coefficient of the fringe share equation. R^2 is not well defined in the GLS context, so the values are reported in quotation marks.

and other characteristics. The differences in the returns, which include the constant term, are often taken as a measure of discrimination.

In Tables 9.3 and 9.4 I present the results from the decompositions using the male–female regression results found in Tables 9.1 and 9.2. First I comment on the full-year, full-time sample (Table 9.4): the decompositions are done for the male–female differential in the average log of annual earnings. The total log-differences of 0.274 (fringe benefits excluded) and 0.283 (fringe benefits included) correspond to male–female wage ratios of 1.31 and 1.32 respectively.

Table 9.2 SUR regressions for 1989 using different wage measures. Full-year, full-time employees aged 16 to 64[a]

	All		*Female*		*Male*	
	Money wage	*Total wage*	*Money wage*	*Total wage*	*Money wage*	*Total wage*
Intercept	10.896**	10.894**	10.672**	10.672**	10.859**	10.849**F
	(0.032)	(0.032)	(0.050)	(0.051)	(0.045)	(0.046)
Woman dummy	–0.255**	–0.261**F				
	(0.010)	(0.010)				
Education level dummies						
Basic ed.	0	0	0	0	0	0
Lower voc. ed.	0.091**	0.090**	0.091**	0.090**	0.094**	0.094**
	(0.012)	(0.012)	(0.016)	(0.016)	(0.018)	(0.018)
Upper voc. ed.	0.261**	0.270**F	0.211**	0.212**	0.288**	0.304**F
	(0.014)	(0.014)	(0.018)	(0.019)	(0.021)	(0.022)
Short non-univ. ed.	0.475**	0.489**F	0.429**	0.434**F	0.517**	0.540**F
	(0.021)	(0.021)	(0.026)	(0.027)	(0.031)	(0.031)
Undergrad. ed.	0.576**	0.592**F	0.547**	0.557**F	0.598**	0.625**F
	(0.029)	(0.029)	(0.033)	(0.033)	(0.051)	(0.052)
Graduate ed.	0.768**	0.780**F	0.775**	0.776**	0.766**	0.787**F
	(0.021)	(0.021)	(0.029)	(0.029)	(0.030)	(0.030)
Work experience	0.038**	0.038**	0.036**	0.036**	0.039**	0.040**
	(0.002)	(0.002)	(0.002)	(0.002)	(0.003)	(0.003)
(Work exp^2)/1,000	–0.603**	–0.606**	–0.606**	–0.606**	–0.621**	–0.626**
	(0.043)	(0.043)	(0.054)	(0.054)	(0.064)	(0.065)
Child dummies						
1 child	0.007	0.008	–0.033*	–0.036*	0.034+	0.035+
	(0.012)	(0.012)	(0.016)	(0.016)	(0.018)	(0.018)
2 children	–0.008	–0.008	–0.053**	–0.053**	0.021	0.021
	(0.013)	(0.013)	(0.017)	(0.017)	(0.018)	(0.019)
3 children	–0.005	–0.006	–0.126**	–0.129**	0.065*	0.065
	(0.020)	(0.020)	(0.029)	(0.029)	(0.028)	(0.028)
At least 4 children	–0.069+	–0.069+	–0.218**	–0.206**F	0.007	–0.001
	(0.038)	(0.039)	(0.057)	(0.058)	(0.051)	(0.052)
Overtime dummies						
Overtime1	0.023+	0.020+F	0.026+	0.025+	0.022	0.020
(< 50 h/y)	(0.012)	(0.012)	(0.015)	(0.015)	(0.017)	(0.018)
Overtime2	0.060**	0.060**	0.122**	0.121**	0.025	0.028
(50–99 h/y)	(0.017)	(0.017)	(0.023)	(0.023)	(0.024)	(0.024)
Overtime3	0.138**	0.134**F	0.145**	0.144**	0.133**	0.128**F
(> 100 h/y)	(0.016)	(0.017)	(0.024)	(0.024)	(0.022)	(0.023)
Industry dummies:						
Food, drink,	0.028	0.032	0.037	0.041	0.042	0.047
tobacco	(0.031)	(0.031)	(0.049)	(0.050)	(0.044)	(0.045)
Mining, petroleum,	0.048	0.067+ F	0.045	0.053	0.052	0.076 F
chemical	(0.037)	(0.038)	(0.064)	(0.064)	(0.048)	(0.049)
Metal, mechanical, shipbuilding	0	0	0	0	0	0
Textiles	–0.144**	–0.143**	–0.125*	–0.124*	–0.088	–0.088
	(0.038)	(0.039)	(0.049)	(0.049)	(0.093)	(0.094)
Timber, furniture	–0.075*	–0.076*	–0.014	–0.010	–0.084*	–0.086*
	(0.033)	(0.033)	(0.068)	(0.069)	(0.040)	(0.040)
Paper, printing	0.147**	0.144**	0.160**	0.164**	0.147**	0.142**
publishing	(0.026)	(0.027)	(0.049)	(0.049)	(0.033)	(0.034)

Table 9.2 Continued

	All		*Female*		*Male*	
	Money wage	*Total wage*	*Money wage*	*Total wage*	*Money wage*	*Total wage*
Other manufacturing	0.032	0.028	0.063	0.064	0.021	0.014
	(0.033)	(0.033)	(0.061)	(0.062)	(0.041)	(0.042)
Construction	–0.025	–0.025	0.000	0.012 F	–0.031	–0.032
	(0.023)	(0.024)	(0.055)	(0.056)	(0.027)	(0.028)
Gas, electricity, water	0.077+	0.073+	–0.086	–0.086	0.094+	0.090+
	(0.042)	(0.042)	(0.101)	(0.102)	(0.049)	(0.050)
Transport, communication	0.035	0.032	0.101*	0.106*	0.016	0.012
	(0.023)	(0.024)	(0.046)	(0.047)	(0.029)	(0.029)
Wholesale, retail	–0.025	–0.013 F	–0.030	–0.025	–0.004	0.016 F
	(0.022)	(0.022)	(0.041)	(0.041)	(0.029)	(0.029)
Finance, insurance, real estate	0.119**	*0.158***F	0.161**	*0.209***F	0.096*	*0.124***F
	(0.027)	(0.028)	(0.043)	(0.043)	(0.043)	(0.044)
Professional and scientific services, education	–0.016	–0.005 F	0.065	0.079+ F	–0.082*	*–0.074** F
	(0.024)	(0.025)	(0.042)	(0.043)	(0.034)	(0.034)
Other services	–0.036	–0.030 F	0.009	0.018 F	–0.058+	–0.055+
	(0.022)	(0.022)	(0.039)	(0.040)	(0.032)	(0.032)
Agriculture, forestry, fishing	–0.164**	–0.159**	–0.103+	–0.090*F	–0.194**	–0.192**
	(0.031)	(0.032)	(0.061)	(0.060)	(0.039)	(0.039)
Private sector dummy	0.036*	*0.045***F	0.042*	*0.049***F	0.030	0.042+ F
	(0.014)	(0.014)	(0.016)	(0.016)	(0.022)	(0.022)
South dummy	0.044**	*0.049***F	0.036*	*0.039***F	0.048**	*0.054***F
	(0.010)	(0.010)	(0.012)	(0.012)	(0.014)	(0.014)
# of observations	3,993	3,996	1,846	1,846	2,147	2,147
"R^2"	"0.4960"	"0.4996"	"0.4803"	"0.4845"	"0.4201"	"0.4271"

[a] Dependent variable ln(yearly wage). Coefficients for the fringe share equation ln(1+k) calculated as the difference ($\hat{\beta}_{(total\ wage)} - \hat{\beta}_{(money\ wage)}$). Standard errors in parentheses.
[b] + significant at 10% level; * significant at 5% level; ** significant at 1% level
[c] Italicized coefficients in the total wage equations significantly differ from the corresponding coefficients in the money wage equation according to the computed F-tests. The hypothesis of equal coefficients is rejected at the 5% level and below. Coefficients followed by an F indicate a significant coefficient of the fringe share equation. R^2 is not well defined in the GLS context, so the values are reported in quotation marks.

Since we are analyzing the male–female differential, a negative sign indicates that the factor, or the sum of the factors, is working to decrease the differential. A positive sign, on the other hand, indicates an increase in the differential.

The results show that a large part of the differences in average wages between men and women can be explained by differences in the average returns. Different endowments of personal and job characteristics explain only 7 percent of the gender wage differential. This seems to be typical for the Finnish wage gap. A comparison of the Scandinavian gender wage gaps (Asplund *et al.* 1996) shows that for Finland the largest part of the gender wage gap stems from gender differences in the coefficients, which is not the case for the other three Scandinavian countries.

The positive contributions from differences in the returns to the traditional human capital variables indicate that they are working to broaden the wage gap. For women there are penalties for having children, which also increase the gender differential. The only equalizing factors that work in favor of women are the differences in the sum of the coefficients for the industry, sector and the southern region dummies.

The results from the decomposition do not change much from using female weights – this leads only to a small reallocation between the share of the wage differential ascribed to differences in coefficients as opposed to that ascribed to differences in average characteristics.

What are the effects of including fringe benefits? The only marked change from incorporating fringe benefits is a 10 percentage points increase of the relative share of the total wage differential that can be attributed to differences in the returns to human capital. The change in the returns to education and experience from including fringe benefits serves to widen the gender earnings differential. This also indicates that an exclusion of fringe benefits leads to bias in the estimate of the average return to human capital: that is, the fringe benefits are correlated with the human capital variables. The other gender differences in coefficients remain the same after incorporating fringe benefits.

In the second sample, which includes employees working at least one month in their main occupation, the gender earnings differential is much smaller than the one from the regressions based on the full-year, full-time sample (compare Tables 9.1 and 9.2). This is due to the fact that the employee group is much more heterogeneous, which was discussed above. The decomposition (Table 9.3) shows that the difference in average endowments of the characteristics are in the women's favor, except for overtime. However, there are differences in the returns to human capital in this sample, too. In particular the coefficients for the experience variables clearly work to widen the wage gap, but this is probably partly due to the use of potential instead of actual experience: that is, to an underestimation of the female returns to experience. Differences in the returns to working overtime seem to broaden the wage gap, which is not the case for the full-year, full-time sample. The coefficients for the part-time variable contribute in the expected way: they broaden the wage gap, as do the coefficients for having children. However, the relative share of the wage differential due to the difference in the coefficients for the part-time dummy is smaller when using female weights (6.9 instead of 20 percent when fringe benefits are excluded, and 5.7 instead of 16.6 percent when fringe benefits are included).

It should be noted that the total contribution due to gender differences in the average characteristics is negative in the decompositions for this sample, and thus narrows the wage gap. The inclusion of fringe benefits does not seem to affect the contributions from differences in the returns to any greater extent, at least not in any definite direction. This can partly be due to the fact that both the share of employees with positive fringe earnings and the mean fringe values are slightly lower in this sample. Although the decompositions, for both samples, show that the gender differences in the returns to the human capital variables account for an evidently larger part of the total wage differential than do the differences in the average characteristics, I cannot conclude that the former part can be entirely attributed to discrimination. Most likely there are also effects of omitted variables, i.e. the estimated models may not have fully controlled for productivity factors.

Table 9.3 Decomposition of differentials in average monthly wages of male and female employees working at least one month in their main occupation using male and female weights respectively (percent of the total differential in parentheses)

Differences in the coefficients for the:	*Fringe benefits excluded*	*Fringe benefits included*	*Fringe benefits excluded*	*Fringe benefits included*
	Male weights	*Male weights*	*Female weights*	*Female weights*
Constant terms	0.088	0.097	0.088	0.097
	(53.1%)	(56.0%)	(53.1%)	(56.0%)
Education level dummies	0.026	0.025	0.024	0.022
	(15.8%)	(14.4%)	(14.6%)	(12.7%)
Experience + experience squared	0.105	0.106	0.107	0.107
	(63.7%)	(61.4%)	(64.9%)	(61.9%)
Children dummies	0.042	0.047	0.045	0.048
	(25.7%)	(27.3%)	(27.0%)	(28.1%)
Part-time dummies	0.033	0.029	0.011	0.010
	(20.0%)	(16.6%)	(6.9%)	(5.7%)
Overtime dummies	0.013	0.011	0.018	0.016
	(8.1%)	(6.4%)	(11.2%)	(9.1%)
Industry, sector, south dummies	–0.121	–0.117	–0.126	–0.118
	(–73.2%)	(–68.0%)	(–76.2%)	(–68.3%)
Total due to coefficients, constant term excluded	0.100	0.100	0.080	0.085
	(60.2%)	(58.0%)	(48.4%)	(49.2%)
Total due to coefficients	0.188	0.197	0.168	0.182
	(113.3%)	(113.9%)	(101.2%)	(105.2%)
Differences in average characteristics; the endowment of:				
Education degrees	–0.012	–0.012	–0.010	–0.009
	(–7.1%)	(–7.1%)	(–6.0%)	(–5.4%)
Experience	–0.001	–0.002	–0.002	–0.003
	(–0.3%)	(–1.2%)	(–1.5%)	(–1.6%)
Children	–0.001	–0.001	–0.003	–0.002
	(–0.5%)	(–0.5%)	(–1.9%)	(–1.2%)
Part-time work	–0.008	0.010	0.030	0.029
	(–5.1%)	(5.9%)	(18.2%)	(16.8%)
Overtime work	0.025	0.024	0.020	0.019
	(15.4%)	(13.9%)	(12.3%)	(11.3%)
Industry, sector, south	–0.043	–0.043	–0.038	–0.043
	(–25.7%)	(–25.1%)	(–22.7%)	(–24.9%)
Total due to differences in average characteristics	–0.022	–0.024	–0.002	–0.009
	(–13.3%)	(–14.0%)	(–1.5%)	(–5.2%)
Total difference	0.166	0.173	0.166	0.173

Table 9.4 Decomposition of differentials in average annual wages of male and female full-year, full-time-employees using male and female weights respectively (percent of the total differential in parentheses)

Differences in the coefficients for the:	*Fringe benefits excluded Male weights*	*Fringe benefits included Male weights*	*Fringe benefits excluded Female weights*	*Fringe benefits included Female weights*
Constant terms	0.190 (69.3%)	0.179 (63.3%)	0.190 (69.3%)	0.179 (63.3%)
Education level dummies	0.024 (9.0%)	0.031 (10.9%)	0.021 (7.5%)	0.026 (9.4%)
Experience + experience squared	0.048 (17.4%)	0.070 (24.7%)	0.044 (16.1%)	0.066 (23.3%)
Children dummies	0.048 (17.5%)	0.046 (16.4%)	0.056 (20.4%)	0.054 (19.0%)
Overtime dummies	–0.01 (–3.6%)	–0.009 (–3.2%)	–0.013 (–4.9%)	–0.012 (–4.4%)
Industry, sector, south dummies	–0.047 (–17.1%)	–0.052 (–18.5%)	–0.03 (–10.9%)	–0.036 (–12.7%)
Total due to coefficients, constant term excluded	0.063 (23.2%)	0.086 (30.3%)	0.077 (28.2%)	0.098 (34.6%)
Total due to coefficients	0.253 (92.3%)	0.265 (93.6%)	0.267 (97.4%)	0.277 (97.9%)
Differences in average characteristics				
Education degrees	0.001 (0.5%)	0.001 (0.3%)	0.005 (2.0%)	0.005 (1.8%)
Experience	–0.012 (–4.5%)	–0.013 (–4.7%)	–0.009 (–3.2%)	–0.009 (–3.3%)
Children	0.002 (0.6%)	0.001 (0.5%)	–0.006 (–2.3%)	–0.006 (–2.1%)
Overtime work	0.007 (2.7%)	0.007 (2.5%)	0.011 (3.9%)	0.010 (3.7%)
Industry, sector, south	0.022 (8.2%)	0.022 (7.7%)	0.006 (2.1%)	0.005 (1.9%)
Total due to differences in average characteristics	0.021 (7.5%)	0.018 (6.4%)	0.007 (2.5%)	0.006 (2.1%)
Total difference	0.274	0.283	0.274	0.283

SUMMARY

The goal of this chapter was to analyze the gender wage gap and the changes in men's and women's returns to human capital due to the inclusion of fringe benefits in the earnings equation. The conclusion is, first, that including fringe benefits in the traditional extended earnings equation significantly increases the gender wage gap in both samples. Second, for males the returns to education at the four highest levels, beyond the reference level, increase when fringe benefits are included. The hypothesis that fringe benefits are a constant proportion of the money wage is thus rejected for men. Excluding fringe benefits from the wage measure underestimates the returns to education for males but not for females, which means that gender differences in the returns to human capital estimated from the money wage equations do not reveal the true gender differences. The bias from not using an extended wage measure is quite small, however. On average, the male returns to different levels of education increase by about 5.5 percent. The gender wage gap increases by 3–4 percent due to fringe benefits.

The tests for correlations between the disturbances of the money wage and fringe share equations reveal that there are gender-specific (male) unmeasured factors that relate money wages to fringe benefits. This may be an effect of unobserved ability bias that can be different for men and women due to different preferences for fringe benefits.

In order to analyze the character of the gender wage gap when fringe benefits are excluded and included respectively, the conventional Oaxaca–Blinder decomposition method was used. The decompositions of the earnings differentials show that an inclusion of fringe benefits causes an increase in the gender differences in the returns to human capital that works to broaden the gender wage gap. This is the case at least for the full-year, full-time employee group.

These results show that even small fringe shares broaden the gender wage gap, and create gender effects in the returns to education. Gender effects due to fringe benefits are revealed both in measured and unmeasured factors of the earnings equations: it appears that indeed there is a gender effect associated with fringe benefits. Because the fringe shares can be expected to increase in the future, paying attention to fringe benefits in the wage measure is important.

NOTES

1 There are only a few Finnish studies of fringe benefits: Ruuttu (1990), Torvi (1991), Asplund (1993).

2 However, in this chapter I do not analyze the qualitative data on different fringe benefits. An earlier version of this chapter, and a paper in progress, "Who Receives Fringe Benefits? Logit Analyses on Finnish Micro Data," show, for example, that men and women receive different types of fringe benefits. Men receive the more valuable benefits like a car and housing, while women receive meal benefits and theater tickets.

3 For example, Asplund (1993) uses tax roll data on fringe benefits.

4 See Granqvist (1996) for a more extensive presentation of the model. In a statistical sense it is not adequate to compare coefficients from different OLS regressions if the samples cannot be treated as independent. However, in this case there are no differences in the estimated parameter vectors of using GLS instead of OLS, because the X vector is exactly the same in every equation. Nevertheless the variance–covariance matrix is different from that of the separate OLS regressions, provided that the off-diagonal elements are not zero (see Jäntti 1994 for a discussion of this issue).

5 An adequate interpretation of percentage changes in dummy variables is $\exp(\beta_i)-1$.

6 See Judge *et al.* (1985: 476) for a description of the statistic.

REFERENCES

Asplund, R. (1993) *Essays on Human Capital and Earnings in Finland*, Helsinki: The Research Institute of the Finnish Economy.

Asplund, R. *et al.* (1996) "The male–female wage gap in the Nordic countries," in E. Wadensjö (ed.) *The Nordic Labour Markets in the 1990s*, Part I, Amsterdam: North-Holland.

Blau, F.D. and Beller, A.H. (1988) "Trends in earnings differentials by gender 1971–1981," *Industrial and Labor Relations Review* 41, 4: 513–29.

Blinder, A. (1973) "Wage discrimination: reduced form and structural estimates," *Journal of Human Resources* 8, 4: 436–55.

Breusch, T.S. and Pagan, A.R. (1980) "The Lagrange multiplier test and its applications to model specification in econometrics," *Review of Economic Studies* 47: 239–53.

Currie, J. (1993) "Gender gaps in benefits coverage," *NBER Working Paper Series*, 5265.

Chauvin, K.W. and Ash, R.A. (1994) "Gender earnings' differentials in total pay, base pay, and contingent pay," *Industrial and Labor Relations Review* 47, 4: 634–49.

Fornwall, M. (1994) "Early labour market careers of young business economists in Sweden," Licentiate thesis, Department of Economics, Uppsala University.

Granqvist, L. (1994) "Fringe benefits in Finnish micro data," Congress paper, 1994 meeting of European Society for Population Economics, Tilburg, The Netherlands.

—— (1996) "Fringe benefits, human capital and the gender wage gap," Meddelande 4/96, Stockholm: Swedish Institute for Social Research.

Jäntti, M. (1994) "A more efficient estimate of the effects of macroeconomic activity on the distribution of income," *The Review of Economics and Statistics* 76, 2: 372–78.

Judge, G.G., Griffiths, W.E., Hill, R.C., Lütkepohl, H. and Lee, T.C. (1985) *The Theory and Practice of Econometrics*, New York: John Wiley.

Kim, M.K. and Polachek, S.W. (1994) "Panel estimates of male–female earnings functions," *The Journal of Human Resources* 29, 2: 406–28.

Knudsen, K. (1991) "Kön och 'fringe benefits'," *Sociologisk Forskning* 1: 61–74.

Lazear, E. (1995) *Personnel Economics*, Cambridge Mass.: MIT Press.

Leibowitz, A. (1983) "Fringe benefits in employee compensation," in J.E. Triplett (ed.) *The Measurement of Labor Cost*, NBER Studies in Income and Wealth 48.

Oaxaca, R. (1973) "Male–female wage differentials in urban labor markets," *International Economic Review* 14, 3: 693–709.

Rein, M. and Wadensjö, E. (1997) *Enterprise and the Welfare State in Western Economies*, Cheltenham: Edward Elgar.

Ruuttu, H. (1990) "Tilastoyhteenveto Palkansaajien Luontoiseduista Sekä Päivärahoista ja Muista Matkakustannusten Korvauksista Vuonna 1989," Helsinki: The Research Department of the Finnish Taxation Board.

Smeeding, T.M. (1983) "The size distribution of wage and nonwage compensation: employer cost versus employee value," in J. E. Triplett (ed.) *The Measurement of Labor Cost*, NBER Studies in Income and Wealth 48.

Ståhlberg, A.-C. (1990) "Skillnader i försäkringsförmåner eller icke-kontanta löneskillnader mellan kvinnor och män," in C. Jonung and I. Persson (eds) *Kvinnors roll i ekonomin*, Stockholm: Allmänna förlaget.

Torvi, K. (1991) "Luontoisetujen Vaikutus Hintatasoon," in *Korkean Hintatason Suomi*, Helsinki: Paulon Säätiö.

Townsend, P. (1979) *Poverty in the United Kingdom. A Survey of Household Resources and Standards of Living*, Harmondsworth: Penguin.

APPENDIX

Table 9.A1 Means of variables used in the estimations for two subsamples: employees aged 16 to 65 who worked at least one month in 1989 in their main occupation and employees aged 16 to 65 who worked full time for the whole year (standard deviations in parentheses)

	Employed at least one month in main occupation during the year			*Full time employment for the whole year*		
	All	*Female*	*Male*	*All*	*Female*	*Male*
Yearly money wage (fim)	83,445 (52,698)	69,812 (40,051)	96,374 (59,557)	106,340 (45,462)	89,905 (32,218)	120;582 (50,169)
Monthly money wage	8,513 (5,285)	7,408 (4,293)	9,561 (5,890)	8,867 (3,788)	7,492 (2,685)	10,048 (4,190)
Fringe earners %	26.6	29.1	24.3	30.3	32.6	28.4
Fringe benefits, (total value/year)	1,670 (5,184)	1,074 (2,699)	2,236 (6,694)	2,043 (4,731)	1,324 (2,972)	2,662 (7,162)
Fringe benefits, (total tax-value)	996 (4,276)	445 (1,735)	1,518 (5,676)	1,239 (4,764)	568 (2,051)	1,816 (6,108)
Basic education (<=9 years) %	34.7	33.8	35.6	33.3	34.0	32.7
Lower vocational (10–11 years) %	29.4	27.1	31.5	30.9	28.4	33.0
Upper vocational, (12 years) %	22.2	25.1	19.4	18.9	21.1	17.0
Short non-university (13–14 years) %	5.5	5.6	5.5	6.5	6.3	6.7
Undergraduate (15 years) %	2.4	3.3	1.6	3.0	4.1	2.0
Graduate (> 16 years) %	5.7	5.0	6.4	7.4	6.0	8.5
Schooling, years (constructed)	10.9	11.0	10.9	11.1	11.0	11.1
Work exp., years (potential)	18.7	19.2	18.3	21.5	22.1	20.9
Age (years)	36.6	37.1	36.2	39.5	40.1	39.0
Children # (under 18 years old living at home)	0.94	0.92	0.96	0.93	0.86	1.00
1 child %	23.5	24.1	23.0	22.6	23.5	21.8
2 children %	20.8	20.7	21.0	22.5	21.6	23.3
3 children %	6.5	6.2	6.8	6.3	4.9	7.6
At least 4 children %	1.8	1.7	2.0	1.5	1.1	1.9
At least one part-time month %	6.9	10.4	3.6			
Overtime1 (< 50 h/year) %	18.0	16.9	19.0	21.8	21.1	22.4
Overtime2 (50–99 h/year) %	6.6	5.1	8.1	8.7	7.2	9.9
Overtime3 (> 100 h/year) %	6.9	4.4	9.2	9.0	6.4	11.2
Industries						
Food, drink, tobacco %	3.1	3.2	3.0	3.1	3.4	2.9
Mining, petroleum, chemical %	1.8	1.1	2.4	1.9	1.2	2.4

Table 9.A1 Continued

	Employed at least one month in main occupation during the year			*Full time employment for the whole year*		
	All	*Female*	*Male*	*All*	*Female*	*Male*
Metal, mechanical, shipbuilding %	6.2	1.9	10.3	7.5	2.5	11.7
Textiles %	1.9	3.3	0.6	1.8	3.3	0.6
Timber, furniture %	2.4	0.8	4.0	2.6	1.0	4.0
Paper, printing, publishing %	4.2	2.9	5.5	5.0	3.4	6.4
Other manufacturing %	2.4	1.3	3.5	2.6	1.4	3.6
Construction %	8.8	1.6	15.5	8.1	1.9	13.5
Gas, electricity, water %	1.3	0.4	2.2	1.4	0.4	2.3
Transport, communication %	6.8	4.3	9.1	7.8	4.4	10.7
Wholesale, retail %	11.3	12.2	10.5	10.9	11.2	10.6
Finance, insurance, real estate %	4.5	6.3	2.8	4.9	6.9	3.2
Professional and scientific services, education %	10.0	12.5	7.7	10.8	13.4	8.5
Other services	29.0	44.0	14.8	28.4	43.9	15.1
Agriculture, forestry, fishing %	6.2	4.0	8.2	3.2	1.7	4.4
Private sector %	68.1	56.1	79.5	66.4	54.2	76.9
Living in the southern part of Finland %	56.4	57.5	55.5	59.5	60.5	58.6
# of observations	6,118	2,978	3,140	3,993	1,846	2,147

10

GENDER, WAGES AND DISCRIMINATION IN THE USSR

Katarina Katz

BACKGROUND

Methodological starting points

The general consensus was that women in the USSR earned about one-third less than men (McAuley 1981; Zakharova *et al.* 1989), although more detailed data on the earnings of men and women were lacking. Econometric analysis of women's wages and labor supply in the USSR[1] has either been based on regional data or on surveys of emigrants from the USSR. This study is an attempt to make a detailed analysis of men's and women's wages in the USSR. It is based on data from a survey of a Russian industrial city, undertaken in 1989. This was the first set of household data collected in the USSR itself to be made available for econometric analysis.

The results bring to light some particular features of work and wages in the Soviet system. The foremost is the importance of "gendered work" for relative wages in the USSR. Another is that many women coped with their "double burden" by working less than the standard work week, legally or illegally, with the tacit agreement of the employer.

Soviet wage setting included both centralized and decentralized elements.[2] Formally, wage scales were set according to centrally decided principles. Basic pay was determined by the education and skills required, and by the economic sector. The sectors considered "most important for the national economy," such as heavy industry, had higher rates than the less prioritized. There were also wage supplements for those working under particularly difficult conditions, e.g., in physically heavy work, hazardous work environments or in certain regions.

A general problem in the analysis of Soviet wages is the importance of non-monetary work rewards, which are difficult to measure. Among the most important were access to housing and scarce goods, holiday resorts, better quality child- and healthcare, but also opportunities for extra income and for leverage in the networks of mutual assistance, barter and corruption which no Soviet citizen could do without. Side incomes – legal or illegal – were important in all service sectors, including the socio-cultural, and very much so in trade and catering. These, however, are impossible to quantify.

This institutional context is obviously not even approximated by a theory which assumes perfect competition and profit maximizing enterprises. Yet, the enterprise had some discretion in wage setting, through promotion, job labeling and grading, through norm setting (for piecework) and through the distribution of bonuses. Hence there was scope for the impact of managerial preferences (and prejudices) as well as for supply and demand factors. The enterprise had to attract a labor force which was, in the main, free to choose between jobs, and always in short supply.

Further, Western studies in the economics of gender have also found it necessary to use an institutionalist and interdisciplinary approach, to integrate feminist (and other) research in sociology, history and other disciplines and to question basic assumptions of neoclassical economics such as the exogeneity of preferences. (England 1982; Blau and Ferber 1987; McCrate 1988; Ferber and Nelson 1993).

For these reasons, the approach in this study has been to make descriptive use of a statistical model, and to defer the theoretical discussion until it is time to make inferences about social, economic and institutional relations from the empirical-descriptive results. Among other things, this implied trying a large number of variables which might be correlated with the size of the wage and a large number of specifications, in order to let the data, as far as is possible, determine the choice of model.

Women and work in the USSR

Formally, Soviet women and men had equal rights on the labor market and were entitled to equal pay for equal work. The exception was certain rights for mothers and "protective" legislation which barred women from certain jobs deemed unsuitable for them. Female labor force participation was almost as high as that of men. Further, according to the 1989 census, 78 percent of employed women had secondary or higher education and 15 percent had university schooling, as compared with 74 percent and 14 percent, respectively, of employed men. There were, however, great differences between what women and men studied, and between the jobs held by men and women. For instance, men were much more likely to have technical-vocational school (*profesional'no-teknicheskoe uchilyshche*, PTU), leading to skilled blue-collar work. Despite women's full-time jobs, household chores and responsibilities were as unevenly divided in the USSR as in Western countries. (Niemi *et al.* 1991; Katz 1994: 197–202).

An overwhelming majority of nurses (98 percent) and technicians (82 percent), and a majority of physicians (67 percent) and engineers (56 percent) were women, while most head doctors and chief engineers were men, as were most senior academics. Of textile workers 83 percent were women, but only 21 percent of building workers. Women dominated trade and catering and light industry and the low-paid "socio-cultural sphere" of teaching, childcare and medicine, while men were predominant in the higher paying heavy industry and energy sectors.

THE DATA

This study is based on a survey from the Russian city of Taganrog, a medium-size town (300,000 inhabitants) dominated by heavy industry, much of which was connected to "the military industrial complex."

A random sample of 1,200 households was selected from a stratified register of dwellings in such a way that all households except those living in student or worker hostels (*obshchezhitiia*) should have an equal probability of being selected. Non-response was about 1 percent. In each household one person was chosen as "the respondent" in a non-randomized manner. There is, however, no reason to expect a systematic difference between the wage functions of "respondents" and other household members.[3]

If we take as reference the urban population of the European part of the USSR, I consider the shortcomings of this sample to be less grave than in any other data collected in the USSR during the Soviet period, which have been available for this kind of study. Previous econometric studies were based on samples of emigrants, with inevitable selectivity in terms of who could and who wanted to emigrate.

Among the respondents, 931 reported a wage from the state sector[4] for the preceding month. For 370 men and 527 women all the data required by the wage model were available. Average monthly net wages were Rbs242 for men and Rbs158 rubles for women. The hourly rates were Rbs1.33 and Rbs0.97.[5] Hence the female to male ratio was 65 percent for monthly wages and 73 percent for hourly wages.

The men worked on average 42.4 hours per week, including overtime. If teachers (who appear to have counted only hours in the classroom) are excluded, the difference between men and women was just over two hours.

VARIABLES AND MODEL

A number of specifications for a log-linear wage equation were estimated separately for men and women, for both hourly and monthly wages.[6] The following section will focus on one specific model for hourly wage rates.[7]

Usually estimates of wage equations for women need to be corrected for selectivity, since potential wage offers for those who are not employed cannot be observed (Heckman 1979). In this case, the rate of employment of women aged 20–54 (the standard pension age for women) is 87 percent. If we add the 6 percent caring for children under eighteen months old, the figure differs only by 0.5 percent from the male participation rate. Conversely, nearly all mothers stay at home until the child is one year old and most of them until it is eighteen months.[8] Hence, a selection bias does not seem likely and OLS regression was used.

Definitions of the independent variables and variable means are reported in the Appendix, in Tables 10.A1 and 10.A2, respectively. As can be seen, the differences between men and women in age, work record (*stazh*) and seniority do not indicate a large difference in labor force attachment, beyond the five-year higher pension age for men. Full-time and other kinds of higher education[9] were treated separately (highed1 and highed2). This was necessary because returns to part-time education were found to be considerably lower than to full-time. Specialized secondary education (or incomplete higher education) was coded as "specsec" and ordinary secondary education (with or without vocational school) as "second." Vocational-technical school, with or without full secondary education, was coded as "PTU." The reference group consisted of those with incomplete secondary school or less, i.e. eight years or less of schooling.

The coding of the survey included six "qualification levels" of the jobs held by the respondents. These have been aggregated into four. "Highqual" refers both to managerial staff and to higher level employees in jobs defined as "linked with the creative process" (university teachers, researchers, artistic work). A broad group ("midqual") includes all other white-collar workers and professionals. "Physqual" stands for skilled work with some physical element. The reference group is unskilled manual workers.

Women do unskilled physical work twice as often as men, while men do skilled manual work twice as often as women. Also, two-fifths of the women do low-to-middle level white-collar work, compared with only a quarter of the men. About half of the women in this group have higher education, while about half have secondary education. Of the men, in this group, three-quarters have higher education.

Fifty-two percent of the sample work in industry, as compared with 40 percent in the Soviet urban workforce. Male respondents are strongly concentrated into heavy industry, while the employment of female respondents is more varied in terms of economic sectors.

The model also included variables for pensioner status and marital status[10] and for four work conditions (heavy work, heat, nervous strain, and at least one of the following "bad" conditions: work-hazards, gas or fumes, and noise).[11]

Early estimates as well as institutional considerations suggested that "having a less than forty-one hour week" was important. My hypothesis was that this could reflect four different phenomena which were operationalized in the following way: official part-time ("offpart") meant working and being paid for a part of the normal time for the job, unofficial part-time ("unoff") meant to be hired and paid for a full week but work much less.[12] For those in jobs for which the legal work week should be less than 41 hours, the variables "reduc" and "reduc-ed" measured the number of hours by which this "reduced work-week" fell short of 41: "reduc-ed" for those working in public education and "reduc" for others. In order to attach these labels to respondents, job type, hours and pay were combined with answers to: "Do you work a full work week?" In about 60 cases, in addition to the coded job type, the actual occupation was found from the questionnaires.

REGRESSION RESULTS

In the following we report the results from estimating two different wage models, one that includes work time variables (Table 10.1) and one without such variables (Table 10.2). Both models are estimated for hourly as well as monthly wages. We start by discussing the results for hourly wages in the first model and complement the picture obtained from these estimates by adding information from the second model and from estimates based on monthly wages.

Returns to education

According to the estimates for hourly wages, the reward for full-time higher education over incomplete secondary education is 37 percent for women and 22 percent for men (see Table 10.1). For women the difference between highed1 and highed2 is not dramatic, but for men the latter has an (insignificant) negative parameter. That the return to higher education is greater for women agrees with the results of Ofer and Vinokur (1983), and so do, roughly, the orders of magnitude.

Both kinds of secondary education have a higher return for women than for men. Men, however, are more likely to have vocational school (PTU) education, which has a higher wage return for them, than general or specialized secondary school education. Many PTU programs for highly skilled jobs in industry or construction were closed to girls.[13] It is, therefore, not surprising that the pay-off for vocational schooling is larger for men than for women.

Wage-growth with age and experience

The age parameters in Table 10.1 correspond to quite small wage–age derivatives. Note however the large and significant[14] negative parameter for "pens" ("being a pensioner"). It corresponds to a loss of 27 percent in hourly wages for men and 24 percent for women, even though we control for age. In other words, the age–wage curve turns sharply downwards at pension age, or thereabouts.

Seniority is significant for women's hourly wages but not overall work experience (stazh), although the parameters are of approximately the same

Table 10.1 Model 1 of hourly and monthly wages

	Hourly wages				*Monthly wages*			
	Men		*Women*		*Men*		*Women*	
Variable	*Parameter*	*t-value*	*Parameter*	*t-value*	*Parameter*	*t-value*	*Parameter*	*t-value*
INTERCEP	–0.323	–1.324	–1.137	–5.030	4.820	17.48	3.825	17.33
HOURS					0.004	1.297	0.005	2.268
AGE	0.011	0.949	0.033	3.003	0.006	0.560	0.035	3.627
AGESQ	–0.0002	–1.479	–0.0004	–3.242	–0.0002	–1.396	–0.0004	–3.751
STAZH	0.008	1.570	0.005	1.540	0.011	2.339	0.002	0.819
SENIOR	0.004	1.941	0.005	2.601	0.004	2.245	0.006	3.487
PENS	–0.318	–4.069	–0.269	–3.650	–0.367	–4.837	–0.243	–3.711
MTS	0.068	1.412	0.042	1.423	0.055	1.181	0.024	0.916
REDUC	0.055	7.705	0.031	6.748	0.035	4.689	0.0004	0.102
REDUCED	0.0256	2.511	0.037	8.696	–0.003	–0.296	0.012	2.784
UNOFF			1.147	10.85			0.148	1.391
OFFPART	0.587	2.809	0.323	4.385				
PARTY	0.059	1.568	0.039	1.083	0.042	1.162	0.041	1.276
HIGHQUAL	0.290	2.522	0.330	3.399	0.353	3.178	0.338	3.919
MIDQUAL	0.034	0.451	0.049	1.037	0.047	0.640	0.026	0.618
PHYSQU.	0.100	1.673	0.112	2.717	0.106	1.841	0.112	3.048
HIGHED1	0.201	2.709	0.316	5.041	0.211	2.960	0.305	5.466
HIGHED2	–0.077	–0.860	0.276	3.373	–0.053	–0.608	0.214	2.942
SPECSEC	0.053	0.929	0.143	2.683	0.066	1.194	0.138	2.905
SECOND	0.048	0.874	0.106	2.064	0.041	0.771	0.081	1.766
PTU	0.114	2.153	0.075	1.255	0.112	2.197	0.058	1.085
TRANSP	–0.066	–1.114	–0.078	–1.144	–0.018	–0.320	–0.021	–0.351
CONSTR	–0.054	–0.848	–0.073	–1.126	–0.076	–1.241	–0.037	–0.633
LIGHT	–0.025	–0.324	0.002	0.038	–0.027	–0.366	0.036	0.739
SERV	–0.228	–3.098	–0.001	–0.024	–0.217	–3.057	0.021	0.428
TRADE	–0.358	–2.894	–0.331	–6.245	–0.370	–3.108	–0.266	–5.600
TEACH	–0.054	–0.604	–0.094	–1.748	–0.034	–0.393	–0.054	–1.125
HEALTH	–0.117	–1.005	–0.157	–2.681	–0.089	–0.795	–0.124	–2.383
ART	–0.141	–1.003	–0.236	–2.195	–0.177	–1.305	–0.332	–3.475
SCIENCE	–0.092	–1.209	–0.201	–3.022	–0.089	–1.216	–0.156	–2.636
GOVT	–0.228	–1.066	–0.060	–0.602	–0.055	–0.265	–0.027	–0.301
OTHER	–0.132	–1.862	0.107	1.566	–0.160	–2.349	0.018	0.298
HEAT	0.167	2.805	0.187	2.212	0.179	3.129	0.176	2.340
HEAVY	0.013	0.275	0.144	2.726	0.011	0.237	0.134	2.852
NERVOUS	–0.134	–3.633	–0.084	–2.492	–0.107	–2.990	–0.035	–1.157
BADCOND	0.051	1.369	0.102	2.453	0.048	1.332	0.119	3.217
adj. R2	0.34		0.49		0.31		0.39	
N	370		526		370		526	

size. For men, the parameter for work record (stazh) is larger than that for seniority, but has only half the precision. Seniority is significant at the 6 percent level. A strong relation between wages and seniority is plausible in the Soviet case, since the shortage of labor made managers very concerned not to lose staff (see, for instance, Komozin 1991 and Malle 1987).

Pay-offs to job characteristics

The parameters for "highqual" have high precision for both men and women and the associated hourly wage differentials are 30–40 percentage points (net of the effect of higher education, which people in such jobs usually have). The pay for ordinary white-collar jobs (midqual) is not significantly different from that of unskilled workers, but "midqual" is a very broad and diverse category.[15] The pay of skilled manual workers (physqual) is approximately 11 percent higher than for unskilled workers.

The work condition variables were all significant for women, and all except "heavy work" were significant for men. These variables, apart from "nervous strain," measure conditions that should be compensated according to the official regulations (by higher wages and/or by other means such as longer holidays or special allowances of foodstuffs or medicine). While the physical disadvantages of the jobs resulted in positive parameters, nervous strain had significant negative coefficients.

Few of the sector – or industry – coefficients are significantly different from zero, despite the substantial differences in average pay between sectors, in the sample and according to Soviet statistics.[16] One reason for this is the small number of observations in sectors other than the reference group, heavy industry. However, the sector averages also reflect differences in educational requirements, work conditions, hours and – not least – gender composition of the workforce.

Importance of short work weeks

Officially, reduced work weeks were intended for workers whose jobs were such that they needed more rest to recover after work (Terebilova 1981). Therefore a shorter work week was not supposed to result in lower monthly wages (the usual unit of income). In fact, we see in Table 10.1 that for each hour by which the respondent's work week falls short of 41, every hour they do work is paid at a 3 percent higher hourly wage rate for women, and at a 6 percent higher hourly wage rate for men, for non-teachers.[17]

The parameter for "unofficial part-time" is very large, larger than one. My interpretation of this is that it reflects the particularly acute shortage of labor for certain jobs, usually low skilled, low status and low paid. If managers had not tacitly allowed workers in such jobs to work fewer hours than their contracts stipulated, it would have been impossible to recruit workers for them. In this sample, ten out of eleven respondents coded as "unofficial part-timers" turned out to be cleaners – a job which it was hard to find anyone willing to do.

When the hourly wage function was modified by omission of the four "short work week variables," the explanatory power of the model was considerably reduced. R^2 was reduced by a third for men and by more than a half for women (see model 2 in Table 10.2).

Table 10.2 Model 2 of hourly and monthly wages

	Hourly wages				*Monthly wages*			
	Men		*Women*		*Men*		*Women*	
Variable	*Parameter*	*t-value*	*Parameter*	*t-value*	*Parameter*	*t-value*	*Parameter*	*t-value*
INTERCEP	–0.288	–1.078	–0.495	–1.830	5.075	18.42	3.943	19.61
HOURS					–0.0004	–0.132	0.002	1.165
AGE	0.012	0.897	0.003	0.239	0.004	0.316	0.035	3.704
AGESQ	–0.0002	–1.449	–0.000002	–0.016	–0.0002	–1.291	–0.0004	–3.834
STAZH	0.010	1.820	0.003	0.779	0.014	2.911	0.002	0.747
SENIOR	0.002	0.905	0.002	0.719	0.003	1.694	0.006	3.497
PENS	–0.302	–3.524	–0.323	–3.568	–0.381	–4.876	–0.254	–3.883
MTS	0.054	1.042	0.059	1.617	0.030	0.643	0.026	0.963
PARTY	0.058	1.414	0.032	0.736	0.047	1.273	0.047	1.485
HIGHQUAL	0.219	1.740	0.335	2.900	0.355	3.110	0.297	3.546
MIDQUAL	0.007	0.080	0.022	0.390	0.029	0.387	0.018	0.442
PHYSQU.	0.043	0.660	0.059	1.171	0.074	1.258	0.104	2.838
HIGHED1	0.269	3.317	0.320	4.165	0.240	3.277	0.319	5.724
HIGHED2	–0.089	–0.909	0.219	2.173	–0.030	–0.334	0.212	2.901
SPECSEC	0.096	1.528	0.101	1.545	0.100	1.766	0.143	3.002
SECOND	0.082	1.356	0.059	0.938	0.059	1.078	0.082	1.788
PTU	0.121	2.076	0.160	2.185	0.121	2.293	0.059	1.107
TRANSP	–0.035	–0.547	–0.039	–0.472	–0.002	–0.038	–0.014	–0.226
CONSTR	–0.062	–0.892	–0.081	–1.006	–0.086	–1.365	–0.034	–0.575
LIGHT	–0.032	–0.379	–0.021	–0.309	–0.032	–0.423	0.041	0.831
SERV	–0.220	–2.725	0.012	0.174	–0.203	–2.781	0.024	0.484
TRADE	–0.382	–2.817	–0.307	–4.713	–0.389	–3.175	–0.259	–5.470
TEACH	0.024	0.280	0.167	2.990	–0.075	–0.974	0.009	0.226
HEALTH	0.012	0.096	–0.086	–1.232	0.004	0.037	–0.134	–2.640
ART	0.070	0.465	–0.169	–1.286	–0.067	–0.487	–0.347	–3.631
SCIENCE	–0.105	–1.261	–0.201	–2.454	–0.078	–1.036	–0.149	–2.511
GOVT	–0.254	–1.080	–0.092	–0.743	–0.021	–0.099	–0.028	–0.306
OTHER	–0.084	–1.082	0.240	2.864	–0.134	–1.923	0.021	0.347
HEAT	0.147	2.259	0.184	1.767	0.173	2.925	0.170	2.253
HEAVY	0.006	0.123	0.151	2.320	0.008	0.170	0.142	3.016
NERVOUS	–0.147	–3.642	–0.117	–2.840	–0.105	–2.838	–0.021	–0.691
BADCOND	0.059	1.433	0.125	2.441	0.056	1.496	0.122	3.294
adj. R2	0.21		0.22		0.27		0.39	
N	370		526		370		526	

The majority of those with legally reduced work time are white-collar employees, usually with higher education, and not blue-collar workers with heavy or hazardous work. This is confirmed by the shifts that take place in education and qualification parameters when the "shorter work week" variables are omitted. This reward in shorter work time rather than in wages should be kept in mind when discussing relative wages for Soviet manual and non-manual staff and for groups with different levels of education.

Among men, skilled manual workers are less likely than either unskilled workers or white-collar workers to benefit from shorter work weeks. In education, healthcare and the arts, short work weeks raise hourly wages to the level of wages in industry.

For women too, the parameters for working in healthcare and the arts rise considerably when the variables for shorter work weeks are omitted and are no longer significantly different from the reference sector (heavy industry). Hence, in terms of hourly rates the disadvantage of working in these sectors is partially offset by the advantage of having the reduced hours which are common to them. For the education sector the parameter should be interpreted with caution since we do not know how many hours teachers work outside the classroom.

It is worth noting that the short work weeks make a great difference for the models for hourly wage rates, but not for the models for monthly wages. For the latter, it makes very little difference for the coefficients for other variables whether the work hour variables are included or not. Further, if these variables are included, most coefficients in the equations for hourly wages are very close to the corresponding coefficients in the equations for monthly wages. All of this indicates that these models reflect the institutional framework of centralized wage setting quite well. The decision to reduce the official work week for a profession was not supposed to change monthly earnings relative to the monthly wages considered normal for a Soviet woman with those qualifications.

One answer to the question of why Soviet women chose such jobs as physician or teacher despite the low monthly earnings and the many years of study could be the reduced work weeks. It would have required careful socio-psychological research to determine the relative importance of this factor and of other qualities of the occupation in the explanation of why Soviet women chose jobs in healthcare and education. On the impact of prestige, intrinsic interest and the contradictory demands of Soviet gender roles, see Aage (1984); Liljeström (1993); Katz (1994).

The reduced work-weeks made it possible for a number of women to trade earnings for hours on relatively favorable terms. On the other hand, it would have been harder for the authorities to impose such a low level of earnings without the short work week.

DECOMPOSITION OF THE GENDER WAGE GAP

In studies of wage discrimination, it is standard practice to decompose wage differences between gender or ethnic groups. One part is attributed to differences in the variable values (the endowments) for the two groups, and one part is attributed to differences between the coefficients (Oaxaca 1973; Oaxaca and Ransom 1994).

As is well known (Neumark 1988; Oaxaca and Ransom 1994) such decompositions suffer from an "index" problem: how, or according to which wage function, should the endowments be evaluated when their impact on the wage gap is measured?

The wage function by whose parameters the characteristics are weighted, in the term of the decomposition ascribed to differences in endowments, is implicitly set up as a "non-discriminatory wage function." It is usual to report results using the male and the female wage functions respectively (corresponding to "only discrimination" and "only nepotism"). Neumark (1988) and Oaxaca and Ransom (1994) propose the parameters estimated from an OLS regression on the pooled sample of men and women. This weighting conveys an intuitive idea that discrimination against women and nepotism in favor of men should somehow "even out," in the sense that the existing overall wage structure would also prevail in the absence of either discrimination or nepotism. The theoretical basis for this assumption remains unclear. It forecloses a priori the disputed issue of whether discrimination is only a redistribution between employees or whether employers might gain by it. Hence, this weighting in the endowment term is no less arbitrary than using the male or female parameters as weights.

There are also conceptual problems, irrespective of which wage function is taken as a benchmark. Simply to identify the term attributable to differences between the coefficients in the wage equation as "discrimination" may be said both to overstate and to understate the case. In the absence of a perfect model, it is always possible to claim that some part of the discrimination term would disappear if there were more, or more specific variables, and that therefore, the impact of discrimination is exaggerated.

The claim that the measure underestimates discrimination invokes a broader definition of the concept. Nearly all the "endowments" can be seen as at least partly endogenous (Blau and Ferber 1987). They are the results of choices made and circumstances encountered within a certain social context: the anticipated results for a man or a woman of choosing an occupation or an education, of acquiring seniority and experience depend on discrimination inside and outside the labor market (including "pure" wage discrimination). Hence difference in choice is due not only to difference in preferences – and even preferences are partly endogenous (McCrate 1988).

Further the concept of wage discrimination can be extended to individuals doing different jobs "of comparable worth." "Comparable worth" studies in the West have found a great number of cases where female-dominated jobs have been undervalued in relation to male-dominated ones. In the USSR the sectors defined as most important for "the national economy" were traditionally male-dominated ones like energy, mining, construction, metalworking, and so on. Hence wages in these sectors of the economy were higher. Occupational segregation (resulting in lower average pay for women at each level of education, experience and exertion) is an essential and logical outcome of a discriminatory system: thus, to control for such segregation in the model means defining away a large part of the problem under study.

The decomposition of the gender wage gap by the Oaxaca method "explains" the gap only in a very limited sense, but it tells us something about the form and the mechanisms of the wage difference. From this we can draw conclusions about the importance of different variables (and the forces that affect them, in their turn) for male–female differentials.

RESULTS OF THE DECOMPOSITION

Decompositions of the gender differences in hourly wages were performed on the Taganrog sample. For the decomposition a larger model was used, in order to make use of as much information as possible and to keep down the contribution of endowments of "omitted variables" to the unexplained difference.[18]

The model used accounts for 32 percent of the variation in (the logarithm of) hourly wages for men and 44 percent for women. Yet, as Table 10.3 shows, gender differences in the variable values in the model can account for only 15–16 percent (27 percent for monthly wages) of the gender wage gap, if either the male or female wage function is used as a benchmark. If the wage function estimated from the pooled sample of men and women is used, a larger part of the wage gap is attributable to differences in endowments, 48 percent of the gender difference in hourly wages and 56 percent of that in monthly wages.[19]

Table 10.3 Decomposition of the gender wage gap according to Model 3 (percent)

	For hourly wages			*For monthly wages*		
Weights	*Male*	*Female*	*Pooled*	*Male*	*Female*	*Pooled*
Education	2.7	1.8	6.0	2.2	0.4	4.6
Age	–4.6	–1.4	–3.2	–5.2	–2.4	–3.1
Pensioner	0.8	0.7	0.8	0.7	0.4	0.6
Experience	9.1	8.1	13.4	9.9	4.3	9.4
Job types	8.4	8.6	14.1	6.2	8.1	11.8
Work conditions	2.2	6.5	6.4	1.8	5.9	5.7
Sectors	9.1	8.0	11.8	6.5	4.6	8.2
Hours/week				3.3	3.1	5.3
Short-week variables	–14.7	–20.9	–20.0	–1.8	–3.1	–3.8
"Family" variables	0.5	3.7	15.3	2.4	5.0	14.9
Party	2.0	1.0	3.1	1.0	1.1	2.5
Total due to difference in endowments	15.4	15.9	47.7	26.8	27.4	56.2
Due to difference in the wage function	84.6	84.1	52.3	73.2	72.6	43.8

Despite all the qualifications made above concerning the interpretation of "discrimination terms," we have a strong indication of discrimination. Otherwise we must assume that what distinguishes women from men in the Soviet "labor market" was fundamentally different from the differences within each gender group.

Another way of using the decomposition is to ask how big the difference between men's and women's wages would be if they and their jobs had the same characteristics. Depending on whether we apply the "male" or "female" wage function, we find that men's hourly wages (in this sample) would still have been 32–33 percent higher than those of women. This can be compared with a Swedish study using a similar model (le Grand 1991), which found a corresponding difference of 8 percent in the hourly wage.

Beyond this division into "endowment" and "discrimination" terms, it is interesting to see which variables account for how much of the "explained" difference.[20] Table 10.3 shows this for aggregates of variables.[21]

For both hourly and monthly wages, experience, qualification and sector of employment each account for 4–9 percent of the wage difference, using either male or female weights. Work conditions contribute, but much more using the female than the male equation (6 percent versus 2 percent). One can see why women workers were strongly tempted to accept heavy work under noxious work conditions (Shapiro 1992; Filtzer 1993). The part of the wage gap which is due to differences in education is small – 0.4–2.7 percent. However, while gender differences in PTU add 2–3 percent to the gender gap in hourly wages and gender differences in higher education add 1–2.5 percent, depending on the weighting, gender differences in general secondary school contribute a small negative term, i.e. serve to decrease the gender wage gap.

In Taganrog, even though the parameters were not significant when taken one by one, marriage, children and housework together account for 5 and 4 percent of the gender gap in respectively monthly and hourly wages, when weighted by the female equation. They make a much smaller contribution using the male equation. It is for women that having families is a career impediment.

Reduced work hours and "unofficial part-time" increased hourly wages and were more frequent among women than among men. Hence, the decomposition of the gender difference in hourly wages includes a large negative component due to "endowments of short work weeks." Because of this, the discrimination term comes out as a larger proportion of the gender gap in hourly than in monthly wages.[22]

GENERALIZING BEYOND TAGANROG

Although the level of wages varied very much between regions of the USSR, the centralization of wage scales justifies inferences about an (urban European)

Soviet wage function from a local sample such as this. It is riskier, however, to generalize either the female–male wage ratio or the decomposition of the wage gap, since the average wages as well as the "endowment" and "discrimination" terms involve not only parameters but also variable means which may be fairly specific to Taganrog. For instance, in the Taganrog sample, in 1989 57 percent of the women worked in the relatively well-paid industry, transport and communications or construction sectors, compared to 37 percent of the Soviet female workforce.

Therefore a wage function estimated from the Taganrog data was applied to variable means for the USSR. The difficulty of finding such data in the official statistics meant that the specification of the wage function had to be determined by their availability and also that some imputations had to be made.[23]

The average hourly wages for Soviet men and women predicted by this model for the Soviet population means were Rbs1.16 and Rbs0.82 respectively. (Hence, the female to male wage ratio was 71 percent.) Endowment terms could account for 18 percent of the gender gap when the parameters from the female wage function were applied as weights, but only 7 percent if the parameters of the male function were used.[24] According to these estimates, if Soviet women workers had remained paid according to the same "female" wage function but acquired the same labor market characteristics as men, this would have raised their average hourly wage by 3 percent.

CONCLUSIONS

We have found a gender gap in earnings in Taganrog in 1989 of comparable size to that in many market economies, like the UK or USA, but larger than in the more egalitarian Western countries such as those of Scandinavia (Rosenfeld and Kalleberg 1991; Blau and Kahn 1992). Given that a larger share of the female workforce in Taganrog than in the Soviet urban population worked in the highest paying sectors, one can confidently assume that in the country as a whole the wage gap was not smaller than this.

That the gender gap was found to be smaller for hourly than for monthly wages reflects the possibilities of reduced work hours for certain categories of workers and employees. It seems that the attempt by women to cope with the "double burden" by working fewer hours was encouraged by wage policies, at least for white-collar workers. This – very partial – alleviation of the "double burden" was apparently either considered more desirable or more realistic than a change in gender roles and gender division of labor (including that in the household) which would have been more genuinely egalitarian.

It should also be noted that the smaller gap in hourly wages does not necessarily reflect the "real" state of gender equality better than that in monthly wages. That would assume that women had a perfect "free choice" of work hours, while in fact they were very constrained. First, tradition, ideological pressure and inequality in the household restricted women's choices by assigning the great bulk of household responsibilities to them. Second, even if a woman did decide that a higher monthly wage was worth the longer hours of work, it is very likely that she would have found the road blocked by discrimination in education, employment and promotion.

As the reader will know, it is far from unique to the USSR to find women doing most of the unpaid housework and working only part-time at a paid job, and therefore earning less. But in the USSR this division of labor worked behind a screen of officially proclaimed "equal participation in the national economy" which made it harder to challenge.

Decomposition of the gender wage differential shows that, given the Soviet wage structure which was in itself male-biased, gender differences in experience, education, qualification level and work conditions account for roughly one-third of the gender difference in hourly wages. Different forms of reduction in work hours move in the opposite direction, decreasing the endowment term by 15–21 percentage points (depending on the weighting).

Taken one by one, few parameters differ significantly between the male and female wage equations, even at a 10 percent significance level. The really striking difference is between the intercepts. In other words, both in absolute terms and relative to other women, Soviet women could improve their wages through choice of education or job and by accepting bad work conditions. Yet, their choices would make a rather small difference to the wage differential relative to men with the same personal and job characteristics. Indeed, according to the decomposition, if women in Taganrog had had the same endowments as men in terms of the 51 variables in the model (but retained their "female wage function"), their average wage would have been only 5 percent higher than it was.

It appears that the more factors that are taken into account, the more we are left with the simplest of conclusions: Soviet women were paid less because they were women.

ACKNOWLEDGMENT

This chapter first appeared, in a slightely different form, in the *Cambridge Journal of Economics* (September 1997) and is published by permission of Oxford University Press.

NOTES

1 See the *Journal of Comparative Economics* 3/1987 (special issue); Ofer and Vinokur (1992).
2 For the principles of wage setting in the Soviet Union, see Nove (1986), Oxenstierna (1990), Rofe *et al.* (1991) or Katz (1994).
3 The interviewers endeavored to obtain a reasonable variation in sex, age, etc., while at the same time choosing whenever possible an employed member of

the household. However, the choice was not systematic. Some information was available for all household members. A regression of (log) monthly wage, using fifteen such variables (for levels of education, marital and pensioner status, children and age) was run both on the entire sample and on the respondents. Using an F-test on the "male" and "female" equations separately, the hypothesis of equality of the parameters for respondents and other household members was not rejected at the 5 percent level for either sex.

4 Since the object of the study was the Soviet wage system, I did not include self-employment or work in the newly emerged cooperative sector. For a comparison of this sample with one aimed at cooperators (using the same questionnaire), see Nivorozhkina (1992).

5 To impute average hourly wage rates ("w"), I have assumed that the yearly wage is twelve times that of the preceding month ("wage") and divided that by hours of work per year. Hence:

$$w = 12*wage*\frac{7}{365}*\frac{1}{h}$$

where "h" is reported "usual hours of work per week" (both wage and h include overtime and second jobs if these are in the state sector). For a detailed discussion of issues of measurement, see Katz (1994).

6 An F-test comparing the "male" and "female" equations led to rejection of equality at the 1 percent level.

7 Tests of the model specification (tests of equality of parameters for subgroups of the sample, for heteroscedasticity, for sensitivity of parameter estimates to "outliers," and for normal distribution of the residuals) are reported in Katz (1994) and available from the author on request.

8 Furthermore, of women aged 25–60 about 90 percent have children.

9 In Soviet terminology, "higher education" means university. This could be acquired in day (full-time) courses or evening and correspondence courses.

10 Models including the number of children born to the respondent, children in the household and hours of housework per week were tried, but the parameters for these variables were not significant.

11 The choice was made so as to get as many significant parameter estimates as possible.

12 This, of course, was not said by respondents. It is my interpretation. But the existence of the phenomenon has been confirmed by every Russian I have asked.

13 In this particular sample a large proportion of the very few women with PTU training work as cleaners or in other unskilled manual work with "unofficial part-time." This is not so likely to be typical, and because of the small number of observations no conclusions about this educational group should be drawn.

14 Unless otherwise stated, "significant" means at the 5 percent level.

15 For women, a model with interaction effects shows that for "midqual" jobs with higher education, the wage effect is considerably larger than for white-collar work with only secondary school.

16 The design of the survey questionnaire made it difficult to measure the bonus component of wages. Comparison with another Taganrog sample indicates that this might have led to an exaggeration of wages in construction and transport by up to 3–4 percent, and in heavy industry by twice as much. For a thorough discussion of this problem and the evidence that it would not noticeably affect other parameter estimates than those for sectors, see Katz (1994: Chapter 5).

17 See Katz (1994) for a fuller discussion of hours, wages and wage rates for teachers.

18 In this model education and "qualification" levels are more disaggregated than in the previous one. More work conditions are included and also variables for

number of children and hours of housework. See the Appendix.

19 I find it intuitively more appealing to report shares of the differences between the (geometric) averages of wages, rather than (as is usual) of the differences between the logarithms of these. (In this case it makes little difference. Endowment terms make up 14 and 15 percent of the difference between the logarithms of the male and female average wage rates, i.e. almost the same as their share of the difference between the averages themselves.)

20 No such attempt to attribute the "unexplained" difference to differences in specific parameters (unequal returns to specific characteristics) was made. Such a decomposition is not invariant under linear transformations of the explanatory variables.

21 More detailed decompositions are available from the author on request.

22 It may therefore be objected that the decomposition should be made with a wage function which does not include these variables, in order not to exaggerate the discrimination component. If this is done, gender differences in endowments account for 18 percent of the wage gap.

23 Definitions, sources and methods of imputations, as well as coefficients and estimated means for Soviet workers and employees, are described in detail in Katz (1994) and available from the author on request.

24 If it is correct to assume that the wage function is more or less the same in different parts of the USSR, then we can conclude that the specificities of Taganrog have led to a small underestimate of the impact of discrimination, since in the Taganrog sample endowments accounted for 23 percent of the gender gap when weighted by this female function, and 19 percent when weighted by the male one.

REFERENCES

Aage, H. (1984) "Uddannelse, prestige og inkomst for forskelige ehrvervsgrupper i Sovjetunionen og i Danmark – nogle forelobige data," *Nordic Journal of Soviet and East European Studies* 1, 1.

Blau, F.D. and Ferber, M. (1987) "Discrimination: empirical evidence from the United States," *American Economic Review* 77, 2: 316–20.

Blau, F.D. and Kahn, L.M. (1992) *The Gender Earnings Gap: Some International Evidence*, National Bureau of Economic Research, Working Paper No. 4224.

Cotton, J. (1988) "On the decomposition of wage differentials," *Review of Economics and Statistics* 20, 2: 236–43.

England, P. (1982) "The failure of human capital theory to explain occupational segregation by sex," *Journal of Human Resources* 17, 3: 358–70.

Ferber, M. and Nelson, J. (eds) (1993) *Beyond Economic Man*, Chicago: University of Chicago Press

Filtzer, D. (1993) *Soviet Workers and the Collapse of Perestroika. The Soviet Labour Process and Gorbachev's Reforms 1985–91*, Cambridge: Cambridge University Press.

Heckman, J.J. (1979) "Sample bias as a specification error," *Econometrica* 47, 1.

Katz, K. (1994) *Gender Differentiation and Discrimination. A Study of Soviet Wages.* PhD thesis, University of Göteborg.

Komozin, A. N. (1991) "A work career from the standpoint of the life cycle," *Soviet Sociology* 30, 5: 49–61.

le Grand, C. (1991) "Explaining the male–female wage gap: job segregation and solidarity wage bargaining in Sweden," *Acta Sociologica* 34: 261–78.

Liljeström, M. (1993) "The Soviet gender system: the ideological construction of femininity and masculinity in the 1970s," in M. Liljeström *et al.* (eds) *Gender Restructuring in Russian Studies*, Tampere: Slavica Tamperensia.

McAuley, A. (1981) *Women's Work and Wages in the Soviet Union*, London: Allen & Unwin.

McCrate, E. (1988) "Gender difference: the role of endogenous preferences and collective action," *American Economic Review* 78, 2: 235–9.

Malle, S. (1987) "Planned and unplanned mobility in the Soviet Union under the threat of labour shortage," *Soviet Studies* 39, 3: 357–87.

Neumark, D. (1988) "Employers' discriminatory behavior and the estimation of wage discrimination," *Journal of Human Resources* 23, 3: 279–95.

Niemi, I., Eglite, P., Mitrikas, A., Patrushev, V.D. and Pääkkönen, H. (1991) *Time Use in Finland, Latvia, Lithuania and Russia*, Central Statistical Office of Finland, Studies 182.

Nivorozhkina, L.I. (1992) "Kachestvennye parametry truda v gosudarstvennom i chastnom sektorakh ekonomiki," in N.M. Rimashevskaia and V.V. Patsiorkovskii (eds) *Sotsial'no-ekonomicheskie issledovaniia blagosostaiania, obraza i urovnia zhizni naseleniia goroda. Proekt Taganrog- III*, Moscow: Institute for Socio-Economic Population Studies.

Nove, A. (1977) *The Soviet Economic System*, London: Allen & Unwin.

Oaxaca, R. (1973) "Male–female wage differentials in urban labor markets," *International Economic Review* 14: 693–709.

Oaxaca, R.L. and Ransom, M.R. (1994) "On discrimination and the decomposition of wage differentials," *Journal of Econometrics* 61, 1: 5–21.

Ofer, G. and Vinokur, A. (1983) "The labor-force participation of married women in the Soviet Union: a household cross-section analysis," *Journal of Comparative Economics* 7, 2: 158–76.

—— (1992) *The Soviet Household Under the Old Regime. Economic Conditions and Behaviour in the 1970s*, Cambridge: Cambridge University Press.

Oxenstierna, S. (1990) *From Labour Shortage to Unemployment? The Soviet Labour Market in the 1980s*, Stockholm: Almqvist & Wiksell.

Rofe, A.I., Shunikov, A.M. and Yasakova, N.V. (1991) *Organizatsiia i oplata truda na predpriiatii*, Moscow: Profizdat.

Rosenfeld, R.A. and Kalleberg, A. (1991) "Gender inequality in the labor market. a cross-national perspective," *Acta Sociologica* 34: 207–25.

Shapiro, J. (1992) "The industrial labour force," in M. Buckley (ed.) *Perestroika and Soviet Women*, Cambridge: Cambridge University Press.

Terebilova, V.I. (ed.) (1981) *Kommentarii k zakonodatel'stvu o trude*, Moscow: Yuridicheskaia literatura.

Zakharova, N., Posadskaia, A. and Rimashevskaia, N. (1989) "Kak my reshaem zhenskii vopros," *Kommunist*, 4/1989: 56–65.

APPENDIX

Table 10.A1 Definition of variables

wage	Wage from the state sector (including overtime and second jobs) reported by the respondent for the previous month.
w	Hourly wage rate imputed from "wage" and "usual" hours per week of work in the state sector, reported by respondent, including overtime and second jobs (see text).
lwage	Natural logarithm of "wage".
lw	Natural logarithm of "w".
Age	Age in years.
Agesq	Age squared.
Stazh	Work record (*Obshchii stazh*).
Seniority	Seniority, i.e., years at present place of employment, (*Stazh na predpriiatie*).
Pens	=1 if respondent states his/her occupation as pensioner/working pensioner or if he/she is above normal retirement age, otherwise =0.
Mts	Marital status, =1 if respondent has spouse living in the household, otherwise=0.
Reduc	Reduction in work time (41 minus "h") if respondent is not a white-collar employee in a school and states usual work hours below 40 and if this is compatible with the "normal" hours for his/her job, otherwise = 0.
Reduced	Defined as "reduc" but only for those working in the education sector as non-managerial, white-collar employees (i.e., probably teachers).
Offpart	=1 if the respondent says that s/he works "not a full" work week or day and the hours stated are below the standard and the wage appears too low for a fulltimer in this job, otherwise=0.
Unoff	Work hours too low for full-time in the job and wage too high for part-time.
Party	=1 if respondent is member of the CPSU or Komsomol, otherwise=0.
Lowqual	Blue-collar worker in unskilled work (ref. category).
Physqual	Blue-collar workers in highly skilled work, physical or with physical elements.
Midqual	All white-collar workers, except those in "highqual".
Highqual	Managerial staff or highly qualified staff in work "linked with the creative process" (university staff, artists, etc.).
Highed1	Higher education, acquired in full-time program.
Highed2	Higher education from evening or correspondence courses.
Specsec	Specialized secondary or incomplete higher education.
Second	Secondary education, general or combined with PTU.
PTU	PTU with or without secondary education.
Lowed	Incomplete secondary education or less (ref. category).
Heavyind	Heavy industry (ref. category).
Transp	Transport and communications.
Constr	Construction.
Light	Light industry (including food).
Serv	Services in utilities, consumption and housing.
Trade	Trade and catering.
Teach	Schools (not institutes of higher education).

Table 10.A1 Continued

Health	Healthcare and physical education.
Art	Art and culture.
Science	Research institutes and higher education.
Govt	Economic administration, government and social organizations.
Other	Other branch.
Heat	Hot workplace.
Heavy	Physically heavy work.
Nervous	Nervous strain.
Badcond	One or more of the following: work hazards, dust, fumes, noise or vibrations.

Table 10.A2 Variable means

Variable	*Mean for men*	*Standard dev.*	*Mean for women*	*Standard dev.*
W	1.33	0.543	0.974	0.491
LW	0.220	0.355	–0.105	0.400
WAGE	242	84.1	158	50.4
LWAGE	5.43	0.335	5.01	0.327
H	42.6	5.83	39.5	7.72
AGE	41.6	10.7	39.6	10.1
AGESQ	1,848	917	1,674	866
STAZH	22.7	11.2	19.0	9.56
SENIOR	13.2	10.1	11.3	8.23
PENS	0.0757	0.265	0.0835	0.277
MTS	0.865	0.342	0.725	0.447
REDUC	0.497	2.27	0.744	3.10
REDUCED	0.211	1.78	0.908	3.890
UNOFF	0	0	0.0190	0.137
OFFPART	0.00540	0.0734	0.0342	0.182
PARTY	0.316	0.466	0.192	0.394
HIGHQUAL	0.0351	0.184	0.0266	0.161
MIDQUAL	0.254	0.436	0.421	0.494
PHYSQUAL	0.622	0.486	0.372	0.484
LOWQUAL	0.0892	0.285	0.180	0.385
HIGHED1	0.232	0.423	0.215	0.411
HIGHED2	0.0595	0.237	0.0437	0.205
SPECSEC	0.327	0.470	0.329	0.470
SECOND	0.222	0.416	0.287	0.453
PTU	0.135	0.342	0.0550	0.228
LOWED	0.0919	0.289	0.110	0.314
HEAVYIND	0.5432	0.499	0.429	0.495
TRANSP	0.0811	0.273	0.0398	0.196
CONSTR	0.0649	0.247	0.0417	0.200
LIGHT	0.0432	0.204	0.0626	0.243
SERV	0.0486	0.215	0.0626	0.243
TRADE	0.0189	0.136	0.070	0.256
TEACH	0.0514	0.221	0.123	0.329
HEALTH	0.0189	0.136	0.0569	0.232
ART	0.0135	0.116	0.0152	0.122
SCIENCE	0.0541	0.226	0.0436	0.204
GOVT	0.00541	0.0734	0.0171	0.130
OTHER	0.0568	0.232	0.0380	0.191
HEAT	0.0865	0.281	0.0247	0.155
HEAVY	0.151	0.359	0.0797	0.271
NERVOUS	0.265	0.442	0.205	0.404
BADCOND	0.2956	0.456	0.135	0.342

Table 10.A3 The model used for decomposition

The model used for decomposition of the gender wage differential (Model 3) includes more variables than Model 1. The differences are the following:

1 **Age and experience:** Model 3 includes second-order terms for experience and seniority and a third-order term for age.
2 **Family and household:** Besides marital status, Model 3 includes the number of children born to the respondent, the number of children of pre-school age and the number of children of school age in the household, and an estimate of the respondent's housework in hours per week.
3 **Job types:** In Model 3, skilled workers ("physqual" in Model 1) are divided into those with predominantly physical work and those with only elements of physical work. Further, the "highqual" category of Model 1 is divided into one group with managerial work and another with highly qualified, creative work.
4 **Education:** In Model 3, incomplete higher and specialized secondary education are treated separately, as are PTU with and PTU without secondary schooling.
5 **Conditions of work:** While Model 1 includes four work condition variables, Model 3 includes ten: hot workplace; hazardous work; dust or fumes; hard work tempo; heavy work; dirt; noise or vibrations; sharp changes of temperature; nervous strain; and lack of light or space.

INDEX

For Product Safety Concerns and Information please contact our EU representative GPSR@taylorandfrancis.com
Taylor & Francis Verlag GmbH, Kaufingerstraße 24, 80331 München, Germany

www.ingramcontent.com/pod-product-compliance
Ingram Content Group UK Ltd.
Pitfield, Milton Keynes, MK11 3LW, UK
UKHW010959180926
475701UK00004B/453

* 9 7 8 1 1 3 8 8 6 6 1 7 1 *